NO
PLACE
FOR A
WOMAN

THE LIFE AND
NEWFOUNDLAND STORIES
OF ELLA MANUEL

Compiled and edited by
ANTONY BERGER

BREAKWATER
P.O. BOX 2188, ST. JOHN'S, NL, CANADA, A1C 6E6
WWW.BREAKWATERBOOKS.COM

COPYRIGHT © 2020 Antony Berger
ISBN 978-1-55081-836-9

A CIP catalogue record for this book is available from Library and Archives Canada

We acknowledge the support of the Canada Council for the Arts.
We acknowledge the financial support of the Government of Canada and the
Government of Newfoundland and Labrador through the Department of
Tourism, Culture, Industry and Innovation for our publishing activities.
PRINTED AND BOUND IN CANADA.

   Canada Council   Conseil des arts   Newfoundland
for the Arts   du Canada   Labrador

Breakwater Books is committed to choosing papers and materials for our books that
help to protect our environment. To this end, this book is printed on a recycled paper
and other controlled sources that are certified by the Forest Stewardship Council®.

TO ELLA'S GREAT-GRANDDAUGHTERS
MAHALA, LILA, AND SADIE

CONTENTS

PART I

ABOUT ELLA MANUEL

~

PREFACE

MY MOTHER, Ella Manuel, was very guarded about her private life, so when, not long after she died, I came across a package of letters in a sealed manila envelope on which she had written in bold, "Please, please destroy without reading," I was uncertain what to do. Why had she kept them? Had she forgotten about the contents, or did she mean them to be read one day? Without thinking it through, I did as she had directed. As the letters disappeared in flames I caught brief sight and then lost track of an intimate part of her life, never to be revealed. But there was also a slim diary from her university days, and, in a small bundle tied round with a faded blue ribbon, the letters she wrote to her parents in Lewisporte between 1927 and 1943 from England and the USA. About those years, Ella would say little, save that she had blocked them from her memory. So when I found those letters, that world sprang clearly to life. These were my main guides to a time she rarely spoke about, when this young woman from a mercantile family in Lewisporte studied in Boston, travelled to England and beyond, married my English father and through him encountered an odd assortment of artists, writers, power-brokers, revolutionaries, and eccentrics. I began to understand how her fierce independence led to my parents' divorce and drove her feminism.

In later years, Ella became such a colourful influence on many younger women that the story of how one independent Newfoundlander in the early days of feminism managed to forge her way in a male-dominated world still resonates today. Though she did not realize it at the time, she was helping to drive a wedge into the side of a paternalistic society, opening space for women. Her way with words led her to journalism, and with her marvellously expressive voice she became well-known for her stories and commentaries broadcast on radio. In this biography, I set out something of her opinions about the role of women, and most of all, her desire to contribute to Newfoundland culture and society. My father and his circle opened for her the world of political thought and social action, so I have included brief portraits of some of the people she met and worked with in England.

Ella was an intriguing woman with strong and often controversial opinions. Her stories were written after her experiences in England and the USA, after her divorce and the birth of two children. She returned to Newfoundland in 1945 with two small boys about the time of Confederation with Canada, when to be a single mother was near enough a scandal. It was then that she began to find her métier as a writer and broadcaster. She wrote for newspapers and magazines and published a well-regarded children's novel, *That Fine Summer*, about a strong-willed girl who spends the summer fishing with her grandfather.

This book contains a selection of her Newfoundland stories, all based on actual people and events, especially those in western Newfoundland's Bonne Bay, where she eventually found her home. Her writings convey something of the traditional culture of Newfoundland and Labrador. They portray the lives and values of people who have long since faded from the scene, so that the stories have now acquired the patina of history, and yet also resonate with those who delight in the rural life. Her love of the land, the bays and rivers, the hills and the forests, the birds and fish, emerges as the background to her stories, most of which have never before been published.

TELLING HER OWN STORY

So now here is Ella telling a little about herself, leaving out much of what I shall shortly put back.

WHEN I was asked once years ago to be interviewed for radio, I realized that here was an opportunity to try out my ideas about being from Newfoundland. I began by saying that my strongest recollection of early years was the terrible anxiety I used to feel in late fall when the fog came down and stayed for weeks, and the weather was cold. When the coastal steamer left on its last voyage for the year, hooting through fast-making ice, pennants fluttering, and when the snow fell steadily for days, I had the impression of being forgotten in the middle of a grey, black ocean in which we were on an island so shrouded that nobody would know we were there, and the world would go on about its exciting business without my being able to take part. But that was only when we were very young and keenly aware of the excitement of a big world we were shut off from.

I found that didn't happen, and as soon as I could make a choice and leave for foreign parts, I began to have a feeling of great superiority about being a Newfoundlander. I never realized I had a curious accent, and any differences I put down to other people's errors. And since my forebears have been on the island since before 1750, coming mostly from Dorset, I had pretty deep roots in a culture I could cherish and respect.

Because they were obsessed with education, my parents sent me at the age of fifteen to an aunt in Boston—so that my life until then revolved around saving enough to send me to college. And so, after a year in high school there, I went to Boston University and got my degree. I graduated in the Depression and went to England to find work—a job in the Welfare Department of Marks and Spencer. This sent me travelling all over England, sometimes to little villages most Englishmen hadn't seen. It was a liberating experience, for it brought me close to the roots of Newfoundlanders and made me see ourselves in a new context. At the same time, I was not above telling tall stories of icebergs, fog and seal-meat, just to get attention. After all, not everyone could boast such an exotic background!

I had a variety of jobs, from looking after war refugee children, and working in a library, to helping make films and writing the odd fishing story. It all led a few years before Confederation to the radio microphone in the attic of Glynmill Inn in Corner Brook, the studio of the Voice of Western Newfoundland (VOWN), part of the Newfoundland Broadcasting system. I began with children's stories and graduated to information programs on cooperatives and agricultural matters. For a time, I was known locally as the "Manure Lady" until I developed a program called *Citizens' Forum*. Later, I wrote about local affairs for *The Western Star* in a column called "Think it Over."

When Confederation came, everyone on the mainland wanted to hear about us. Any articulate native could have demanded a hearing on radio, and there was I, burning to explain my history and culture to everyone. My hackles rose when I heard certain writers and playwrights speaking in my name, presenting us to the world. Their words said nothing to my experience as a Newfoundlander, less to my cultural background. So I supposed it was up to me to speak up— to tell my myth. But before I had that chance, I had to move to Halifax, because our male-dominated provincial radio network neither approved of nor trusted me. In the end, I was able to speak for

Newfoundland across Canada, and on the BBC and the Australian Broadcasting System.

Though my political education started early, my radical training started late in life. Around 1960, I became a member of the Voice of Women, then the main peace movement engaging women in Canada. Working with VOW members across Canada with vastly different backgrounds, I found that my Newfoundland experience gave me a sharp edge in problems concerning the Third World, and so I became Vice-President of the movement, which occupied me completely for several years.

There were limits, of course. Women were neither presumed to be wise in politics nor analytical, since their opinions were based, it was thought, on intuition rather than reason. Just to hold their own, women were obliged to be far more certain of their facts than men and far more articulate. I had no idea what a feminist was then, but what I lost being a woman, I think was made up being a Newfoundlander. It is only here that I find a landscape to which I belong and a people with whom it is a joy to live.

A LEWISPORTE CHILDHOOD

THE FIRST Manuels came to Newfoundland in the mid-1700s from south-western England. After a brief stay at Greenspond, in northern Bonavista Bay, they moved to Notre Dame Bay, to Twillingate, and then to the island of Exploits. Here they prospered, most as merchants and shipbuilders, and here Ella's father, Robert William Manuel, was born in 1871. As a young man, he fished off Labrador and later moved to the new settlement of Lewisporte on the nearby mainland, for many years the commercial center for northern Newfoundland and the shipping port for Labrador. The town lies on the side of Burnt Bay where the branch railway line from Notre Dame Junction ended at the government wharf. Here my grandfather built and operated a general store and hotel.

When he married Jessie Sophia Reader from Musgravetown, she looked after the family and the hotel, while Grandfather tended to the store and to other business interests. They were well-known throughout the length and breadth of Notre Dame Bay. Grandfather sold the business in the early 1940s, but the name Manuel Hotel was retained for another thirty years or so. In the 1980s, the business was sold again and the premises were finally torn down, leaving in its place just a patch of grass and the fading memories of people who had passed through looking for adventure, work, or simply escape.

Many young men stayed in the hotel on their way to and from the Great War in Europe. For example, on October 16, 1916, William

Blackhall from St. John's "together with Lieut. Hicks and a dozen other heroes from the front held a grand patriotic meeting here tonight." As the War wound down, Les Jones, a seaman from Fogo just back in late 1918 from service with the Royal Newfoundland Regiment, called it "a rotten affair," and Norman Pardy noted that he was heading home to Twillingate "discharged, permanently unfit." William Whiteway from Musgrave Harbour was more interested that the "girls in this hotel are as nice as pie," and Sam Fasey from Twillingate "wanted a wife—any chance of one here at this hotel?" His neighbour John Barrett claimed that he was on his way "to Timbuctoo to evade the Spanish flu." Another soldier heading to Gander Bay from the war was Sergeant Blake "en route for home after 4 years chasing the Hun." And among the discontented was A. Zundell from New York whose entry in the ledger in December 1919 said firmly, "Am quite sure I will not take this trip again if I can help it."

Ella was born in Lewisporte on March 24, 1911, and her sister, Louise, on March 7, 1913. It was a strange childhood, being raised in a busy household centred around the needs of the hotel guests. The family had its own apartment in the hotel, but the girls were familiar with the hubbub around them, which helped them develop a sense of the world outside and of ease in meeting strangers. Their parents, being squarely of the merchant class, had more money and influence than most of their generation, and the two sisters thought no children anywhere had as much fun as they had growing up. Indeed, Ella once toyed with the idea of writing a book called "Young and Happy, Outport Style."

The hotel had a battery-run radio with a huge horn-shaped speaker from which they picked up broadcasts from Schenectady and Havana. Late at night they would listen to wonderful music, which was always interrupted when the steam train pulled into the station, a stone's throw from the family sitting room. Those arriving late at night could help themselves by taking a key from the unattended front desk, occupying a room for the night, eating breakfast, and only then paying their bill before departing. A great many people travelling to

Labrador or northern Newfoundland passed through the Manuel Hotel, including Sir Wilfred Grenfell and the Twillingate-born opera singer Toulinguet Stirling.[1] On her way home, Stirling sang for the two little girls "I Dreamt I Dwelt in Marble Halls." Ella marvelled how cold her feet must have been on a marble floor.

Robert Manuel was a good, if somewhat dogmatic, man who neither drank nor smoked, a serious Methodist for whom the Bible was his guide through life. The church and "the hell of Sunday" loomed large in the girls' lives, with its procession of prayer meetings, Lenten testimony meetings, and "the excitement next day of hearing who got converted." Their father found it hard to express affection for his daughters, and Ella felt it difficult to live up to his expectations. Many years later, she realized that she was "as good a person as he in my feeling for humanity, love of them, sense of responsibility and awe. Saying this, I suddenly felt free—I had severed a cable that awakened my guilt: such a floating, peaceful feeling of everything falling into place."

Lewisporte was rich in ghosts and storytellers, fierce goats, and trim little vessels. Though the town had no library, the girls read all the books that relatives sent them—Dickens, Walter Scott, Louisa May Alcott, and vivid stories from the Bible. When Ella was eight, her father bought a little rowboat, a rodney, which he tethered to the wharf by a long rope. The two girls learned to handle the boat by rowing to the end of the rope and back again. They fished off the wharf for connors and tomcod and, later, they would row out into Burnt Bay and down to the little brook at the bottom where they could fish for trout. Ella's passion for the sea, small boats, and fishing remained strong throughout the rest of her life, and was the basis for many of her stories.

---

[1] Born Georgina Stirling, she became a minor opera singer in Europe under the stage name Toulinguet Stirling, following the spelling of a small cluster of islets off the coast of Brittany, from which Newfoundland's Twillingate Islands derived their name.

TO BOSTON UNIVERSITY

FOR YEARS her parents had been saving for their girls' education, though local people thought they were quite mad to send their daughters away to college. Because her mother's sister had settled in Boston, Ella was sent there to live. She previously had no sciences, so she had to do a make-up year in a Boston high school before gaining entry to Boston University in the fall of 1927. Here in the big city she haunted art galleries, libraries, and concert halls. Performances of the Boston Symphony Orchestra inspired her to study music, and during these years she learned to play the piano quite skilfully.

Summers she returned home to Lewisporte where the days were filled with friends, picnics, long walks, boat rides, swimming, and—best of all—boys. Beautiful, talented, brash, a little conceited, her affections in Newfoundland swung from Ted to Howard, and when they weren't around, there were others to amuse her. In Boston there were even more, as she danced with Stan and Roddy, Chappie, Hinkle, Dick, Ray, Fred, and Jackson:

> Boy, were they funny. George kisses marvellously as ever and said "I love you." He is darn cute, but he sure is jealous. Rolly is in love with me. Art begs for a break. I go round in circles. Maybe emotions are an essential part of one and not a weakness. Maybe I have kept myself bottled up. Or maybe it just belongs to the process of grow-
> i   n   g

up. One by one I've slipped from the old customs and ways. I suppose next year I'll be at a nightclub!

Just before graduating from college, Ella wrote her mother that George, a young lawyer, had proposed to her, but that she had no intention of accepting him:

> The attitude of practically all college students of my acquaintance is that marriage is the only thing, and there is a perfect epidemic of engagements this spring. They feel that they owe it to life to be well educated in order to help their husbands and bring up their children properly. For several years I have been sending away worthy young men, educated and cultured who have in their heads the silly idea that it would be very nice for me to get their meals. I don't propose to be a fool and wait for a man who lags along after me, because I have an alert mind inherited from my parents, and a good sound background, thanks also to you. Do you think that I would throw that away on a man? Well, hardly.

Meanwhile, her powers of expression were rapidly developing. At home in Lewisporte she wrote in her diary:

> Went down to the point to read. The all-enveloping silence is lovely. I can lean against my rock and hear not a sound but the wind sighing through the trees, and birds whistling at intervals. The wind in the spruce and fir in the near distance plays an accompaniment to the melody of the waves lapping and the light leaves rustling. The blue of the water shows through the trees and seems to meet in the blue of the sky in a circle which encloses the deep beauty of the world. Glorious feeling of solitude, not loneliness.

In 1931, Ella graduated from Boston University with a B.Sc. in

---

2 She quickly abandoned chemistry in the jobless years of the Depression and instead developed her fascination with words, but she followed with interest her two sons' careers in the earth sciences.

chemistry.[2] The Depression was then deepening, and she began to suspect there was something wrong with the existing social and economic scheme. Back home, Newfoundland was at a crisis point, which led to the country voluntarily handing governance back to England. As for many of the leaders of that time, Ella wrote, "I think sometimes that there is only one thing more contemptible than a man who corrupts his political office and that is the people who allow him to do it with impunity."

There were few jobs available to her in the US, so Ella returned to Lewisporte where she worked for her father and taught piano. By mid-1933 she had saved enough to buy passage—$25 it was—on a ship bound from Botwood to London with a cargo of paper. This would be a time to decide what to do with her life, and especially with her long, on-and-off again romance with Ted. What she thought would be a relatively short visit to England turned into one of the most exciting and important periods of her life.

ENGLAND, MARRIAGE,
AND SOCIAL ACTION

ELLA REMAINED in England for the next five years and left a changed woman, with her own family, and a new outlook on life. Her letters home, which described important events and famous people, conveyed a sense of what it must have been like in pre-war England as a young woman from a distant colony on the geographic and economic margin. They sometimes referred to the favourable impression she made with other people. She made friends easily, though she did sometimes think the English were "slow-acting, pig-headed folk." People showed interest when she said she was from an old part of the Empire. In southwest England, she found the local fishermen were the only people who had any idea where Newfoundland was, for many of their fathers and grandfathers had made the journey every year. They all thought Ella must be Cornish, since her accent resembled their own.

Soon after arriving in London, Ella took a course in "Superior Household Science," a fancy name for housekeeping and cooking, specializing in British cuisine, such as it was. She always retained a half-hearted interest in nutritious foods, and was inclined to culinary adventure, but certainly not excellence. Once out jigging in the bay, my brother and I caught that most ugly of marine fish, a sculpin, which we dragged back home. Ella cut it open to discover—and later feed us unsuspecting kids—some tasty white meat she found hidden deep inside its revoltingly horny exterior. One of our favourite desserts as children was her wondrously soggy invention of honey graham crackers floating in a bowl of milk.

As an attractive single girl, she met many interesting young men in London. One of them took her to a political meeting where a man with a great sabre scar all down his face gave a speech that appalled her. This was William Joyce ("Lord Haw-Haw"), a prominent fascist, who after the war was executed by the British for his treasonous broadcasts from Nazi Germany.

On Armistice Day, 1933, Ella and a friend found in an old churchyard "a Flanders field" with a Newfoundland plot where the two girls planted "little crosses in memory of the boys whose mothers and fathers could not be there to do it for them." There were markers for the Ayre family of St. John's who had lost four young men in that terrible conflict. "We stood with bowed heads and said our little prayers for them." And there were warnings of things to come. Among the "tub thumpers" she heard at Speakers' Corner in Hyde Park was a young Jew who spoke of murder and death in Nazi Germany.

Wandering around London, Ella felt at first something of a failure. Despite her education, she did not know what she wanted to do in life. She wrote her parents that "when conditions are at their very worst and I am almost in despair, I can remember that this is the very world in which my father and mother are struggling." Then everything changed for her.

Ella answered an ad in the *London Times* for a "Young lady, 20-25, required to take charge of boy age 9 during the daytime for the Christmas holiday month: must be cultured, intelligent, of good appearance and personality." Joseph Berger, now divorced, was seeking someone to look after his son, Peter, for whom he had custody. Ella was promptly hired. Then in his mid-thirties, Joe held a senior executive position with the department-store chain of Marks and Spencer (M&S), a job with a high salary and much prestige. So when Peter returned to his boarding school, Joe arranged a job interview for Ella with M&S.

Ella was hired by the company's new Welfare Department. This had its origins a few years earlier when Flora Solomon, a well-to-do

émigré Jew from Russia, met an old acquaintance, Simon Marks, the
Director of M&S. "You know you have a shocking reputation in the
country; your labour conditions are notorious," she said to him. Quite
taken aback, Marks challenged her to do something about it, and
hired her to head his Welfare Department, reporting to Joe Berger, who
understood Flora's objectives and invariably supported her, being,
as she wrote in her memoirs, "a pacifist in every fibre, and extremely
left-wing."[3] The idea was to improve the working conditions for
employees, especially the shop girls. That meant setting up subsidized
staff canteens in every store, where a hot meal at noon would be
available for sixpence, with a proper English tea for four pence. Free
uniforms would be available, and there would even be holiday camps
for those who could not afford to leave home on their own. When
Marks complained to Flora that she had recruited two women at a
weekly salary of three pounds ten shillings, violating his rule that no
employee should start at above three pounds, she argued that, like Ella,
they were highly qualified because they had university degrees. "Oh,"
he grumbled, "that means they ought to earn more than me. I haven't
a degree."

Ella and later her sister, Louise, were part of the team that fanned
out across England to check conditions and to persuade store managers to appoint their own welfare officers. Imagine a group of
women activists—including two Newfoundland "colonials"—led by
Flora Solomon, herself still with a thick Russian accent, telling the
English shop managers what to do! Ella's work with M&S took her
around the country, inspecting their shops and ordering materials for
the new canteens. She was soon promoted to Welfare Supervisor for
the north of England, where times were particularly tough. George
Orwell's The Road to Wigan Pier always reminded her of the bleak
living conditions of working-class people that she saw in Lancashire
and Yorkshire.

She was now in charge of the well-being of some 5000 people
employed by one of the largest department-store organizations in

[3] Baku to Baker Street: The Memoirs of Flora Solomon. London: Collins, 1984.

England. It was exhausting but exhilarating work. She might return from the north to London on a Friday night, then go to the office on a Saturday morning, and to an exhibition in the afternoon to look at gas stoves and cupboards. Monday at the office until 5:30, then on the evening train for Leeds, where the manager was at loggerheads with the girls, and the girls among themselves:

> So I called a meeting after work and talked to the girls, about 100 of them. I told them that we were all for them, that we would do anything we could for them, that if they would like I would find a place nearby where they could get discounts for their hairdressing. I left feeling that if there is anything the matter they'll come and tell me.

When a new store opened in Kent, Ella had to arrange the new kitchen and secure decent prices from local butchers, bakers, and green-grocers. She wrote home, "Can you imagine me telling the cook and cleaner what to do every minute of the day, and seeing that the place is clean? Every one stares at me when I present my card. They expect to see a middle-aged, hard-looking lady. I try to look older to fool them."

She felt that she was now much more balanced and happy. In a few months she had found an important reason for living—to help people and to "change as much as I could this ridiculous, tragic system of society." Meanwhile, Peter had told his father that he really liked Ella. "That is good," Joe replied, "because I am going to marry her." She was obviously flattered by his attentions, and over the next year their affections deepened. Of course, they had to keep the affair very quiet since she was one of his employees, way down in the company structure.

Joe came from a family of middle-class Jews. His Trieste-born grandfather, Joseph Charles Berger, had migrated to England in the early 1800s, setting up business in Liverpool. He had a large family,[4]

---

[4] One of his granddaughters married American Aldo Leopold, who wrote so elegantly about ecology and environmental philosophy, and a great-grandson was the well-known writer and art critic John Berger.

most of whom either drifted away from any kind of conservative
Judaism, or converted to Christianity. In 1917, at eighteen years of
age, Joe Berger joined the British army. Here he found himself in
close contact for the first time with working-class men, from whom
he learned that bravery, compassion, and courage were not restricted
to the middle and upper classes. After the war, he graduated as a
chartered accountant, and set up a practice into which he took young
men whose parents could not afford to pay the usual fees for such
training—a move which brought him into conflict with the regular
accounting establishment. Dissatisfied with his work, Joe left his
company to his junior partners,[5] and put his somewhat radical ideas
about economics into practice by setting up the Gresham School of
Economics, which taught not only book-keeping but also economics,
politics, economic history, and geography, aiming to give students
a better understanding of the differences between capitalism and
Marxism. The school collapsed financially in 1930, victim of the
Depression, but Joe refused to declare bankruptcy, which would
have meant being struck off the lists of the Institute of Chartered
Accountants. Determined to repay his debts, he joined M&S in
London later that year. In a short time, he rose to become the joint
secretary and chief accountant (chief executive officer) of the
company, which by the end of the decade employed some 20,000
people.

That summer of 1934, Ella returned to Lewisporte for a few
weeks to sort out her feelings, and to tell her parents about Joe.

> He is one of the most charming, educated men I have
> ever met, and the whole firm thinks the world of him.
> That is perhaps why I am so flattered by his confidence
> in me. Of course, since I joined the firm, I have told
> nobody that I know him outside business—except Mrs.
> Solomon, who knew that I looked after Peter. There is a

---

[5] Including John Diamond, later Baron (Lord) Diamond. He was a senior member
of Harold Wilson's Labour Government in the 1960s and later became a leader of
Britain's Social Democratic Party.

vast difference between being a Jew by faith and one by birth, and Joe is one by birth only.[6] He has the most marvellous philosophy by which he lives. It has explained to me why there should be so much poverty and disease and heartbreak when we are taught to think that God is a loving father. I cannot explain in writing just what this philosophy or, more correctly, this translation of the Christian teaching, consists in. But I can tell you it has made it easier for me to view dispassionately the death of people near to me. And after all, if a philosophy does that for one, surely it must be valuable.[7]

Late that year, after her return to London, Ella wrote her parents that she was going to marry Joe. She had known him for a year now, and they had spent much time together. She was not going to depend on him for a living, but would continue working, perhaps in some new venture at "whatever we decide most important to be done." She felt he understood her and shared her ambitions: "Nobody has ever been so good to me. He makes me have meals with him whenever I am in town, because he says girls living alone don't eat properly—which is true. Last week when I came home he brought me a lovely handbag, because he saw mine was worn out."

Not surprisingly, her father and mother were worried. Joe was considerably older, from a different culture, religion, and economic class, and, especially, a divorced father. Ella explained to her parents that Joe and his first wife, Ena, had become engaged when she was sixteen and he nineteen, and were married three years later. Ena was attractive, energetic, with a flair for dramatics, but after Peter was born, she became involved with another man, and the marriage fell apart. Many years later, Ella and Ena met and apparently got along well. In some ways they were alike, occasioning many a speculation about Joe Berger's choice of women.

[6] However, when he was young his family thought he might become a rabbi, and his first marriage was in a synagogue.

[7] I have no idea what his philosophy was, and her letters never refer to it again.

Ena was always active on the left of the political spectrum, and decades after her divorce from Joe, she married Tom Driberg, journalist, MP, and later Lord Bradwell, Chairman of the Labour Party. Tom was promiscuously gay long before homosexuality became legal in England, and would have needed a cover during his parliamentary career.[8] Ena provided that, thinking she might change him, but there was not a chance. *Ruling Passions*, Driberg's sordid autobiography, published posthumously, is a crusading defence of homosexuality, in which he gave no hint of a marriage and no mention of Ena.

To let the Manuels judge his suitability as a future son-in-law, Joe decided to visit them. So, in early August of 1935, he took Peter to Lewisporte, returning to England by ship at the end of the month. The trip was a success, and any doubts about the marriage were dispelled. Louise accompanied Joe and Peter on the return journey, and just after her arrival, she wrote home, "Oh Mom, I'm absolutely crazy about Joe, now especially when I have seen him in his natural setting. I wish I could tell you how highly he speaks of both of you." Joe's English family quickly accepted Ella, but had difficulty conceiving of any place being "so undeveloped and backward" as Newfoundland. With Flora Solomon a witness, Ella and Joe were married in a London registry office that October. Apparently, news of the wedding was broadcast at home on the *Gerald S. Doyle News Bulletin*. Ella's reaction when told? "What a joke. Just as well people have something harmless to talk about."

Joe and Ella soon found a flat in Highpoint, one of London's newest and most fashionable apartment buildings, with a fine view over Hampstead Heath.[9] Describing it to her mother, Ella wrote, "It is very modern, with heating in the floors and ceiling and constant hot water. You'd love the kitchen, all done in the latest style with built in cupboards, a zinc-lined sink with two drain boards, white tiles and

---

[8] Francis Wheen. *The Soul of Indiscretion: Tom Driberg, Poet, Philanderer, Legislator and Outlaw*. Harper Collins: 2001.

[9] Highpoint, an apartment building in Highgate, has been labelled "the only pre-war Modern building in Britain."

tiled floor, and a service hatch into the dining room."[10]

During her years in England, Ella travelled whenever the opportunity arose. There was a memorable trip with her sister to Leningrad and Moscow. She wrote her parents that the church in Russia "was nothing but pure and simple despotism," and that the Russians now had a "new religion, which is better, stronger and more useful." Like many others then, Ella and Joe were both impressed with the accomplishments of Soviet communism, but the emerging news of Stalin's terrible purges made them think again. Despite her left-wing views, Ella would later admit that in the voting booth at home she had to resist her hand going automatically to the checkmark for the Liberals, the party of her parents.

Once in Paris she stayed in a flat owned by Flora Solomon, who warned her to leave immediately if a strange man opened the door. When such an event did occur, Ella was forced to exit hurriedly through the fire escape. The stranger was Aleksandr Kerensky, socialist revolutionary and the last prime minister of Russia before the Revolution when Lenin took the reins of power. Kerensky and Flora had a long relationship in the 1930s. Later, it was Flora who tipped off British intelligence about Kim Philby, a member of MI6. It turned out that Philby had also been working for the Soviets, and had attempted to recruit her too. Philby fled to Russia in 1963, never to return.[11]

Despite worrying times in mid-thirties Europe, Ella was happy with Joe. They were obliged to do a lot of entertaining, which she dreaded: "I want to wear the oldest thing I have, and dirty my hands at rough work as a visible rejection of this sort of life." Though she enjoyed her new and comfortable life, she was perturbed that she had

[10] Their neighbours at Highpoint were a fine assortment of the famous and the about to be: Aldous Huxley—writer, Sir William Rothenstein—artist, Beatrix Lehmann—actress, Geoffrey Vevers—keeper of the Whipsnade Zoo, and Gray Walter—neurophysiologist and pioneer brain scientist. She and Joe were good friends with Peter and Doris Drucker and witnessed their wedding. Drucker moved to the US and became the guru of right-leaning economists and management people, and the author of many popular books on the subject.

[11] It was Flora's son, Peter Benenson, who founded Amnesty International, one of the world's leading international human-rights organizations.

done little to deserve it. She tried to persuade her parents to visit England, thinking they might even retire there:

> It isn't every day your oldest child gets married and has a home so beautiful that it must be written about in a magazine. We'll meet you in Liverpool complete with conveyance to conduct you to our home, the highest spot in London. Marta is dying to cook for you and give you tea at odd moments.

Her mother did eventually come, but nothing could stir her father to leave his business in Lewisporte, until he sold it years later and moved to Corner Brook, where the Manuels spent the rest of their lives.

As one crisis followed another in Europe and the clouds of war gathered, Ella felt that England was "idiotic and completely incapable," and was angry that the League of Nations had not stopped Italy from its war on Abyssinia (Ethiopia). During a trip to Holland, Joe and Ella found themselves near the border with Germany. Out of curiosity, they crossed over to find that, by comparison with the Dutch, everyone looked shabby, the food was poor, and the shops almost empty of goods. "Everyone heiled Hitler on every possible occasion, but we looked politely blank and merely said 'Good morning'."

As she wrote years later, Ella and Joe were then:

> Like all aspiring socialists, as close to the centre as we could get. London was full of such people. There were the ones who came to Highpoint once a week and read and discussed *Das Kapital*. Not that it did me much good for I never got beyond the tenth page. I remember being asked to sell the *Daily Worker*[12] outside the Highgate tube station—and me living in Highpoint! I didn't do it, but I did buy a copy and flaunted it as I walked home. I taught Peter "The Internationale" and sang it walking up and down Highgate Hill. I was a

[12]   The Communist Party newspaper.

real bourgeois socialist living in luxurious surroundings, fretting about clothes and how to fill my time.

Joe and Ella were furious with the British Government, which was trying to stop people from going to Spain during its civil war to help fight the fascists. As she wrote, "It is perfectly legal for Hitler to send 30,000 troops and Mussolini nearly 20,000. But the English mustn't interfere. Their hypocrisy makes an honest person sick." The Left Book Club, which was much more than a publisher of fiction and non-fiction, had booked a hall seating a thousand to show a movie taken in Madrid of the fighting there. As a club member, Ella was busy putting up posters and collecting money to send medical supplies to Spain. She and Joe were also helping to bring children to safety in England from war-torn Spain and from Nazi Germany.[13]

Early in 1937, Ella wrote home of her intention to write a book about Newfoundland. She felt that she could see her island and its problems more objectively from a distance. What she had in mind was a critique that would, she reckoned, antagonize many readers, for she intended to say things that she felt stood in the way of progress: "If I should live my life without doing everything in my power to help our people, then it is much better that I never lived and ate the food which might keep someone else alive." She worked on the manuscript for several years, and was waiting for the end of the war to finish it, but by that time she was out of touch with events in Newfoundland. What might have seemed obvious to her from pre-war England was now much less so, and talk of union with Canada was starting up again. I never heard her speak of her planned book in later years, and it was not until I discovered these letters after her death that I knew anything about it: no trace of a manuscript could be found among her papers.

---

[13] The British government was persuaded to allow in a certain number of Spanish children, as long as sponsors could be found. Many people donated money and offered to provide homes for the refugees, mostly from the Basque region, and sometimes for the priests and teachers who accompanied them. Nearly 4000 were brought by ship in 1937, most of whom returned to Spain when the civil war ended. Joe and Ella were also part of the British Movement for the Care of Children from Germany (Kindertransport), many of whose Jewish parents sent them away for safety before losing their own lives in the Holocaust.

Ella's life was about to change once more. I was born in the London Clinic on Marylebone Road in November 1937.[14] Business at M&S was now booming, but for most people, life in England was not improving. As the cost of food was rising, Ella wrote home:

> When I look at my fat, healthy child, my heart aches for the poor women who must watch their ailing and hungry children and suffer because of lack of means. There must surely be some justice somewhere, but certainly not in our state of society. I can't think what I've done to justify my fortunate economic position, any more than the woman who slaves away in a badly furnished, ill equipped house on no money.

Joe and Ella saw war coming and felt the conflict was unnecessary. They believed that England ought to have opposed Hitler on his way to power, when political means could have destroyed him. Moreover, Joe had fought—and very nearly died—in the First World War, and had seen the havoc caused by military leaders who were isolated from the realities of war in the trenches. One war was enough for him. Like so many other politically active people, the purges in the Soviet Union had shaken their interest in communism, and they could see nothing but danger and bloodshed ahead for Europe.

In 1939, they decided to leave England, and Joe resigned from Marks and Spencer. He was now earning 3,000 pounds per year, plus an annual bonus of 600 pounds—a huge income in those days. To Simon Marks he wrote:

> I know that you will realize that my resolve has been taken only after the most careful consideration. My reasons are such as far to outweigh all thoughts of personal profit or advancement. I know that you are not out of sympathy with these considerations, and whilst you may be of the opinion that some of my reasons have

---

[14] My godmother was Flora Solomon: it is my loss that I neglected to look her up when I lived in England in the 1960s.

been exaggerated, you are wise enough and broadminded enough to accept my sincerity and judgement of my personal future life.

As for Ella, the years in England changed her way of speaking, her outlook on life, and awakened her interest in politics. She left determined to make a difference, but any dreams she may have had of a brilliant career were soon to come up against the difficult challenges of war and domestic life.

CONNECTICUT: THE WAR YEARS

ABANDONING THEIR comfortable flat and financial security, my parents packed their belongings for the United States, and sailed from Liverpool to St. John's with Peter and me in April 1939. After a brief stay in Lewisporte, they settled in Madison, Connecticut. They were not planning to return to England after the war, for Joe immediately applied for American citizenship. At first, he set out to support his family as a consultant and lecturer on the American university circuit, but he was open to any business opportunities that appeared, including the marketing in England of Newfoundland lobster, bakeapples, and lumber. None of these ventures went very far, and there were times when Joe was not sure how he would continue to support his family. American institutions were not impressed by an English expert in business management, and Newfoundland companies were slow to respond to new opportunities. Moreover, with war now come to Europe, normal commercial life was disrupted. It did not take long for Joe to find a new direction, and for most of the rest of his life he worked to bring refugees and others fleeing war to safety.

The newly formed US Committee for the Care of European Children sent him to Montreal in July 1940 to meet, clear through immigration formalities, and bring to the United States the first boatload of English children who were being sent by their families to escape German bombs. He worked for the National Council of

Jewish Women in New York in their efforts to help fellow Jews who were being rounded up for the concentration camps in Europe. In 1944, he became the executive director of the experimental refuge, established at Oswego, NY, by President F.D. Roosevelt for the first large group of "displaced persons" liberated by the American army in Italy. In one way or another, Joe helped to care for thousands of refugees who found their way to the US from war-torn Europe.

From her new home in the USA, Ella regarded the war then raging in Europe as a terrible commentary on Christianity:

> While accepting and trying to live by the teachings of Jesus, I can have no part in official churches. I will teach Antony the Bible and his prayers, and try to make him a good follower of Christ, but I don't want him to be what we know as a good churchman.

She succeeded beyond her wildest dreams.

The war years passed her by in a blur of hated domesticity. Joe and Ella soon had a house full of children and little money. In addition to me, there were sixteen-year-old Peter; Joe's fourteen-year-old half-sister, Lee[15]; Pam (10) and Tony Vevers (14), who had been sent to safety by their father in London; and before long a second son, Jonathan. There was a maid from time to time, but the domestic strain of managing the household with two small children and four teenagers taxed Ella to her limits. After the Vevers went to live with another family in 1942, Joe and Ella moved to Greenwich, Connecticut. Despite the war, her escape from the suffering of others did not soothe her, and she was miserable at her loss of freedom. She had no time to herself, no chance to think or to work on her book, and she never became reconciled to the loss of freedom. She rarely referred to these years, except to say that she had worked hard to put them out of her mind.

After the war, Joe wrote prophetically to Louise about the state

---

[15] Lee's father and mother (Joe's step-mother) lost their lives in early 1941 when the ship taking them to live with their two daughters in Australia was attacked in the Irish Sea.

of affairs in Europe, and I suspect Ella would have agreed:

The sad pattern of European division continues. It looks as though we are to have two worlds after all, one dominated by America (with, hopefully, some kind of United States of Western Europe, economically at least) and the other dominated by the USSR. Which of these two economies will ultimately bring greater comfort and material wealth to its inhabitants, I don't know. But if it be the USSR, I fear the price demanded in the surrender of human liberties is too high, and I for one am not willing to pay it. I cannot ignore the weight of evidence, and all points to life in the USSR as being one of little, if any, personal, spiritual and intellectual freedom, checked by all the trappings of a police state. As you know, for long I looked upon the USSR as a tremendous experiment to give a fuller life to the ordinary peoples of the world. But I now know that you cannot measure the fullness of life in terms of economics alone—the personal freedoms do count. And anyone who doubts this need only live in an occupied country such as Germany to find out for himself. If I have strayed from the good o   l   d line, I've done it consciously and painfully and after much thought. I regret nothing of my past sympathies, but today in 1947 I think the perspective is different. I believe with Bergson that the essence of life is the dynamism that makes new beginnings.

NEWFOUNDLAND:
SEPARATION AND DIVORCE

IN AUGUST of 1944, Joe and Ella took Jonathan and me to Newfoundland. Peter had by now been drafted into the American army, and Lee had married. When Joe returned shortly to the US to take up his new appointment at Oswego, we remained behind. It was agreed that Ella would take this opportunity to see what she could make of her writing. That fall, she found much to do in Corner Brook, where we lived with her parents, who had retired there a few years earlier. She chaired a public meeting on wildlife conservation, at which she reminded people that "the fish and wildlife of our country belong to all of us. They are a part of our heritage just as much as the hills and rivers." She was now beginning to host radio programs on cooperatives and farming, and to write for the local daily, *The Western Star*. She was bursting with energy after the five-year lull in creativity. But first there was a major decision to make.

In the spring of 1945, she suddenly wrote Joe that she wanted a divorce. After many months away from him, and with the strong feeling that she was at last able to work productively on her own, she told Joe:

> I write this with sick misery but knowing there is nothing else I can do. I can't come back to you. For months I have thought of little else in my free moments. I have weighed everything and my decision is made. My work

means more to me than anything else in the world, and I must pursue it or die of frustration. I can manage living the way I do and looking after the boys, sharing with them their life and mine, but I have nothing left after that except for my work. If I had to take on again the responsibility of making a home for you, I should no longer be able to work or create. I can foresee my own development, and I can plan the things I must do, but they can only be planned around me and the boys. I must go on alone, Joe, and it fills me with more sadness than you will ever believe. Yes, I've thought of all the implications. Now that we have been apart for a year, there is no point our coming together again. It would only make matters worse for you, me and the boys, and it would be hellish being together with nothing between us. I know I am doing something terrible, for which I shall probably have a sense of guilt all my life. But I can't pay the price of going on living with you feeling as I do. I have to be alone, to be me, myself. I know it will just about finish you, but Joe what can I do? You wouldn't want me back knowing the way I feel. Let's finish and be done with it. Forgive me the inhumanity of my decision. I can't do anything else.

Joe's reaction was one of utter surprise and horror. He had already gone through one marriage and desperately wanted this one to last. He begged Ella to reconsider. In an attempt to patch things up, he spent a week with us in Corner Brook that summer, but the visit changed nothing. She was steadfast in her determination:

Is it to be a full life for me alone, or is it to be a half-life together? I am what I am, what generations and experience and life have made me. I know what you see for the future, and that will not suit me. To go back to what was would put me completely off balance for the whole of my life. Many things I did with you were done because I believed you knew best. As it was your money,

it was up to you to decide how we'd live on it. Now
I'm not financially dependent, and I know what I am and
what I want.

I don't know how she later acquired the letters she sent to Joe,
but I doubt she ever reread them. At fifteen, I had been begging her
to tell me something more about my father—I had just discovered
through a chance remark at school that he was a Jew—she gave these
letters to me, and was afterwards sorry for it. These shadows of a
personal tragedy confused and hurt me, as did his death when I was
eleven. Though I was young and inexperienced, I came to understand
something of what those years cost her. My love for her helped me
to grapple with the reasons why my parents separated. I was torn
between empathy for her and tears for him, his loss—and mine.

To complicate matters, in 1945 Joe accepted an offer to join
UNRRA, the new United Nations agency whose task was to care for
and resettle the millions of people displaced by the war. This took
him to Germany where he took charge of a huge refugee camp near
Munich, one that included the infamous Dachau concentration camp.
Here with up to 20,000 "displaced persons" under his management,
he had little time to worry about his personal problems. To Louise he
wrote:

> If Ella insists on breaking up, I can't or won't stop her.
> I love her too much for that, and I only hope she will
> find the satisfaction she seeks. Those of us who believe
> we are finding a road to inner peace have such a great
> responsibility—to be true to ourselves and to be sufficiently
> patient as to have faith in personal behaviour and in the
> power of example.

Ella had proposed that Jonathan and I remain with her for the
next few years, but that Joe could have us whenever he wanted.
We boys missed our father but, she judged, not enough to thrive in a
family without love and affection. So in March 1946, Ella travelled
to Nevada for a "no fault" divorce. Jonathan and I were placed in
joint custody "until such time as the parties agree otherwise." A few

months later, in Germany, Joe married one of his co-workers, Françoise Lawrence, a young English woman with French roots. They remained in Germany after leaving UNRRA, and Joe became a civilian financial manager with the American army in Europe. Alas, at the end of 1948, he died suddenly of a haemorrhagic stroke at the age of forty-nine.

ELLA ON THE RADIO,
AND THE LOMOND VENTURE

BERGER WAS not a Newfoundland name—still isn't—so Ella quickly dropped it. She knew the only way she would get anywhere in Newfoundland was as Robert Manuel's daughter. There were few single mothers and fewer divorcees then in Corner Brook, and she was the target of much gossip. Undaunted, she was soon reading children's stories on the VOWN radio station in Corner Brook. Her new life was now well under way, and the outpouring of articles, stories, essays, and broadcasts over the next few decades brought her a sense of fulfilment.

Ella was now re-acquainting herself with Newfoundland and discovering people and places new to her. One of her early stories, "Among the Scots of the Codroy," describes the rich Scottish heritage of people she met in the Codroy Valley in 1945 on an assignment for the Newfoundland Agricultural Division. She began to regale her listeners with tales retold in her own characteristic style, such as the famous St. John's duel as recorded by Lt-Col Robert "McCrea in Fish-and-Fog Land," and the rescue of people who had spent "Six Months Adrift on the Ice."

With the divorce now settled and with opportunities for newspaper and radio work beginning to come her way, Ella made the surprising decision to set up a seasonal sports-fishing operation in Lomond. This was influenced by her growing friendship with prominent American sportsman Lee Wulff.[16] He had been hired before the war to advise the Newfoundland government on ways to promote sports fishing. He argued that game fish were too valuable to be caught only once, a statement that grew into today's widely accepted catch and release policy. In 1940, Wulff published *Leaping Silver*, a classic portrait of the Atlantic salmon, with many examples from Newfoundland. He was also a prolific writer, graphic artist, and photographer, who made many films about Newfoundland and Labrador. In the fall of 1945, Lee hired Ella to assist him in the making of *Silent Menace*, a movie for the Newfoundland government about tuberculosis, long plaguing the country.[17]

By war's end, Lee had begun to think of setting up camps at River of Ponds and Portland Creek where there was excellent fly-fishing to be had. But to get there would require a long trip by boat from Bonne Bay, then at the end of the road north from the railway station at Deer Lake. A kind of way station here, where superb salmon and trout fishing could be had on the Lomond and Upper Humber rivers, would make sense. Whether or not Wulff inveigled Ella to join him in this venture, the need on the west coast for adequate sports-fishing facilities she described in "A Chance Meeting, A New Idea."

In the summer of 1946, Ella made her move. In Lomond, at the eastern end of the Main Arm of Bonne Bay, there was a rather palatial but empty house. St. Tecla had been built in 1920 for George Simpson, the manager of the St. Lawrence Lumber Company in Lomond.[18] When the company finally disappeared from the scene in 1942, the Bowater Paper Company took over the property and later leased it

---

[16] An impressive documentary video entitled *Lee Wulff: A Remarkable Life* has recently been produced by Director Jeff Pill. Included are many scenes from Newfoundland and Labrador.

[17] In the February 1946 issue of *Atlantic Guardian*, Ella described this as "Newfoundland's first homemade movie," for it had been made without any foreign actors.

[18] For the story of Lomond and the Killdevil venture, see James Candow's *Lomond: The Life and Death of a Newfoundland Woods Town* (Harry Cuff, 1998) and my *The Good and Beautiful Bay: A History of Bonne Bay to Confederation and a*

to Ella. She renamed it Killdevil Lodge, after the steep-sided mountain across the Arm.

She was taking a big risk. Save for growing up in the family hotel in Lewisporte, surrounded by people coming and going throughout the year, she had no experience in hosting guests and dealing with their needs and wants. There was neither encouragement nor support from the Commission of Government, which had little interest in tourism beyond Eastern Newfoundland. Even after Confederation in 1949, Premier Smallwood was in no hurry to encourage visitors, arguing that the necessary infrastructure was lacking, as was a cadre of trained locals to cater to tourists.

Over the next few years, Ella and her team of local people ran the summer-time operation. One of these was Emma Tapper, first her guide and then lifelong friend. Ella was now immersed in a man's world. As she tells in "No Place for a Woman?" fly-fishing was a man's sport, and women were not welcome: letters would arrive in Lomond addressed to Mr. Ella Manuel. Still, those were marvellous summer days in Lomond. Jonathan and I fished from our rowboat, played on the big Bowater wharf with village boys, and once chased after a wandering bear. In "My Killdevil Days," our mother recaptures the pleasures of Lomond and Killdevil Lodge of long-ago.

Ella's venture did not flourish. It was just too difficult to cope with the poor roads, lack of telephone connections, inexperience of local household staff, and complete disinterest on the part of the authorities. She tried to improve business by obtaining a license to sell beer, there being no other legal outlet in Lomond. However, the regulations required drinkers to order food, so a cook was needed, and men who got obstreperous had to be dealt with. By the mid-1950s, Ella had had enough. She sold Killdevil Lodge to the Anglican Church, which continues today to operate it as a popular visitor and conference centre.[19] In the early 1960s, she returned to Bonne Bay, this time to Woody Point, where she built her house, and where most

---

[19] For an account of the later days of Killdevil, see Stewart Payne, *The Killdevil Lodge Experience in Gros Morne National Park* (Flanker, 2019).

of the stories in this book were written. But it was in Lomond, now
a quiet campground in Gros Morne National Park, where she first
fell in love with Bonne Bay.

TO NEW YORK WITH LEE WULFF

LEE WULFF's passion for and extensive knowledge of the outdoors must have influenced Ella.[20] They were also powerfully attracted to each other,[21] and were married very quietly in early 1947. The following school year, we all lived together in Lee's house in upper New York State on the banks of the Battenkill River, known simply as the 'Kill. I remember him as tall, rugged, austere, and not very talkative, except perhaps about fishing and photography. I can still see his house and its setting so clearly. Ranch-style, it sat in a little hollow below the road, with a curving driveway and a big yard in front. It was here that Lee taught Jon and me how to cast a line, and to tie flies, Jon's bright red hair making a fine dry fly.

The marriage did not go well. Lee wanted someone to prepare his meals and to keep the house tidy. He complained that Ella was a haphazard cook and not fastidious enough with her clothes, not a smart dresser like his previous wife. I don't recall them fighting when we lived together that one year, but after one serious disagreement, Ella wrote, "It appears that just by being myself I have lost Lee's love, and I know it will never come back. I know he'll do nothing

---

[20] Lee's posthumous memoir of his time in Newfoundland, edited by his son Barry, includes a brief but not altogether accurate description of Ella at Killdevil Lodge (*Bush Pilot Angler: A Memoir*. Camden, ME: Down East Books, 2000).

[21] Wulff cut a handsome figure. It was said that when he entered a room he "oozed testosterone," which may help to account for his five marriages.

about it like counting up the things I am, against those I'm not." By the summer of 1948, it was all over. That fall Ella moved to Vermont, where Jon and I attended boarding school. Many people in Newfoundland knew of the relationship with Lee, but not the marriage—adding another bit of mystique to her presence.

Things were kept so quiet that even after Ella died, her sister Louise was not certain that Ella and Lee had ever been legally divorced: they had been. Ella's ability to sweep unpleasantness under the carpet came in handy, for she never mentioned him again, not in her writings about Lomond or in private to her family. And that was it for marriage, though she did later have close relationships with several men. Years later she wrote:

> On one level I have lived intensely and peace flows into
> me. As for the rest, the deep hurts and loneliness I can
> keep buried most of the time. How could I have been
> so unwary, letting my guard down, and making critical
> errors, albeit in good faith? I suppose I'll pick up again
> the familiar shell and put it around me. I have to confess
> the shell is comfortable as long as I'm sure not to let
> anyone close.

Jon and I still have pleasant memories of our short time with Lee Wulff. Years later, Jon was on a small plane from Puenta Arenas, Chile, to the Falkland Islands, where he was installing a seismic station. His fellow passengers were showing each other the dry flies they planned to use in the Falklands. One leaned across the narrow aisle to say, "I don't suppose you know anything about fly fishing." To their astonishment, he replied, "Oh yes, that one's a Grey Wulff. Lee showed me how to tie it," and returned to his book in silence, while the others sat there open-mouthed, waiting for an explanation which never came.

SETTLING DOWN IN NEWFOUNDLAND

AS NEWFOUNDLAND entered Canada in the spring of 1949, we returned to Corner Brook to live once again with Ella's parents. The next two decades were to be productive ones for Ella, as she continued to develop her Newfoundland voice. She wrote extensively on local topics for newspapers and magazines, produced book reviews and reported on provincial fisheries conferences. She continued her broadcasts and began to assemble a mass of material in her private journals and type-written scraps. She also renewed her exploration of the west coast by car, coastal boat, and on foot, recounting her journeys on the CBC.

In the days after Confederation, when Canadians were discovering Newfoundland and Labrador, Ella was disdainful of those who held the romantic view that Newfoundlanders led simple lives: "On the contrary, life here is elemental and complex, for in order to live in safety and a tolerable degree of comfort, we have to develop special skills and learn from the experiences of our forebears," who always understood the need to be prepared for cold, storm, and isolation. A woman who could knit a hundred pairs of socks from the wool of her own sheep and a man who could grow a big crop of potatoes were highly respected. She was critical of people who dreamed of escaping the "modern world."

They do not understand an existence where romantic ideas of the sea cannot be tolerated, nor do they understand our intuitive feeling for land and water, our preoccupation with rain, wind and frost. They cannot accept the extent to which the sea is our rising and falling stock-market, our food and shelter. Our old people have been beating to windward all their lives. They know that suffering is part of the human condition. This does not make them hostile, but rather sympathetic with the suffering of all others. Isolated from one another most of their lives, they share no conventional manners; they behave naturally, according to their emotions and frequently their manners are truly aristocratic. They have learned from early childhood to respect other humans and they expect the same respect for their humanity.

So Ella began to write more about the people she met and the stories they told her of their own lives. Some she identified fully, but even those described only by a first name, real or fictitious, might still be identified by people old enough to remember. She would say on the radio, "Now I am proud to introduce you to some of my Newfoundland friends and neighbours." "Around the Island for 75 Cents" is an amusing account of one young Labradorian's long and resourceful Christmas trip home from one village to another nearby, and "The Zeppelin over Famish Gut" is based on a story recounted by another old friend. The older people from villages around Bonne Bay told her of the early settlers, as in "Hugh McKenzie's Grand-daughter" and "Nan Harding Remembers." She wrote delightedly about "More of My Favourite Uncles," using this traditional term to express the wish that they, and her "Aunts," "did, in truth, belong to us in blood relationship, and at the same time to infer the respect in which we hold them." "Jim Shears of Rocky Harbour" and "Cantankerous Uncle George" describe two such uncles. And she was half in love with an adventurous Englishman "Victor Campbell: Explorer, Sailor, Farmer," who made his home on the banks of Harry's River.[22]

Not long after the death of her parents in the 1950s, Ella decided to spend the summer in Woody Point and wrote of the experience in "Getting My Bearings Again." She was once more entranced by the sheer beauty of Bonne Bay and the surrounding hills, and soon began to dream of having her own place in this lovely village. A few years later, this started to become a reality. In "Building My House on the Hill," she describes how she found the perfect spot for a cottage, and how her plans befuddled the local builders. But that was nothing compared to the troubles getting connected to the power supply, as she tells in "The Electricity Kerfuffle." In the late spring of 1963, she finally settled in, and soon found herself looking after two kittens, descendants of the famous feline depicted in "Jinny-Down-By-The-Bow." She described her early years in Woody Point in four pieces set around the seasons of the year: "Spring: Back Home Again," "A Summer of Wonders," "Autumn in the Bay," and "Winter on the Hill." She worked with others to further the idea of establishing a national park around Bonne Bay and was delighted to see it develop, with the new trails that she loved to hike.

Ella delighted in her rediscovery of the people and landscapes of western and northern Newfoundland. As the road along the west coast north to St. Anthony was being built, she walked the old coastal mail track, a journey revealed in "Down to Sally's Cove," where she met three remarkable brothers. In "The New Road Northward," Ella observes the changes brought to those who could now, for the first time, quickly and safely reach the cottage hospital in Norris Point, and continue on by car or truck to the railhead in Deer Lake and the many shops in Corner Brook. She would often return to the rivers to fish for trout and salmon, as in one memorable occasion she described in "Centennial on the Upper Humber." And she learned firsthand about the fishing industry, and narrated this experience in "Chasing the Herring."

[22] More about Emma Tapper, the Curlings, the McKenzies, the Hardings, the Shears, and other early settlers of the Bay can be found in my *The Good and Beautiful Bay: A History of Bonne Bay to Confederation and a Little Beyond* (Flanker, 2014).

WRITING APACE AND
RETURNING TO SOCIAL ACTION

ELLA'S FASCINATION for the sea led her, on one occasion, to
regale her radio audience with readings from *The Newfoundland
and Labrador Pilot*. She travelled by steamer along the coastal route
around the Northern Peninsula and down into Notre Dame Bay,
and was intrigued by "The Skipper on the Baie Verte Run," as he
manoeuvred his vessel in and out of the outports along the way.
"When Ships were Ships and not Tin Pots" was based on the re-
collections of roguish Bill Barnes, another seaman. From time to time,
Ella returned to Lewisporte, but found little to remind her of her
childhood days until she returned to Exploits Islands by motor boat,
a journey retold in "Back to Exploits." She retold an amazing story
of shipwreck and survival—one of the earliest recorded along the
west coast—in "Shipwrecked off Green Gardens," and cautiously
recounted the disappearance at sea of a local man in "Murder at Sea:
Or was it?"

In the mid-1950s, Ella had a regular column in *The Western Star*
in which she tackled many topics, including the paving of roads,
women workers in Newfoundland, fisheries science, the dangers of
censorship, the taste of scallops, women leaders from India, and
English humour. She also wrote for the *Atlantic Guardian*, the
Newfoundland Journal of Commerce, the *Family Herald* and *Weekly
Star*, about oil exploration in St. Paul's Inlet, fishing for herring in
Port au Port Bay, electrification of the Humber Valley, and many other

topics of current interest. She often rode her high horse into national issues, and was particularly angry over the international opposition to the seal fishery, as she wrote in "Spring: Back Home Again."

Ella was intrigued by the odd assortment of missionaries who came to Newfoundland in the nineteenth century. Her grandmother often spoke to Ella about the English "parsons" she had known during her long life in Notre Dame Bay. Many had a profound influence on the lives of their isolated parishioners, bringing spiritual succour, worldly knowledge, and frequently medical help. "James Lumsden: Parson but no Skipper" and "Out from Greenspond with Julian Moreton" are two of her portraits. The missionaries, she wrote, "were imbued with the passion, rife in Victorian England, to save our souls and 'illuminate our darkness.'" Some wrote about their lives here, sometimes resisting the temptation to "embellish their experiences to make them all the more wondrous or heroic to their European readers." But so little was said at that time of Newfoundland women that they might as well not have existed. One medical man's diary entry for October 18, 1877, reads, "Gale from the northeast. Married." He did not even record his bride's first name. As Ella wrote, "It is shameful that these men so rarely related the experiences of women, but in those days nobody did, and now it is too late."

During this most productive phase in her Newfoundland writing, the memory of her political experiences and activities in pre-war England bothered her conscience, for she was doing nothing to contribute to a world once again threatened by war. So in 1965, she joined the Voice of Women, founded five years earlier,[23] and quickly became its national vice-president. VOW members—about 6000 of them before long—were then very active lobbying government officials, attending peace conferences, and publishing broadsides against nuclear testing. They were inclined, Ella remembered later, to regard themselves as "superior and to despise many politicians and statesmen. It seems to me that we were living out feminism

---

[23] The Canadian Voice of Women for Peace is regarded as the oldest national feminist peace group in Canada.

without knowing it. We refused to be silenced because we were women. And we engaged in political action, believing we could use our experience to influence the men to support the peace and anti-nuclear movement." Oddly, within this peace movement, Ella and her good friends, Kay MacPherson and Muriel Duckworth, were sometimes referred to as "the big guns." Ella stayed with VOW for a few years, but found it hard to take the long rambling discussions and the frequent clashes between the leaders, with their strong personalities and opinions. In later years, she would frequently fulminate against political knavery and inaction, swearing at what she saw as ongoing stupidity. She would rant about an approaching collapse of society, while smoking furiously or roaming around her house munching on whatever scraps were to hand.

In 1968, Ella presented a brief to the Royal Commission on the Status of Women in Canada, the only individual to do so. Commenting on the loneliness and isolation faced by rural women, she said, "The world has changed, for women as well as for men, and as long as the community relies on only half its members for meaningful participation in public life, so long will the community suffer." She argued for family-planning clinics and for TV and radio programs on health, child care, and consumer information, particularly for women in rural areas, "caught up in a vicious circle founded on apathy and ignorance."[24] Years later, her brief was quoted in the citation for the Persons Award,[25] which was presented to her by the governor general in 1980. She was also praised for her work to make children "conscious of social issues."

[24] In her submission to the Royal Commission she wrote, "The situation of women in Newfoundland is that of inferior beings in a society of underprivileged citizens." When The Globe and Mail (Sept 17, 1968) and other newspapers reported that she had called Newfoundland women "inferior beings," she was horrified and demanded retractions. The Canadian Press issued a correction, followed by an offer from Chief of Bureau Jack Brayley to come "to Woody Point and face the sophisticates hard-nosed and bare-knuckled."

[25] The Governor General's Awards in Commemoration of the Persons Case were created in 1979 to mark the fiftieth anniversary of the ground-breaking Persons Case, which changed the course of history for women in Canada.

A last word on her thinking about the struggle for the rights of women.

> I always considered myself the intellectual equal to any male I knew. I soon found out that what was called my feminine instincts gave me an advantage when it came to understanding problems we all faced—political, economic, emotional. I knew many women whose family circumstances belied the very notion of "women's place." They were women who ran the house, brought up the children and provided physical and emotional nourishment while, in time left over, looked after animals and dug gardens—because their men were fishing or working in the lumber camps. Many Newfoundland women can say "These were our mothers and grandmothers." Their liberation came with running water, electricity, family allowances, more than from a change in the men's mode of work. Those of us who have gone further, having started with advantages, have a different view. Our situation is clear: the injustice is enormous and destructive, and we are impatient with those who cannot see that.

As she aged, she accepted that "no revolution can bring back our chances. All we can do now is to understand what happened to us in the light of new discoveries and so feel less guilty, less alone. What we can do is to support and look for new life-styles, not anymore being ashamed to rely on others, help the young by thinking, talking, writing about what they are trying to live."

THAT FINE SUMMER AND FINAL REFLECTIONS

IN 1976, Ella began a work she had been mulling over for some time: "Thinking of my grandsons, one day I invented a real old-fashioned grandfather whose dead wife, without knowing it, had been a liberated woman. That called for a grandchild, and in no time Mahala appeared in my head and took over." The place was the Bay of Exploits, the time around mid-century. Eleven-year-old Mahala Jacobs is a head-strong girl who spends the summer with her grandfather and learns to do all the things girls traditionally don't do. *That Fine Summer*[26] recounts the adventures Malie has with Obadiah, a part-Inuit boy from Labrador who is having a hard time being accepted in the community. As they row their small boat around the bay with its many islands, they learn about friendship, self-reliance, and tolerance of others. Malie listens raptly as Grandfather tells stories about her grandmother, a strong and adventurous woman she clearly takes after. Reviewers commented especially on the "rich linguistic flavour" and the strong sense of place in this portrait of a young feminist in the making.

Perhaps Ella saw herself reflected in Mahala as "for a long time she lay, feeling in her bones the strangeness of the middle of the night on a little Island in the immensity of sea and sky. She knew she would

---

[26] First published in 1980 by Jesperson Press. A second edition was issued by Breakwater in 1995, and was reprinted in 1998 by Prentice-Hall for use in Ontario schools.

never forget this as long as she lived." There was another children's book in which Ella played a part, this time as a photographed character rather than a writer behind the text. This was *All Aboard! A cross-Canada adventure*,[27] in which young Kate makes her way across the country by train, starting in Woody Point. Here she has been visiting her grandmother, played by Ella, more or less as herself.

That Fine Summer was Ella's one big success in getting her stories published in book form. For years she tried to find a way to bring them together, and though she often asked writerly friends for advice, nothing quite seemed to work. She wrote reports on various Canadian and international conferences, and produced, on commission, a concise biography of a well-known Newfoundland music educator.[28] Even as her health was rapidly failing, in part because of a life-long smoking habit, she carried with her the typescripts of a handful of her stories which she was hoping to publish. I suspect she had forgotten how many other good stories she had written.

Looking back a few years before she died of heart failure in late 1985, she wrote:

> I cannot now join together the parts separated by blanks that I have been unable to think about or probe. This is not part of my failure in life or my stupid-ignorant choices and misconceptions. The parts just do not fit. There are too many jagged edges, as if part of a broken pot had crumbled leaving a nasty and permanent gap. Yet I can turn life around the way I turn the pot, so that I can enjoy its "wholeness," knowing full well it is flawed.

As a merchant's daughter, she had an air of noblesse oblige, though that did not seem to prevent her from becoming accepted by

---

[27] Written and photographed by Barbara O'Kelly and Beverley Allinson, an OWL book published by Greey de Pencier Books, Toronto, 1979.

[28] *Music Then and Now: A Tribute to Sr. Loretto Croke, Pioneer Music Educator.* Music Council of the Newfoundland Teachers' Association, 1980.

the local Bonne Bay community, even if for some an amusing outsider who lived up on the hill. She might be accused of being patronising in the way she recorded local speech, but she did not laugh at outport Newfoundlanders; rather she worked to share their humour and adventures.

For her sons, she was a free spirit, quite unlike the mothers of the other boys. She seemed pleased when, at the age of about fourteen, I began to call her "Ella," which says something about our relationship. As we boys grew and left for boarding school and university, never again to live with her save for short visits, she treated us as friends, took pride in what we were doing, and was rarely censorious of our mistakes. That did not stop her from sometimes making life difficult for her independent-minded daughters-in-law. In later years, she found it difficult to confide to others her fears and worries, especially about her sons' families.

Had Ella lived into today's world, she would no doubt have had much more to say about the way Newfoundlanders have added to the garbage of the Anthropocene—plastics and other techno-junk. She did write of her desire for better protection and preservation of forest, fish, and flora, and though she read and agreed with Rachel Carson, she died before the idea of "sustainability" became prominent and before the widespread recognition of impending climate and environmental disasters.

In what follows, a few of her stories are exactly as she wrote them. Most I have assembled from her journals and correspondence, adjoined to scraps of text left among her generally undated files, and occasionally adding something of my own. It might seem to the reader of these stories that Ella was living in a rather romantic dreamland, for many avoid mention of hard economic and social conditions. However, she was well aware of the avarice and jealousy found in most any small community, and her newspaper columns and her writings for the Voice of Women were commonly critical of government policies. But poverty and humour are familiar bedfellows, and she preferred to emphasize the latter.

To anyone who would tell her a yarn, Ella always listened as eagerly as did the radio audience to her own stories. As she said, "Every time I hear a good story, I feel rich, so now I want to share them with you, because they are a part of our magnificent culture and heritage."

HER
NEWFOUNDLAND
STORIES:

~

LOMOND

PART 2

HER
NEWFOUNDLAND
STORIES:

LOMOND

NO PLACE FOR A WOMAN?

Growing up in Lewisporte, in northeastern Newfoundland, Ella Manuel acquired a love of fishing that stayed with her for the rest of her life. Here she tells of days on the rivers of western Newfoundland and of her encounters with men who could not accept the idea of a woman fishing expertly. On the Lomond River she glories in the thrill of fly fishing and first hears of the remarkable Emma Tapper, who was completely at home on any river.

JUST ABOUT dusk one evening in late August, two men in fishing clothes sat next to me in the coffee room of a Newfoundland inn. They had been fishing and were rounding off the day discussing their luck. Now I like to fish and I like listening to fishing talk, so I deliberately eavesdropped.

"I've been fishing the Lomond River," said one, "and I had a queer experience in Simpson's pool. I had fished hard two hours or more and hadn't even seen a salmon. Just as I was going to pull out, I saw someone coming down the trail. I waited long enough for him to rig his rod and wade out just above me. Would you believe me, it was a woman. She cast two or three times and hooked a good-sized fish. When she had landed it, I went up to her and said, 'I've been fishing this pool for hours and haven't even seen a fish.' She just shrugged her shoulders. 'There's plenty of salmon in this pool, if you know where to look for them.'"

"I'll be darned," said his companion, "Do you know who she was?"

"No idea. She just picked up her rod and fish and moved off."

I wondered who she was too. Whenever I met an acquaintance who fished the Lomond, I would ask hopefully, "Do you know any women who fish the river?" and they all told me they hadn't seen such a phenomenon. Later, I discovered the mystery woman was Emma Tapper, who could cast a long line before she could read and write. After school she used to walk five miles to the river and five miles back just to get an hour's fishing. Over the years she became my close friend and fishing companion.

In a country where women's accepted place is in the home, the idea of a woman knowing anything about catching salmon was intriguing. I didn't know about male chauvinism in those days, but I soon learned. One of the most maddening statements I've ever heard was that women are not and never can be born fishermen. They learn to love it only through some man—if he happens to love fishing! That statement came from the pen of a venerable fly fisherman in England. All I can say is he ought to come over here.

One time I was on Portland Creek, a river far north in Newfoundland unfrequented by any but the most ardent angler. This particular day, I was doing quite well for myself, all alone and minding my own business, in a pool down by the tidal waters. Then along came an angler whom I knew and who, up to that moment, I had respected.

"Have a look at that fast water, out there between the boulders," he commanded.

I had a look.

"Think you can wade out there?" he asked.

"Sure," I said, "but why should I? I'm satisfied here, unless maybe you want to fish this pool." I was leaning over backwards to be generous and show good fishing manners. "It's not that," he replied, "but I've been looking at that water for two days now, and I'm pretty sure there's fish in it."

"Why don't you try?" I asked.

He said that the local guides had told him that nobody, but nobody, ever fished there. Salmon never lay in that pool.

"I'd look pretty silly fishing out there after what they said," he continued, "but if you went out and tried, nobody would think anything of it. They wouldn't expect anything else from a woman."

I was, for a moment, frozen by his cynicism. Then I got mad. I waded out into the fast water. I didn't even take a good look at the pool. I just cast my line. Once—twice—and the third time, just on the retrieve, I saw a fat salmon come up with a whirl and take my fly. Still too angry to have room for excitement, I went about calmly playing the fish. Then I brought him in to the beach and laid him at the angler's feet.

"Here's your salmon," I told him.

And would you believe it? He went around telling everyone that I had taken a salmon out of a pool where nobody else had ever caught one, but only because he had told me to fish there! Even long afterwards, guides on that river would say to a new angler, "Oh, yes, Ella caught the first salmon out of that pool, but of course, Bill advised her to fish there."

Many years later, after I'd been away earning a living, I returned to the Lomond River, to me, one of the loveliest in the entire world. About seventy miles north of Corner Brook, it lies in a deeply wooded valley surrounded by overhanging cliffs. It is only five miles from head to mouth, but five miles of endless variety: the swift sparkle over green and red pebbles, hurtling white foam over a twenty-foot falls, the widening and deepening to the blackest depth at Dynamite Pool, and the placid rippling in the long Steady. Altogether a most satisfying river.

The night I arrived, it was dark. I woke at daybreak to see a robin perched on a tree by the open cabin door, singing with sheer delirium, and a woodpecker hammering in rhythm. In five minutes I was on the trail. Mist covered the hilltops, but small patches of blue came through with the promise of a fair day. The river splashed along with its high, thin sound, rising in volume as I approached through the tunnel of evergreens where the smell from yesterday's heat lingered. I was going down to the pool below the falls where, if you're lucky, you will see a salmon leap high and hurl himself up the falls into the silk smooth water above. This was the pool—long, rocky and turbulent—where the salmon lay, waiting for the proper water conditions to leap the falls, and where one could always fish with plenty of elbow room.

There came toward me on the trail the river warden, greeting me as a friend properly should, who hadn't seen me for years. "Well, you're back. I thought it was about time." As if I were part of the landscape that accidentally got moved.

He said, "Do you mind the steady where you used to fish? Well, salmon have been moving up river three, four days now, so it should be good upstream a bit."

I hurried along the overgrown trail, criss-crossed with rotting windfalls to snare your feet and spider webs to trail over your face, and always in your ear the purling water of the hidden stream. Then suddenly the trail breaks out on the bank, and there you are, on the Steady, where the river widens imperceptibly and flows shallow over shining pebbles. Trees on either bank overhang, and you have to be careful not to cast a shadow on the water, nor to catch your hook in a back-cast.

It was almost with awe that I looked up and down that stretch of water, as if I was looking for a sign from the place that had stood so long in my mind for peace and solace and continuity. I scooped up a bit of colour floating by and held in my hand the red gleaming bud of a juniper with a crown of green needles. Now, I knew that the juniper tree, old as time and shaky, was still around the bend, still shading the pool, spreading its branches, very much alive. And as I lifted a small dry-fly out of its box and tied it to my leader, I heard the bittern honk. I'd seen him first, ten years ago, winging up the same meadow, only one bittern, always in the same place.

Then a fish splashed, with a tremendous sound in the silence, and

I turned around in time to see the ripples he left behind. I cast out across the gin-clear water and marvellously, after all those years, I put the line out clean, with a little U-loop at the end before the fly snapped and dropped silently into the stream. I let the fly float, retrieved it and moved a step, over and over for an hour or more. Nothing but the silky soft murmur of the river past my boots and the snap of the line.

The sun climbed higher. The shadows of the clouds moved across the water. Robins as big as hawks flew overhead, and sparrows big as robins perched in the trees. A beaver swam across the stream, not ten feet from me, and a woodpecker hammered out a fast military tattoo on a hollow fir tree. A fisherman appeared on the river bank, and I moved along to give him a stretch to cast over, as we exchanged experiences of the day.

We agreed that we really didn't upset the balance of salmon with what we caught, but something did. The paper company was now running pulp logs down this lovely river, gouging out the sandy bottoms and depositing rotting bark. And wasn't it against nature to build dams cutting off the natural water supply? Then we saw how high was the sun and how clear the water, so we reeled in our lines, knowing that even the stupidest salmon would not now be fooled into thinking our flies were real. So, sun-soaked, muscles aching and hungry, we said to each other, "Better luck tomorrow."

I have put this down, about the morning on the river, not because it was so exciting, but because it is so characteristic of mornings on Newfoundland rivers, full of flavour, colour and, for me, the sounds of home.

A CHANCE MEETING,
A NEW IDEA

Some years earlier, as Ella was thinking of ways to earn a living in western Newfoundland, she had a conversation with some fly-fishermen from the southern United States. This might have been one impetus for the sports-fishing venture she later developed at Killdevil Lodge in Lomond.

THERE IS an old saying that misery loves company. We were a miserable crowd that day in Moncton as the rain poured down, and the planes stayed on the tarmac. I had just left Newfoundland that September of 1945 to return to New England, where I was to spend the winter. Now we faced a night's delay instead of a few comfortable hours of flying. A big sunburned man stood beside me when he heard the announcement: "Sorry. The flight to Boston has been cancelled. You'd best catch the next train." He swore softly under his breath, then, glancing at me, said, "Oh, excuse me." We both laughed and the ice was broken.

"That's a fine-looking rod case you have there." I said. "May I look inside?"

"Sure," he replied and opened the case. When I appeared to show an intelligent interest, he said with a gleam of real friendship in his eye, "Say, do you fish too?"

"Why, yes," I replied, waiting breathlessly for this opportunity. "I live in Newfoundland, so naturally I fish."

"You do? Holy Smoke! Hey fellers," and with an all-embracing gesture to the lobby, "come and see the gal who fishes in Newfoundland."

They came, half-a-dozen of them, and the questions they asked nearly floored me, but I had made up my mind to sell them a bill of goods.

"How did you hear about fishing in Newfoundland," I asked.

"Oh," replied one, "some fishing guy wrote a story about General Marshall and General Arnold fishing a river down there. Say, did you ever fish that one?"

"No, but I know the man who wrote the story. And as for fishing, you should see the Lower Humber in August. Now, that's fishing, gentlemen. Last summer one day in the Steady Brook pool one fisherman had a twenty-pounder on his line, while his wife on the opposite bank played one equally large. In fact, once they were both landed, within twenty-five minutes of being hooked, hers was five pounds heavier than his."

Well, they just stared at me. They'd heard such stories before, of course, but they had never seen anyone in the flesh who had been witness to such fantastic goings-on. As we boarded the waiting train and settled down to four hours before the connection to Boston, questions began again.

"What is the average-size salmon?"

"Well, you don't boast about anything under twenty pounds. Of course, grilse come smaller and there are quite a few of them caught."

"What size hooks do you use?"

"Number six, generally."

"Streamer flies?"

"Nope. Only for trout."

"How much backing?"

On and on I floundered, thinking that the next question would be my last, and my abysmal ignorance would finally be exposed. So to play safe, I began to ask them, "Where have you been fishing now?"

"Up in New Brunswick. But the weather has been rotten and the water too high. We got only two salmon between the lot of us. Of course, we don't mind spending money, but it makes a guy sort of mad to spend five hundred dollars and not have the fun of landing at least a grilse."

"Five hundred dollars!" I said, holding on to my seat. "How long were you there? A month?"

"No, about ten days. But you see, what with cabins $18 a day and supplies, and boats and cigarettes and a bottle or two of liquor. And, of course, presents for our wives. And we bought a hundred dollars' worth of flies tied by a local fellow."

All this time I had been making mental calculations: five hundred times six is three thousand... Can't be—not three thousand in ten days. Why, that's nonsense. I started again and, carefully checking the noughts on my fingers, decided the amount was three thousand dollars, without a doubt. Oh well, there is no accounting for the actions of the rich. One man ran several grocery shops, another was a real-estate dealer in a small town. That much I gathered from the conversation.

One man said, "We used to buy all sorts of things in Canada to take home to our families. This time all we could find was cups and saucers. What do you sell in Newfoundland that we can't get anywhere else?"

I thrust out my arm encased in a beautiful Nonia sweater.[29] They were impressed. I pulled from my case a pair of slippers made by the Grenfell people from blanketing and embroidered with flowers. They were fulsome in their praise, and one wanted to buy the slippers from me. I described the many other things we made: Nonia tweeds, Grenfell socks and gloves, moccasins, sealskin mittens and boots, hooked rugs and panels, bone and wood carvings. The prices they couldn't believe. "Nine dollars for that sweater. It's worth twenty-five."

[29] NONIA, the Newfoundland Outport Nursing and Industrial Association, was founded in 1920 to improve health services in outport communities by raising money from the sale of hand-knit garments to pay the salaries of nurses.

I began to think that their desire to visit Newfoundland was half-compounded of wanting to catch a salmon and half of the love of finding bargains. "You could make thousands of dollars on that stuff," they told me. "Everyone would want to buy something to take to his family."

Then one of the men asked, "Say, couldn't we go down there next summer, around the end of July, maybe? How about you giving us the names of people who could put us up?"

"I wish I could. I'd love to have you visit Newfoundland, but there are very few places catering to people like you, and they are full for the whole summer. There just aren't many cabins on the fishing rivers."

That was beyond them. "What! No cabins and nowhere to stay. We don't want the Ritz you know. Outdoor toilets suit us. For Heaven's sake, here you are with everything a fisherman could want, and plenty of us willing to pay for it. But nowhere to go. Why?"

That was the question I couldn't answer, the question that floored me completely.

And then I had an idea....

MY KILLDEVIL DAYS

In 1944, having spent the war years in New England, Ella returned to Newfoundland, a divorced mother of two small boys. She met American sportsman Lee Wulff, who was thinking about setting up fly-fishing camps in north-western Newfoundland, and needed a good base to start from. Encouraged by him and by her earlier conversation with the fishermen from the southern US, in 1946 she suddenly decided to start a sports-fishing venture. In Lomond, the once busy logging town in Bonne Bay, now a quiet campground in Gros Morne National Park, she set up a summer-time operation called Killdevil Lodge. Though it did not thrive for long, she gloried in the beauty of her surroundings, as she tells here.

THAT FIRST summer, I rented a big house in the bottom of the East Arm of Bonne Bay, thirty miles from Deer Lake, the nearest town on the railroad. It was a wonderfully peaceful house, for we were quite alone except for the tiny village of Lomond, a short walk away. Across the bay was the massive form of Killdevil Mountain, heaving itself out of the water to a height of nearly twenty-five hundred feet, and behind the house a pasture of ten acres sloping up to hills, dark green and brooding.

Twenty years earlier, Lomond had been a bustling logging community, with a large sawmill by the water. I asked my friend

Emma Tapper about the village and the twelve families who still lived there. "Who, for Heaven's sake, has that bright blue wall on the outside of their house?"

"Wonderful, isn't it?" she replied. "You won't see a thing like that everywhere! I'll tell you about it. All these were company houses, and when the company went out of business, the people stayed on, paying a small rent of anything from ten to twenty dollars a month, although there wasn't much employment handy. Then, when the pulp and paper company bought the place, lock, stock and barrel, they let everyone stay on at the same small rent, because they needed men to cut the pulpwood, and the people, you can believe me, were glad to work, being near enough to starvation.

"Well," Em continued, "after the paper company had cut all the wood around here and pulled out, they finally sold the houses. Elias bought the house you're talking about for two hundred dollars—two rooms upstairs, two down and a back kitchen. He sold the back kitchen to his brother; just sawed it off, towed it up the lane and set it down on the edge of the woods. His brother hasn't got round to sheathing it up yet, so there it stands — blue wall with pots and pans hanging on it."

"And the house with the boxes of nasturtiums on the roof?" I asked.

"That's Lizzie's. In the early morning a week or so ago the goats got in her garden and ate the whole works. They were commencing on the nasturtiums when Lizzie woke and drove them out. So next day she had her son put the boxes on the roof, out of harm's way. Nice touch, isn't it?"

"But they were hard times," Em continued. "During the Depression there was absolutely no work and damn little dole—about a dollar and eighty cents a month, as I recall. In the winter after we'd moved, I came out here to pack up our house, and I stayed with Lizzie. I remember that all we had to eat, clear of bread and margarine, was salt herring left from the fall catch. Every Friday afternoon, they'd take a net full of fish up to the brook where they'd anchor it in the water to soak, and then bring home the net-full they'd left the week before."

One evening, Lizzie came home and said she had seen a big black animal creeping down to the brook. Off went the men with their guns and came home with a bear carcass. "Well," said Em, "by that time everyone was so sick of herring that they fought over the meat. When we were at the table that night, hardly civilized enough to wait for the Blessing, so hungry were we, Lizzie said, 'I wonder if that's the bear that ate Ikey Morris,' and we threw the lot in the slop can."

The house I rented had been built around 1920 for the Scottish manager of the lumber company. Named by him St. Tecla, it sat solid, four square on its concrete foundation, rising three stories to a gently sloping roof. A narrow platform, approached from inside the house through a skylight, was built on the highest peak of the roof and edged with low-carved pickets and a handrail, like the widows' walks on the old Nantucket whaler homes.

A white pillared veranda overhung with a tall birch tree sheltered a broad oak door, over which was a delicate fan-light. The rooms were square, high-ceilinged and with at least two windows that flooded light over white walls and birch floors. The garden was sprinkled with English daisies, lupins, Canterbury bells, delphinium and larkspur, and under the birches, grey-blue violets grew on long stems. Beyond the garden was a fringe of spruce and fir on the edge of a terrace, which fell abruptly to the mouth of the Lomond River. So we had river and sea at our front door.

The Simpson family, for whom the house was built, must have enjoyed what was for that period sybaritic comfort: central heating—the old coal furnace still in the basement, and huge iron radiators in each room—electricity from their own Delco generator, and water from a spring hidden in the hills half a mile away that gushed from the taps in the second-floor bathroom. If the one possession they left behind—a massive, handmade mahogany wardrobe—could be taken as an indication, the furnishings were of the very best. Unhappily, they did not long enjoy their comfort. By the late 1930s, the mill had closed for lack of business, Simpson had died, and his family had left for good. So I took over the empty house, changed its name to Killdevil Lodge and began a sports-fishing business.

It was quite a struggle to provide food and drink for the people who came over the next few years to fish the Lomond and Upper Humber rivers. Cooks, cleaners, and handymen came and went, and making arrangements to transport my guests around was never easy. One day, a telegram alerted me that my party was arriving at Deer Lake by train in a couple of hours. I jumped in my jeep and drove as fast as I could the long, dusty dirt road to the railway station. At one stretch that allowed a glimpse of the town and railroad, I saw the puff of smoke from a departing train, and drove faster those last few miles. At the station, I rushed out of breath to collect my guests, but the platform was empty.

"Bert," I asked the station master, "did you see any sports get off here?"

"No," he replied. "Were they coming by today's train?"

"Yes. I just saw it pull away from the station."

"Ah, no, my dear. That was yesterday's train, today's is due tomorrow."

Save for growing up in my family hotel in Lewisporte, surrounded by people coming and going all throughout the year, I had had no experience in hosting guests and dealing with their needs and wants. So after a few years, the venture fizzled out, and I turned to other things. But, oh, those marvellous summer days in Lomond, when my two boys were youngsters.

One day the wind, which always rises at dawn and sleeps at mid-day, was whipping the trees and carrying the sound of water slapping into the shallow cove. Emma and I mended the fence, turned over the new-mown hay and transplanted lupins so that they would spread along the edge of the terrace. All morning long, as we worked, we could hear my boys shouting with joy in the cove, as they rescued floating logs in our boat, with *Galloping Ghost* painted on her stern.

The sea gradually smoothed its wrinkles to such clarity that, looking from the hilltop, we could see where the river's muddy bottom merged into pebbles and salt-water seaweed. A gull poised, plummeted in a steep dive and rose with fish in its mouth. An osprey closed in with a swoop and snatched the fish. A bald eagle from its nest on the cliff beyond the river flew over us and sailed across the scars on Killdevil to the lush green of the forest.

An hour later, on the mirror of the bay, the oars of the *Galloping Ghost* rose and dipped as the boys set out to hunt for minerals. In the boat were fishing rods, a matchbox full of hooks and flies that Jonathan had tied with his red hair for dressing, a knapsack for rocks, which must be added to an already enormous collection, and a package of cookies to ward off starvation. The boys were arguing, their voices coming to us clearly, about their first port of call. Then they rowed round the point and out of sight.

Em and I laughed as we stretched out on the warm, splintery wood of the wharf at the end of the village, our chins barely over the edge so we could look down into the clear water, down to the myriad of fish in the seaweed weaving around the sunken piers. When we had been still long enough to blend into the fishes' landscape, little connors ventured to the surface to blow bubbles. Tiny fish with movements imperceptible as nerve thrills came to us, arrow straight, as if they went through air, and the wonderfully magnifying power of water etched them larger than life. When they reached the surface we could actually see their bones.

Em's foot nudged mine. I looked at her without moving and, following her glance, saw that what I had taken to be a shadow was a sculpin lying absolutely still against a pier and gazing up at us with unblinking, wicked eyes. A school of porpoises rolled lazily past the point and into the bay. Em said, "Maybe the boys will be frightened." So we walked along the deserted beach over slippery kelp to the low cliff on which stood a tiny white lighthouse. The sea was deep blue, except where Killdevil's reflection streaked it with grey, green and beige. A cloud gathered and sailed slowly toward Birchy Mountain past a distant waterfall, a thick white streak exposed in velvet sage and green. Beyond us was the *Galloping Ghost*, neatly beached and tied to a boulder.

The sun was now getting hot, and a faint breeze stirred. Voices, fleeting and light, floated over the constant raucous cry of the terns and gulls. The bald eagle left the eastern cliff, with long graceful down-swooping wings and sailed across the scars and patches of green spruce. A three-quarter moon hung in a cloudless sky. The sea was deep blue, save for the reflections streaking it green, grey, beige. Some twenty small terns jostled each other over a shoal of mussels. They wheeled and splashed and slithered, but when they were silent there was only the rustling of some small bird in the long grass.

It was dark when we pulled the *Galloping Ghost* to her mooring and half-carried the tired boys to the house. We slept to the sound of the river and the wind stirring the leaves, and next morning, seated at the big kitchen table drawn up to the window so that we could view the expanse of cleared fields beyond the house, Jonathan said, "Oh, look at that big black dog."

"That's not a dog. That's a bear!" Tony's voice shook.

I laughed not bothering to look, but Em by the window said, "He's right. That's a bear, a young one."

There was a sudden scuffle. I shouted, "Tony! Where are you going?"

"To the barn for my gun," and Vicky, the half-grown dachshund, streaked through the door after him. Em tore after Vicky, and Jonathan, with one look at me, made himself scarce.

When I had convinced myself that all must be well, despite my harrowing fear, they returned crestfallen. "We lost him by the river bank," Tony said, out of breath. "Then we had to hunt for Vicky, and we found a nest with a little bird hanging out of it." He was thrilled to watch as Em skilfully separated with a knife a pair of baby yellowhammers, born Siamese twins.

Laughter from the kitchen meant that Em was spinning one of her many yarns, full of humour and delicate perception. As she talked, her eyes would shine and her face reflected inward pleasure. When one night I could not sleep for the lunatic crying of a loon, Em said, at breakfast, "It was the female. She was calling her old man the whole night long, but he paid her no heed. He was down by the river having a high old time with the twillicks[30]—I saw him totter home at daylight, and while I had my eye peeled so that he wouldn't sneak by without my seeing, I had a ring-side seat for the rabbit dance."

"Rabbit dance?" Jonathan squeaked.

"Sure. There were hundreds of them congregated by the woodpile, all doing a kind of square dance," and Em solemnly promised that should such a miracle occur again, she would wake the boys to see.

She was a good listener too, unfailingly appreciative of the amusing remarks of the children. Five-year-old Jonathan said, "Em is the kindest person I ever knew in my whole life." How the boys loved it when she presented them with a bat lying at the bottom of a mason jar. "I caught him last night when I was out chopping kindling."

Sometimes at night, the boys and I watched entranced while our landscape was transmuted by the catalyst of moonlight to something strange and movingly beautiful. It was as if we had been transported to the mountains of Kashmir, and there came to me a memory buried since my own childhood.

We had camped on the seaward shore of an island a mile from the town in Notre Dame Bay, where I grew up. At night we built a fire of driftwood so slow in burning out that my companions went to the tent, while I was left to tend the dying fire. I fell asleep, for I do not know how long, but I remember that when I woke, I was in a new country. The moon, invisible when I fell asleep, was high in the sky. The stars had faded, all but one ice-blue unwinking planet, and the lights on the far shore were extinguished. I lay with my arms outspread, clutching the earth as it moved slowly, carrying me in its orbit. I felt I was actually sailing across the black of empty space. And for many years, walled off by the sheer mechanics of living, I had forgotten this ecstasy until I saw my own children caught up in it.

That was the never-to-be forgotten magic of summer in Lomond.

[30] A Newfoundland name for long-legged shore birds.

WOODY
POINT

GETTING MY BEARINGS AGAIN

A few years after her Lomond venture and when Killdevil Lodge had been sold to the Anglican Church, Ella Manuel returned to Bonne Bay to rediscover its beauty. This time she decided to explore the South Arm from Woody Point, once styled the "capital of the West Coast."

THERE WAS rain early this morning, drumming on the roof of the house I had rented for the summer. Through the noise I could hear birds singing like mad, a cow lowing and, best of all, a motorboat putting out to sea. When I rose and opened the door, the smell of new-mown hay, damp earth, balsam trees, and good fresh manure was ambrosial.

The first voice I heard this morning was my neighbour's calling to his neighbour with the high, thin voice our men develop for shouting over the wind. He called, "The bay is full of squid-squalls this morning—signs of fish, they say." Squid-squalls are little jelly fish, and indeed the bay was simply heaving with them. The second man said, "I heard tell of that sign, too, but last year we had plenty of fish without the squid-squalls."

I called to my neighbour, "What sort of a day will it be?" And he answered, "Well, now, me maid, I don't know what to say about today. 'Tis a proper wind for rain, and there's mist up on the Tablelands.

But the radio said, fine and warm. Best you watch the sky!"

I did. Mist in shreds. Mist in patches. Mist filling the hollow between the Tablelands and the curiously shaped peak they call the Pickatenny Reef. I thought it strange to call a peak a reef until one day I was leafing through some old *National Geographic* magazines and saw the picture of my reef—but in the Canary Islands. The Peak of Tenerife! And across the arm the corrugated hill is called Gibraltar. Many an old seaman had put into this bay after leaving the Mediterranean and the Canaries, and what more natural than to name these hills for their doubles, there across the Atlantic.

A doctor who had moved here many years ago from Ontario told me, "When they asked me to come to Woody Point back in 1915, they said I could choose one of two vacant houses, but would have to do so immediately since there were so many people wanting them. And in the late fall nearly every house had two families living in it—people moving in from the coast to fish for herring.

"All along the main road," he continued, "were big shops, and I remember how surprised my wife and I were at the variety of things we could buy, goods you wouldn't find anywhere outside St. John's. Local merchants here used to import directly from Halifax and the Old Country food, clothing and furniture, and the people all had money to buy what they wanted. Oh, they had comfort in those day— before the terrible fire of 1922 that took nearly everything along the road clear down to the Haliburton house." Now, years later along the same road, there were several three-storey houses with hardwood floors, marble-topped mantles and stained-glass windows, giving the village an air of comfort and serenity.

I walked down through the meadow to breakfast in the little cafe and bar that hangs out over the water and gives a heavenly view. In what is really the hub of the village, men were already drifting in for a beer, having accomplished hours of work since sunrise.

Bill came tearing into the pub looking for his jigger. "Can't find me jigger anywhere. Wonder if the youngsters took it."

"No, b'y," said John. "I forgot to tell you, I took the line off it to fair up the chimbley I'm building."

Then George arrived and announced that the Simms boys got nineteen mackerel in their net that morning. I asked if they had far to go to set their net.

"Far?" exclaimed George, "Far? No, maid, they ties the net to the leg of the kitchen stove and just hauls her in when they get up in the marnin. Wonderful way to fish."

A stranger came in to enquire about sending a telegram. The answer? "Go down to the new office, down there, not up to the old one. They're all capsized up there." Nobody laughed. Later, I discovered that they were in the process of moving to the new office, and I can think of no better word to describe the chaos they were in.

Later, a woman dropped in, she said, to see if I was comfortable, and if I needed anything, because if I wanted some splits or some wood sawed, her grandson would be only too happy to oblige. Splits—kindling for my wood stove—I did want, but for now I had enough to make a fire under the kettle and brew some tea. I did need help with cleaning the chimney, unused for years.

"For that," she said, "you wants a red devil."

Did I indeed? Then I discovered the devil was a small block of something or other that you put in the stove on top of a hot fire and let it explode up the chimney along with the accumulated soot.

"Only mind you don't have your washing on the line same time," she added.

My visitor, looking through my window at the magnificent sweep of sea and hills said, "My, I remember how my mother used to stand in front of the sink and look out from Wesleyville across the water— the water that stretched, yes, clear to Spain over the Atlantic. She was a tiny, frail woman, my mother, with yellow hair and light blue eyes. When it blew a storm, she would stand there and say, 'That's something man can't tame. Just look at that.' And father would remind her of the men in danger out there, but she wouldn't care. Seems there had to be something in the world that nobody could get the best of, and it was the sea."

As we talked, the mist was creeping down over the green hills, sending little shreds and patches ahead and joining them together until the landscape was blotted out. A moment later, the sun broke through over the hills on the other side of the bay and shone with intensity that warmed you through and through. As the battle between mist and sun went on, we debated as to whether or not we should take in the half-dried sheets from the line.

My friends, who have no fortune, tell me that many on this part of the coast who do made it on smuggling. I like to look at the few surviving old houses with their oak ceilings and their stained-glass windows and wonder how many bottles of contraband spirits it took to build them. And contributing to the building and furnishing of many homes were wrecks. If a vessel went ashore, you'd be silly not to take anything that you and your family were capable of moving. I know a woman who has in her dining room a pedestal on which a massive chair swivels and rocks back and forth—the captain's chair out of some wreck. And all over the place are spoons, forks, knives of silver with the names of long forgotten ships engraved on them, and if you've something the origin of which you want to hide, you always say when asked where you got it, "Oh, I got it out of a wreck." That's warning a plenty that you are to ask no more questions.

I asked Cleve if the water was warm enough for swimming. "Sure. I been in and out of it all summer. Only trouble is I never get time to take my clothes off." Apparently he spends his spare time pulling children out of the bay. He tells it this way.

"The first one I handed out was Jim's boy; he can't be more than two. I was down tying up the dory one evening when I hear the biggest kind of screeching. I knew for sure someone was in the water, but the youngsters were so frightened they couldn't tell me where. So I dove in, boots and all, and what do you suppose? I saw a pair of rubber boots floating under the pier, so I made a grab but missed. Then

I got under the pier and caught the youngster as he drifted in. The air in his boots was floating him upside down. So then I got him up on the pier and I laid him on my knees and rocked him back and forth, head up, then down. When he yelled, I tell you I was some proud. I sang out to his father and told him what happened. Little bugger, if he wasn't down by the wharf again today, all by hisself."

Chris added, "B'ys, there's some changes down in Lomond now, but Lardy is still hanging out there with his new wife."

"You ever hear about when he first got married?" asked John, and not waiting for a reply went on. "Well, you knows Lardy couldn't read very much, and one day he gets a letter from his old girlfriend. He wanted to know what it said, but he didn't want his wife to know. So he took the letter to her to read, but not before he stuffed her ear with tow." This, I soon discovered was the word for cotton wool.

Now it's time for bed—a quarter moon hangs over Pickatenny Reef and on the moon's horn a blue star. The sea is a black mirror—only the white edges of foam in the wake of the motor boat coming back from a day's fishing. I don't suppose there is a more beautiful or more peaceful place in the whole world than this. And I am perfectly certain there are no kinder or more charitable people anywhere. I am reminded of a verse. I wish I knew who wrote it.

"Now on my left a wood, and on my right the sea—the place I am is good, and it is well with me."

BUILDING MY HOUSE
ON THE HILL

Having found in Woody Point the perfect spot, Ella decides to build a house for herself. Little did she know the challenges and frustrations that awaited her as she befuddled the local builders with her plans.

I HADN'T been back but three days before someone asked, "What are you going to do this summer?" And to my utter horror I heard myself saying, "I'm going to build a house." I turned to my friend Emma. "Did you hear what I just said? My God, what came over me?"

I had lived during one summer in a cottage "on the point" behind the public wharf with the smell of seaweed and the coastal steamers bearing down as if they were coming clear into my garden. That house had been sold. Then I'd lived in a tiny cottage at the end of the bay with only a stove, a chair, a table and a bed, but with a wonderful "bridge"—as we call verandahs—overlooking Gros Morne and the purple cliffs across two miles of the deepest blue water. Now that one was taken too. And in the intervening three years I had arranged my life so that I no longer had to live in town, but could spend as much time as I wished in the only place where I could really be contented. But build a house?

Of course I wanted one. I'd wanted one for years, but I always had good reason for not getting one. First it was money, then it was my inability to decide what sort of house I wanted. Now here I was, hoist on my own petard. I knew that news would get round so fast that I'd have no way out.

So I began looking for a place to build. It must have a view, I told myself, because that was why I wanted to live there—to be able to see out and over. But surely there were lots of good views. There were indeed, but nobody wanted to sell me an inch of land, much less a building lot. "Me father left it to me, and me sons might want to have some back when they gets done working in the mill." "The land's not really mine; me brother owns half and he's in Toronto." And so it went. Villagers would stop me on the road. "Hear you're going to stay. Where are you going to build?"

I can't sleep nights. I went round in circles and finally came back to the basic fact that building a house was altogether too much for me. After a week or more of this I asked Emma, "I know you wouldn't sell me a piece of your meadow?" "Oh, yes I would," she replied heartily, "Just go up and stake out what you want."

So that afternoon found me on the hillside, armed with four kindling splits that I'd sharpened with an axe. I walked round what I thought should be enough land for a small house and garden, drove in the stakes and sat on a huge boulder to have a look. The view was nothing less than stupendous. In front of me was the sea, to my right the long, smooth top of the Tableland, all brow and bare, before which was the round green of Birchy Head, and to one side the sharp edge of the Pickatenny Reef. Behind me more hills covered with spruce and fir and birch, and to my left lay the long sweep of the western arm of Bonne Bay, with Gros Morne, round, grey and full of shadow, and the green mountains of the Long Range fading into the distance.

I asked Emma how much she wanted for the land, but all she said was, "I don't want you to move that rock," as if I could. It was as big as a young mountain, and anyhow I had decided that I wanted it just at the corner of the house. That was how I chose the exact spot—four more splits to mark it, twenty by thirty feet. I measured with a tape what I considered a good round figure, though I couldn't picture how much space that would give me inside.

Emma said to me, "Get Taylor to build your house; you'll have something solid then." Taylor was our dear friend, a First World War vet, a wonderful woodsman and raconteur. I'd never thought of him doing anything as ordinary as building a house, but apparently he'd said to Em that he was sorry for me, a lone woman whose sons had "abandoned" her and she without shelter. To me he said, "I guess I can manage to put down the foundation, frame it up and put on the roof before mowing time. But mind you, I wouldn't do it for anyone else but you and Emma," which made the house a special thing even before it was started.

"Now," said Taylor, "you draw up a plan for me." I thought for one moment of the bulging file I had somewhere, collected over many years with all sorts of wonderful ideas for a home, inside and out; but all I could say was—"I want it twenty by thirty, one storey and not too steep a roof." Taylor was all for saving money, so when we got to the question of a foundation he said, "Now if you could get some water-soaked sticks, they'd do as pilings for twenty to thirty years before them lungers[31] rotted. You go down and see if you can get a few off of Jabez."

"Yes, my maid," said Jabe, "you can have any God's amount of them sticks. I'm going to tear off that cribbing on me wharf anyhow, when the Gov'ment gets round to building a new ramp. Let me see now—moon's full on Tuesday. Should be a good low tide on Monday evening. I'll get the sticks off then with me boat."

By the following Saturday, Jabez must have been sick of the sight of me hanging about his wharf that he called for his son to lend a hand. He borrowed a leaky lobster dory with no seats and one oar and managed to lasso the end of one of the sunken pilings of his wharf. He tied the end to the big boat, put the engine full speed and ripped the thirty-foot log off its base easy as wink. Jabe triumphantly towed it to shore, moored it to the bank and surveyed its worm-eaten length. "There you is—it'll make twelve good lungers when 'tis sawed up." I was delighted—my little house anchored to the earth with

---

[31] A lunger is a long pole used in constructing roofs and floors.

logs that had lain in the sea, festooned with seaweed and caressed by connors, sculpins and tomcod, and it cost me nothing—so far.

Getting the log cut and hauled to the site was my next job. Jabe said Bill had a bucksaw, and Bill said I could have the loan of it, if I could find it. I questioned five of Bill's seven youngsters, one by one, before I found the saw behind the remains of an old marine engine which was behind a stack of lobster pots. I dragged it out, and paid Bill's oldest boy to sharpen it. Then I went round the village trying to find Austin, who had an old truck and did odd jobs. After I'd run him to earth, having a mug-up in the galley of a long-liner, he said he'd do the job seven o'clock Monday morning. But he'd need someone to help him because, whether I knew it or not, water-soaked logs were very heavy. And, he added, "'Tisn't everyone would drive their truck up your road." "I know it's bad," I agreed, "and I can't take my car up it either, but come fall we'll get it fixed."

"Come somebody dies," retorted Austin, for my road led only to the cemetery, on the hill behind me. And lying almost in the middle of the road was a pile of logs someone had hauled out the winter before and dumped there, as far as a horse and sled could get. That someone was Dick, I soon discovered. I found him down in the bait depot and threatened him with "Court Works" if he didn't move the wood. I told him that Austin would bring it down if he, Dick, would get up early Monday morning and help in getting my stick up to the house, Austin would help him move his wood. It all fell together like a jigsaw puzzle.

Taylor came off the hill that evening for a beer. I could see something was disturbing him. "My maid," he said, "I been all over your land with a crowbar and I can't get down more than a foot. We won't be able to use them sticks for lungers. We'll have to make them of concrete. And that," he added, "is going cut into your fishing time, 'cause there's no cement within forty miles of Bonne Bay. Now, mind what you said? You wouldn't hold us up five minutes for want of material for the house."

Jabez arrived at this moment, got his bottle of beer and joined us. "Just as well," he said judiciously. He had judicious opinions about everything under the sun and made quite certain that you heard his ideas, from A to Z, whether you wanted to or not. "Way I sees it," he said, "first big blow and you'll come right off that hill unless you're anchored fore and aft—and sticks won't do it." Now Jabe has a high, penetrating voice, so everyone around heard him. Those in favour of my blowing away cited instances of trees uprooted, roofs sailing through the air, poles going down like ninepins after a sou'wester had roared through the funnel of the Gulch behind my land.

"Ah, go on, for glory sake," said Em, "Don't be so fullish, Jabe. That barn up on my meadow—two stories high with a list on her like this"—she put her hands together at a fifty-degree angle—"and it's been that way since I can remember. Why didn't that blow down?" She was disgusted and flounced out.

Ed joined us then. He had a soft voice, you had to listen carefully to hear him, but curiously whenever he started talking, everyone fell silent, as if they expected something unusual. Usually they got it.

"I can mind," he said, "when we were living on the lower road under the cemetery hill, we used to go up on the level to Aunt Jane Crocker's for our milk. One morning in the early fall, I minds, it was blowing a living gale. You could hardly stand up on the back bridge. Mother sent me to get the milk, and all the way I had to hold unto the fence pickets for dear life. My feet went straight out behind me. I was some worried how I was going to get down again with the jug of milk. Anyhow, when I got up, I met Aunt Jane on the road. She was just going up the hill to her house. ''Tis blowing some hard down our place,' I told her. 'I had the work of the world to just stand up.' 'Funny,' she said, 'we ain't had no wind up here.' And sure enough,
w   h   e   n
we got to her bridge, there was vamps and larrigans[32] draped all over the place, and they weren't even stirring in the wind. And up on the hill where Ella's place is, there wasn't even a bending of the grass in the meadow. I'd say she's got the most sheltered spot in Bonne Bay." Thus spoke the sage. Why he was right I don't know yet.

---

[32] Long boots.

But Taylor was taking no chances. When he came to pour concrete for the posts, he added to the mixture a hundred pounds of old iron chain, to anchor down my house. But before that happened, there were several things I had dimly foreseen, ones that had made me shy off building a house in the first place. I didn't want to spend the summer driving over the winding, dusty, hilly, rocky road to Corner Brook for supplies. I wanted to fish and to lie in the sun. But this was not to be.

Taylor said, "We wants six bags of cement day after tomorrow." Fair enough. Albert could bring it down by truck. But no. Albert wasn't going to Corner Brook next day—not enough orders to make it worthwhile. The following day was a holiday in the shops.

"You'll have to go to Deer Lake yourself," said Taylor. "Can't hold us up. Weather might break any time, now."

"Where can I get cement in Deer Lake?" I asked.

"Gates' garage. They got thousands."

"Why would a garage sell cement?"

"Dunno, but you be glad they do," said Taylor. "And while you're at it, see if you can find a forge and get sixteen bolts fifteen inches long, turned up at the ends. Gonna bolt you down good."

I drove. It took me an hour and a half each way. I got home tired, dusty and bad tempered, lugged the bolts up the hill to the house and told the boys to come fetch the cement. By this time Taylor, who had his buddy, George, working with him, said he'd made a mistake. He needed eight bags of cement—forgot the house was higher off the sloping ground in front, and hadn't calculated on that.

"Well, I won't go back," I said. "It's going to take me four days to get over this trip."

George was soothing. He was a wonderfully soothing influence all through this operation, and I never did figure out whether he was a bit afraid of me or was just naturally a gallant gentleman. "Anyhow," he said, "Get the loan of a few bags from Fred. He's got plenty."

Fred was building a concrete-block storehouse. Down I went, hung about a bit, sort of casing the joint, but I couldn't see an ounce of cement. Finally, I shamefacedly admitted the purpose of my visit.

"Never does to order just enough," said Fred. "I've just loaned me last bag to the fellers in the school. They ran out sudden, too."

"Well, damn it," I said and took refuge with Emmie and a cup of coffee.

She said I was some stunned to go to Deer Lake in the first place when Norm over in Norris Point had barrels of cement. And being of a practical turn of mind, she suggested that I make one journey and get my lumber ordered the same time. I asked Taylor what we needed and he spouted a list long as your arm.

Seeing my dismay, George suggested, "You just go down to Shears and tell him what we're doin' of, and he'll send you whatever we wants."

So I put my car on the ferry, chugged across the bay—the only way then to get to Norris Point—and ordered my cement. This time I wasn't to be had. I ordered four bags, not two. Then I drove on to Rocky Harbour and found Mr. Shears. He got pencil and paper and worked out—two-by-twelves, three-by-eights, and six-by-tens. The bill came to $480, and then I knew I was building a house.

The cement came. Taylor discovered he only needed six bags after all, and I'd better do something with the other four, because we couldn't leave them out in the weather. After much arm twisting, Ed said he'd take them off me for friendship's sake, but when we went to fetch them, there they were—gone. Fred had run out, heard there was some to be had on my land, and just helped himself!

Well, we had a spell then, and I caught up with my fishing. The sills went down, the beams and uprights appeared, and the rafters and roof went on.

"Shingles," said George. "Now, if I was you, I'd get those nice blue shiny ones like Taylor got. They'd show up right nice on the hill."

Indeed, they would show up—but how nicely was another matter. Taylor's house stood on the beach, with the sea for a foil to his blue roof. I wanted the most unobtrusive colour you could find so as to blend with the hillside and not be an exclamation point in the middle of the most lovely landscape on earth. Not only did I buy a colour of shingle called autumn brown, but I made the boys paint the eaves brown. And I broke the news that I was going to use cedar clapboard in its natural state.

"Oh, my," said Taylor, "You won't be able to see the house from nowhere."

By this time I was wondering how much more I could get away with. I knew the real battle was to come. But before that George said, "I 'lows first thing you knows, everyone'll want to be up here. I'm going to get a bit of land meself; there's a jib sticking out to westward nobody owns."

"Ah ha," I said, "That's what you think. Em's got it all tied up, and we've agreed only four houses in the field—stacked so's nobody will spoil anyone else's view. And Em's fussy who she sells to."

"Four houses, then?" Taylor joined the discussion. "Well now, that makes the septic tank business easier. See, that tank's going to cost you a bit. Jim's been digging all week thru the rock, and I figure you're going to need nigh on a hundred feet of pipe. That'll cost you some." Then he brightened, "Never mind, though. First bang of the pick and we found water. I reckon your well won't cost you more'n ten dollars. And I got a cut-off valve I'll give you."

Whatever a cut-off valve was, I was duly grateful, for I was running out of money. And the wall board for the inside not yet paid for. It was getting toward mowing time. Taylor was restive. George didn't mind; he had no cows. So Taylor said they would work overtime and cover the house in, good enough for winter. Then, come spring they'd finish it.

"All you have to do," he said, "is mark out where the windows are going, get them ordered, and time you get back, we'll have them in and the clapboard on."

My sister wired me from Corner Brook to come to a sale of windows at a shop which had just been remodelled. I endured the drive up and got two plate-glass mirrors, three small windows and one huge one for ten dollars, counted my change and ordered a double-glass window, six feet high and five feet wide for my view over the bay.

"What are you going to do with two looking glasses?" George

asked. Taylor told him 'twas so I could see meself fore and aft, same time.

"And now," I said, "I'm ready to mark out on the uprights where I want the windows."

"I s'pose you're going to put them in the middle of the wall," said Taylor. "Where else could you put them?"

Whenever I think of the argument ensuing, I go cold all over. Several times I thought all was lost. I couldn't make them understand that having gone to all the trouble of building the house way up on the hill, I wanted to have a free run of the view, and I couldn't do that with windows in the middle of the walls, no matter how queer they'd look from the outside. So I put heavy black marks on the uprights, and I swear the boys moved them a few inches every night.

Many a time I waited all day for the workmen, only for them to appear the next day. After one such delay, I asked, "What kept you, George?"

"Well," he said, "I had to put a yarnel in the church basement."

Never having run across such a thing before, and suspecting that he was trying to pull the wool over my eyes, I asked, "Now, George, what do you do with a yarnel?"

"My dear, I don't know what you do, but I pisses in it!"

Little untoward happened as they wrapped the house in insulation and put on "ten-test" as the wall boards. I had during the previous winter on the mainland found a lovely insulation called "sea felt," and it appealed to me having my house wrapped in the eel grass that fish had nosed in and limpets attached themselves to.

When I bought the windows, I also bought a front door. Taylor made the box, hung it and then came down for a beer and to say, "My maid, that's a very timid door you got. I hung it, but I'll have to make a storm door. That one's not strong enough to stand the winter. And another thing, we'll have to put up partitions."

"I'm not having any partitions," I told him.

"Blessed Lard, Ella, you've got to have partitions. If you leaves them off for the winter, any amount of snow on the roof and the rifters won't stand it."

Well, I must say I admired the aplomb with which he received the news that partitions were impossible. You see I hadn't decided what I was going to do with the space.

The last thing Taylor and George did was put the bathtub—which I'd bought so cheaply I still can't believe it—on the floor against the outside wall, and built partitions at each end of the tub to hold up the "rifters."

Meanwhile the matter of paying for the land on which my house rested weighed heavily on my mind. Every time I broached the subject to Em she'd say, "Now we're not going to row about that. We'll see about it sometime. I want to get it properly surveyed come fall."

I suggested something might happen to one of us, then what a mess our heirs and assigns would be in. So finally we rather sheepishly went to the magistrate. I'm sure he thought we were absolutely off our heads, me, at least, after building a house without title to the land. So he solemnly called someone from the wharf to solemnly swear I was me and Em was she, these were our signatures, and that he'd seen a cheque pass from me to Em. Then a little bit of paper passing hands made me owner of what I'd been thinking of as my piece of land for the past three months.

"Come spring, me maid," said Taylor, "we'll get you to rights. Just take your time deciding what you want inside."

I was now open to suggestion from all. What should I do with twenty by thirty feet, mostly window? Well, the first thing was to take that timid door from off the outside and hang it in front of the bathtub!

Finally the day came when I took possession. I could now stand in the middle of the room and look north, south and east. And that I did for an entire month, until I recovered from my astonishment at having succeeded in getting precisely what I wanted.

THE ELECTRICITY KERFUFFLE

The challenges Ella had to face in building her new house on the hill in Woody Point were as nothing compared with the frustrations in getting electricity.

SO NOW I had my own house, and since there was no electricity in the village, except for two diesel engines that provided power for the merchants' houses, I did not feel deprived. I bought two kerosene lamps that hung on the wall and had tin reflectors so that they adequately lit bathroom and bedroom. And an Aladdin lamp which cast cold white light over the living room and created the blackest shadows I've ever seen. Only later did I discover that the Aladdin required constant attention, for too much or too little gas caused the incandescent mantle to glow dangerously and burn up, or turn sooty and throw smoke into the room. After being close to asphyxiation twice through falling asleep while reading, I condemned this contraption.

But cold! On my stove, which burned oil, heated the water, and the house—the first to boiling, the second no higher than five degrees— I cooked my food. The snag was that I had to go outside to draw oil from my barrel, and so spent most of the morning cleaning and filling lamps and filling my stove reservoir. Then I bought a kerosene heater which, by dint of wrapping oneself around it, gave a little warmth. It was now late fall, and I couldn't at that late date install a wood stove, because that required a second chimney, for the one on my stove was not only inadequate, but I would have had to drape pipes all over the house to reach it. I had visions that I could keep warm by running the hot water through a pipe to my bedroom wall, and tearing down part of the bathroom wall to let in the warmth of the water heater. Somehow I survived.

And then electricity came to the village in the form of a huge, ugly, smelly and noisy generating plant, with wires draped all over the place. My bitterest enemy then became power poles, of which there were soon hundreds in the village, thirty feet high most of them. Em's barn was still standing at the bottom of the field, so I thought I would have my meter installed in it and would lay some wires across the meadow so that I would not have poles around the house to spoil my view. The electricity men took a dim view of that. They never heard of wires going underground and weren't about to learn. So for eighteen months I held out.

Came late fall with its dark days, and I was desperate. So I said "OK. I'll have electricity. Bring it straight up through the woods, along the cemetery road and into the house." Then when I came home one late afternoon, with the sun gleaming on the Tablelands, and shadows in the valley, I looked out my window and said to myself sadly, "It's the last time I shall see this in its purity," for a large hole had been prepared exactly in the middle of my view, and my lovely white birch near the house had been lopped off. That night I couldn't sleep until daybreak when I said aloud, "But I don't have to have electricity," and comforted, I slept. By the start of the workday I said to the electricity men that I'd changed my mind. John Jellico, who was helping out, sighed and shook his head and said, "Can't say as I blames you,"— my friend forever. I'd already demonstrated too much eccentricity for comfortable communication to anyone else in the village.[33]

---

[33] Her phobia about wires obstructing her views of the bay came to the fore during a brief excursion into teaching high school in Woody Point. She asked her students to write an essay about some issue of local concern. Knowing her passionate hatred of electric and telephone wires, they all identified this as the burning problem of the day.

But the nice power company needed my dollars. They suddenly broke down and said if I would lay the wire in a pipe across my fields, and bury it deep, they'd connect me with the power line. So I bought 300 feet of plastic water pipe, hired Jim and Jimmie, and went at it. They spent a day or more shoving the wire through and buried it. Oh miracle of miracles, I now had 110 volt electricity. I spent the next six months gloating. But not too long afterwards, the snow plow came too close to the side of the road, and cut the pipe and the live wire. The operator came close to electrocution.

When I had to go away for a while, I thought it only prudent to have my meter removed rather than pay for unused power. When the meter man came to take it he mumbled something about having to get a permit from Corner Brook before it could be returned to me. Well, I knew the wiring in the house was sound, so I dismissed the matter. Little did I know!

As soon as I returned the next year, I telephoned Corner Brook for an inspector. He came on his own good time all concerned with his authority, looked at the meter and asked me was the wire underground at the customer's request or the company's. Then he said he would have to have a little bit of correspondence with the meter installer. So I spent the next two days, hour by weary hour, phoning the meter man and never finding him. The mail brought an official document from Corner Brook: the power must come off the customer's own pole, and I had to have 220 volt wiring. Then I could have my electricity.

I went into shock. But after a few night's sleep aided by good stiff tots of rum, my courage returned. So I went all the way, 160 miles, to see the inspector, who was more important than ever, and who said there was absolutely no regulation permitting me to put power lines underground, and if I didn't like it, I could write the chief inspector. Which I did, and had a prompt reply to get in touch with the man in charge of my district, which I did. Having waited angrily three weeks for an answer, I climbed into my little VW and drove all the way to St. John's to see the Power Commission officials themselves. That my VW conked out on the trip and I had to get another car is not part of the story—but you can see how it might add to my anxiety and deplete my purse.

Well, I finally reached the Commission office to find the inspector away. See the engineer, I was told. Now, my fear of engineers is softened only by the certainty that a special hell is reserved for those who plan roads and power lines. No wonder my electricity bills are so high—you should have seen their hang-out—all carpets and shiny desks and enough people to run the government. Two small gentlemen, all scrubbed and shiny, awaited me, and what we said to each other I will draw a veil over. It does not show me in a good light, for I am always intimidated by authority when face to face with it. I know too well that one false move, one unkind word, and they can make my life unbearable. But I did leave with a concession or two, such as not putting my meter outside the house but inside a windbreak which has no door and is accessible to the meter man any time.

In the course of the discussion, I said I hadn't had a reply to my letters, so the engineer phoned Stephenville. How that got into the picture I didn't enquire, being pretty sure that someone had made an error. But the news came back that the head lineman had been to my house after I'd gone. A little horrified that anyone should drive over a hundred miles to see me without phoning to see if I was home, I said so and got the startled question, "You really have phones out there?"

"Heavens, we've had them long before electricity."

By this time I had been working on my problem for exactly eight weeks. Evenings were closing in and darkness fell much too early for me to go to bed. So I invited myself to friends to spend the nights. Which in itself presented problems, since my sons rarely wrote, but telephoned after midnight from faraway places. Thank Heaven I was on good terms with the phone operators, who agreed to transfer calls until I could alert family and friends as to what was going on.

In the ninth week a young man came—the chief linesman, and what a joy he was. I expect it must be the French in him, for on being invited in for coffee, he went into raptures about my view. And for the first time I had a glimmer of hope. Of course, he could see my problem, and together we viewed the situation until his eye lit on a big spruce outside the fence and he said, "Well, if we put a pole right beside that it wouldn't spoil things much, now would it, 'specially if you put the cable underground from the pole to your house?"

I agreed, so before I could change my mind again, a truck full of men in red hard hats appeared and began digging a hole. Down they went, all of eighteen inches, not nearly deep enough for a pole, so that was the end of that. Nothing daunted, they returned, built a three-by-three-foot box about three feet deep and piled cement into it. The more I looked, the sadder I got, but I told myself that I would pull away the box as soon as they left, and I would paint the pole a nice green to match the trees.

So off to Corner Brook I went to buy the wherewithal to go between pole and house. I found a contractor who had some cable he'd sell me wholesale, and he gave me the other odds and ends I would need. He said I would need to put in an eight-fuse meter box. "What," I asked him, "the hell would I need eight fuses for?" My house was one room, a bathroom and a bedroom, and I hadn't even an electric stove.

"Ok," he said, "but they won't let you put in a light in a woodshed without an eight-fuse box."

Anyway, the contractor said I couldn't possibly carry the cable home in my small car, but he would deliver it to a large warehouse, where a trucker from the village could pick it up. The truck man was not making a trip on Monday, the day I got home, but he would pick up the stuff on Tuesday. I called the warehouse in Corner Brook and made arrangements. I called the local electrical handyman to come on Wednesday morning bright and early to hitch up the cable.

Well, the truck arrived, but the cable was in the middle of his load bound for Norris Point, and could not be taken off until he returned the next day. Wednesday morning came and went. Looking out my window about noon, I could see the ferry moving across the water and on it the truck and presumably my cable. I phoned the handyman again. The truck went up the road around 4:30 p.m., headed for Trout River without stopping. Ah, I'll get my cable, I thought, when he comes back. But no, he went right by again. I phoned him, and around 10:30 his wife called that she was bringing me the cable in her car. I told her not to bother; the handyman would pick it up in the morning when he came to make the connections.

Next morning I was up early, and I waited. About noon I phoned the handyman again and his wife said he would come after dinner since he was now fixing up a pen for his ducks. When he did come, I will say this for him, the job went like a house afire, but he did not finish until dark. While he continued working I phoned the man in Stephenville, who had gotten mysteriously into the act, and told him I was ready for the linesman. Alas, the man was somewhere out in the wilds of the north, but he would do his best to find him.

Next morning the handyman turned up with a grin and a long piece of metal rod for a ground connection. "I couldn't get the pipe down through the porch floor," he said, "too much rock there. So I swiped this rod this morning from outside the power house." He promptly put the rod in place, finished his job and left. Meantime the linesman had come and strung the wire from a pole by the lower road, over the trees and onto my pole. It sagged alarmingly. Back he came after coffee and tightened up the line. The pole teetered and leaned out over the road. The cement box broke. The foreman came by to break the news that if only I would let them put a guy-wire on my field they could straighten up the pole.

"But that is just what I was trying to avoid," I said despairingly.

He gave me to understand that since there was no topsoil anywhere he couldn't see what anyone could do. However, if I agreed, they'd connect the power immediately.

So the pole and the guy-wire stand like sentinels, but at least my house is now brightly lit. In the evenings, I sit and scheme how I can demolish pole, wire, bureaucracy and everything that pollutes my

---

[34] Eight years after she first moved into her house, and after much palaver back and forth with the Power Commission, they finally acquiesced, perhaps to keep her quiet. The power line would, at Commission expense, be restrung over new poles brought over the hill behind her property and down through the woods to her house. At last, the battle was won, and her views across the bay were clear and unobstructed: they remain so today.

JINNY-DOWN-BY-THE-BOW

In Woody Point, Ella acquired her first cats. She was drawn into the feline world through her friends, the Campbells of Black Duck. Here is the tale of her first two cats, and their ancestry. Another story tells of Victor Campbell's extraordinary Antarctic adventures.

ON THE subject of cats, better people than I have written, but let me introduce you to my two. They are white with an inverted V of deep amber over the nose and up to the ear tips, along the spine with honey-yellow blobs on either side, and on their tails concentric circles of amber and white. They look, in repose, like delicate china ornaments and, in movement, so full of grace as to make one's heart leap at the sight.

They come from a long line of farm cats owned by the Campbells of Black Duck, and I believe that among their ancestors, they count Jinny-down-by-the-bow, though she must be their great-grandmother to the tenth. She was so named for having very long hind legs and extremely short front ones, and her paternity was much in question. Some even said that her father was a lynx. She rode piggy-back on the old sheep dog and was reputed to be the only undefeated enemy of the saucy bull that lived nearby.

Victor Campbell told me the story. "One fine morning I went fishing on Harry's River, and left my small canoe on the beach by the pool. Presently I hooked a very large salmon, and as I was playing him, I saw our bull racing down the shore towards me. He had broken out of his field, you see, and he was very angry. I waded out into the stream until I was nearly up to my waist, trying all the time to hold my line tight, as one must when playing a salmon. When the bull saw he couldn't reach me, he hoisted my canoe on his horns and went careening around the field. Jinny-down-by-the-bow dashed after him, and seeing that his head was covered by the canoe, she made a flying leap and landed on his back. This made him angrier still. Oh, you should have seen the commotion! Finally, the bull ran into a wire fence and I managed to capture him."

Now, I had never in my wildest moments dreamed of owning cats, or any other pets, for that matter. So, you might ask, what came over me? Well, I've always had a lurking interest in the Black Duck cats. It seemed to me an interesting project to maintain such a long line, from Jinny-down-by-the-bow to the present. When I last visited, a month or so ago, I found mother cat with five kittens she was rear-i   n   g   , and was told by the sentimental owners that they were the last of the line, father having disappeared in July and not returned. So the entire litter was being preserved.

Several times during the visit, my host and hostess wondered out loud where they would find "good homes" for three of them, and I, being much obliged to the Campbells for past and present friendship, finally decided to take two in the hope that someone in Bonne Bay would like two special cats—there are thousands of the ordinary kind around here. I was in it up to my neck once the decision was made, for suddenly the matter of names became important. I spent a near sleepless night, what with mother and her five hurtling from one end to the other of the flat roof overhead and my pondering and rejecting names, one after the other.

You see, I was well aware of the importance of naming cats, for had not the great English poet, T.S. Eliot, himself alerted me?

When you notice a cat in profound meditation,
    The reason, I tell you, is always the same:

His mind is engaged in a rapt contemplation
　　Of the thought, of the thought, of the thought
　　　His ineffable, effable
　　　Effanineffable
Deep and inscrutable singular name.[35]

A good thing he warned me, else I would have thought that my cats in rapt contemplation were busy digesting the last bit of herring. I only hope that my two are satisfied with their everyday names of Samson and Delilah, not that they pay attention to the sound of them when invited to come in out of the wet.

And still on the subject of names: there are moments when I am as concerned about the mental health of my cats, as I used to be about humans. Some psychologist recently said that children become what you tell them they are. Look what I have done to Samson. He displays strange characteristics and grows at such a rate that if he won't move temples—in his prime—he will certainly be able to frighten foxes. He grows and grows and grows—and he shoves Delilah from her feeding dish with threatening growls, all the time gobbling like crazy. He swipes his paw across her delicate little nose when he thinks nobody watches. Delilah, on the other hand, eats like a Victorian lady, as if chewing were vulgar. She is slim and lithe with appealing softness of the eye and the voice of a lyric soprano.

Samson is a raucous pop singer. He is also persistent and demanding: "Open the door," he seems to say, "or I'll drive you mad with my yowling." Delilah sits by the door for minutes without a sound, hoping I'll notice her. But once outside, I swear she thinks everyone in Bonne Bay is watching. She climbs on the killick and poses. She runs up and down the boulder, pausing to show herself to best effect, and once I watched her for several minutes as she sat on her haunches for all the world like a rabbit, front paws folded under her chin. I think she was contemplating the long grass moving wildly

---

[35] From "The Naming of Cats," in *Old Possum's Book of Practical Cats*. London: Faber and Faber, 1939.

and beautifully in the wind.

Samson, on the other hand, hurtles himself menacingly on fallen leaves and grabs at the moving reeds. At least, he did until it snowed. Now they both heave themselves through it, roll, play with the flakes they stir up and run in circles as if demented.

Inside the house, Delilah is an occupational hazard. She worries pencils all around the house. She examines books and papers. The particularly strange ones, she even chews, as if to say to me, "That's what I think of your peace proposals, your student uprisings." She has even tried to insert her head into the earpieces of my spectacles, and if she can get on my desk, she will, with delicate and tentative movements, scramble papers into an impossible mess. As to the tape recorder, the wheels going round inside glass rouse her curiosity to a degree only matched by her mystification with water running into the bathtub. As I said, she is an occupational hazard.

Samson, now, assails only the typewriter. No amount of biffs on the claws from retreating or advancing keys can teach him to leave well enough alone. I never cease to be fascinated by the difference in their approach to the hazards—or the joys—of cat life. One day I had a large mirror propped on the floor against the wall. Delilah happened by, gazed for a moment, let out an agonized wail and retreated behind a door. Samson strutted in to see what was going on, looked for a split second, and whipped his paw behind the mirror with a menacing gesture. Then he went all way round the mirror and sought Delilah to tell her it was really nothing threatening.

But it was Delilah who investigated a large basket full of ancient winter garments I frequently use this time of year. Samson shied away from it almost in terror. Delilah leaped lightly in and out while Samson watched, neither taking eyes off the other. Now, both spend a great deal of time holed up in my old homespun sweater inside the basket.

Delilah nibbles flies and wood. Samson chews buttons, no matter what their attachment—and that can be painful when the attachment is one's shirt, and one is lying prone absorbed in a radio program or a book. It can send you almost as high as one of Delilah's spectacular leaps.

This brings me to necessities which have now arisen in my small house. Any knitting in progress must be hidden in an obscure place; the lovely copper daisy which my artist friend gave me and which stands in an old brown bottle is regretfully stacked on the highest shelf. A handsome handwoven Welsh rug had to go in a cupboard and, worst of all, my leisurely and sometimes slovenly habits have changed. No longer can I lie in bed 'til the ten o'clock news or finish the book which fell out of my hands last night. I must let the cats in from the unheated back room or they'd gnaw holes through the door. Then they want out to see what the weather is, and then they want in. If in and I sneak back to bed, one of them immediately inserts a body between me and my book, as if she could read.

And I should like to know how they communicate with each other. I have seen them put noses together; perhaps that is how. But that does not explain how either knew that I was making ready to go to Corner Book overnight, and they were to stay with a friend. That they did know was evident when they disappeared for so many hours that the journey was indefinitely postponed. Perhaps they knew the storm was coming and wished to circumvent me—for it so transpired that the roads that day were almost impassable.

How do they know when I am about to put a needle on a record when they can't see me? They dash for safety, because once I did start a record going with the volume high—and the music took off with a blast from full orchestra, enough to frighten anyone. And when finally they emerged from hiding with tails high, they ignored me pointedly.

And now, excuse me please, I have to let Samson and Delilah out. They've had enough of all this talk.

SPRING: BACK HOME AGAIN

In the following four stories, Ella describes the goings on of a typical year in mid-twentieth-century Bonne Bay, now the heart of Gros Morne National Park of western Newfoundland. The events she relates might well have taken place in many another rural setting, for they illustrate something of the traditions and culture of rural Newfoundland and Labrador. Here, she returns from a winter on the mainland, rants about the protests over the seal fishery, meets old friends again and samples funnel buns.

I THINK I must have been one of the first to come back this year, but maybe I don't count. I return every year, that is when I'm foolish enough to go away in the first place. No matter how many times I do it, coming home is a special experience. I commence to relax and smile, and whistle when I'm driving alone, just about when I reach the causeway leading to Cape Breton. By the time I reach Tompkins, I'm singing at the top of my voice, waving to everyone on the roads and tooting my horn at the trucks that pass. It is the nearest thing to a state of euphoria. It comes from feeling completely part of my surroundings, and from not having to explain myself and my very strange habit of living in Newfoundland.

I shan't forget for a long time the shock I had when I was being interviewed on TV in Toronto, and the commentator asked me why people live in Newfoundland anyhow—as if we needed a certificate of insanity to do it. I took a deep breath and replied that I supposed some people lived there because that was where they were born; some because they hadn't thought of living elsewhere, and many, like me, who couldn't possibly live anywhere else—and we'd given anywhere else a good try! Then—would you believe it after all these years—he asked me how I liked being a Canadian. I told him that, after all, I'd gone to the polls and voted to be one—which is more than other Canadians had done. He was a bit taken aback, having, I believe, thought that we had been annexed by force.

What I could not say, and what I do not myself know, is why the lovely landscape in the Eastern Townships of Quebec gives me no ecstatic thrill, and lacks the drawing power that even the cliffs outside Port aux Basques overwhelm me with, like other hills as perfect in outline. Or why a stunted spruce that, from my window, cutting vertically across the sweep of the Bay, is the most majestic tree I have ever seen. I wouldn't care if I never saw the Laurentians again, but tell me my eyes would never again rest on Gros Morne, and I would perish.

I came home this time in good May weather, when the snow was almost gone and the pussy willows out along sheltered roadsides, and the trees I had so hopefully planted in my garden last fall showing signs of life. But within three days we had a snowstorm and I was marooned for almost a week and had to get around on snowshoes. Of course, I had already performed the special rites of spring, taking off the storm door and windows, and clearing out the accumulation in the cellar to air and dry in the sun, so I was well and truly caught! And so were a lot of other people who should have known better.

One thing I could have missed with pleasure when I was away from home was the stink about the seal hunt. Thousands of words have been written and spoken, thousands of opinions given, most of them quite uninformed. One man told me quite seriously that there was no danger in sealing. Of course not, he'd been put down from a helicopter on the ice near Anticosti, and as he put it, "It was like walking on a skating pond in Place des Armes." I asked how long he'd stayed and he said about fifteen minutes. I suggested that if he'd come back five hours later he wouldn't have found his skating pond. And he's supposed to be the expert on various forms of cruelty practiced on seals and the appalling depths of bloodthirstiness we Newfoundlanders are capable of!

For my part, this whole thing hurts my pride, angers and frustrates me. I am one of those—and I know there are several thousand others—who grew up admiring and being proud of our old sealing skippers and who found excitement and adventure in the hardy deeds of our men and their heroism in disasters that overcame them. We marvelled at the tenacity of sealers for going year after year to hunt for seals and often returning with almost nothing.

The organization I was working with in Toronto had been receiving a flood of letters opposing the slaughter from people who shouldn't get away with it. Neither should the well-meaning "non-cruelty to animals" people, nor the silly ones who take up this cause to salve their conscience for not making a stand on cruelty to people all over the world. Some of our bright young writers should write about the history of sealing and the truth about the hunting methods used.[36]

But back to my homecoming. When I arrived, everything in my house worked properly. The stove burned without smoke, lights went on and the water ran from the tap, though with a curious gurgle. Bill came to investigate, found a broken joint in the outside line and guessed that a horse had breezed on it, or maybe a moose. He mended that, and the gap in my fence where the sheep had got in and nibbled the new shoots off my little trees.

"That was John done that," Bill said, "coming to get the hay and didn't put up the stiles."

"Sleveen," said I.

Bill replied piously, "May God forgive you for not calling him something worse." That remark, I might say, was worth coming home for.

---

[36] These books have now been written, but even so the seal fishery has dwindled to a mere shadow.

Now that things were all right in my little world again, I met at Em Tapper's house for a morning mug-up. She was making bread and thought I might like to try funnel buns.

"Whatever are they?" I inquired.

"Well, if you don't know I'll show you." She unwrapped the bread dough from its blanket, cut a thin slice off the top, flattened it deftly and slapped it against the hot stove pipe, where it soon gave off an indescribably lovely smell of baking bread and toast. Peeling it off the pipe she covered it with butter, and folded it neatly for my delectation.

Later, after we'd fetched the mail and bought our groceries, we watched the little skiffs loaded with lobster pots chugging out on the glass-calm water. Soon it would be the first hauling, though it was still so cold at night that ice formed in the boats and on the long ropes that had to be handled to get the pots off the bottom. Sixty cents a pound, we decided, wasn't too much to pay for the discomfort the men went through.

That morning, Harvey told me that he wouldn't put out any pots this year. "The way I got it figured," he said, "is that if I puts out me pots, I'll only catch lobsters other fellers could have had. So I'm just going to take the lobsters outta their pots and save us all the trouble."

"How are you anyhow after the winter?" I enquired.

"Lovely, me maid, lovely. And did you see anyone on the mainland you liked better'n me?"

"Lord no, that's impossible," I told him, embarrassed at my vehemence.

Now things are back to normal again, except for today's three-foot snowfall, which a day's southwest wind will soon melt.

A long, lazy, lovely summer lies ahead of us.

A SUMMER OF WONDERS

Here Ella tells of watching a house being moved, launches her new rodney, joins a grand party in the old Orange Lodge, and entertains the Rockefellers.

ONE EVENING late in June, my friend Em Tapper and I were sitting at the kitchen table. The sun had set, and darkness crept over the calm black water of Bonne Bay. Although we did not quite define it as such, we were talking of value—of what we thought was worthwhile in life, of what other people apparently thought worthwhile—you know, just talking rather aimlessly, one thing bringing another to our minds. I remembered a man who once said to me, "If I went blind tomorrow, I'd have enough sights in my memory to keep me happy the rest of my life," and he wasn't fifty then.

"As for me," I said, "if someone told me I could either have five hundred dollars or the day on Western Brook we had last week, I'd take Western Brook." No amount of money could buy for me any material thing that could be half as precious as the day of sun and wind when for two hours we walked the bank of the river, waded through its waters, ploughed through the marsh—and saw sights that were like gems in my mind's eye.

My whole summer was like that—day after lovely day—clouds chasing each other through a blue sky, shadows racing across the brown Tablelands, changing their colour every moment. Gros Morne sometimes a soft blue, shot with green, other times a slate grey, the bay every colour that water could show. There was always the sound of a brook or the waves on the beach or the wind stirring the leaves, wherever you went. Those of us who had time to look began to wonder, why does that happen? What are these birds anyhow? And at night, when the sky was close enough to touch, our wonder grew. All the month of July, we went round with cricks in our necks from looking up at the stars, trying to pick out the constellations.

One day, just as we were going for a row, someone shouted to just look at those two great black gulls sailing in among the blue-white herring gulls. "Oh," said a fisherman, "they're saddlebacks—old ones turned dark." But we weren't satisfied with that, so we tied the boat up again and went to fetch our *Birds of Newfoundland* book. This confirmed that these saddlebacks were actually the great black-backed gull, a completely different bird from the others. And the rest of the afternoon we spent looking up other birds in the book and trying to identify ones we'd seen during summer. We thought it a shame that the writers of the book didn't know that the great bald eagle nested in the cliffs at the mouth of the Lomond River, or that they could be seen soaring over the Gregory Plateau and on the inside of Trout River ponds. Or the story Baxter told of the fight between two crows on Norris Point hill. One pecked the other over the cliff, and watched him roll down, then flew after him and pushed him into the water where he floated, quite dead!

It was a July morning that summer, when Harvey told me that Mansell was going to launch his house, and that was something I shouldn't miss. I nearly did, though, for launching day was so warm and sunny that I attended the garden, and by the time I started for the village, the house was already several hundred feet along the road. There it faced me, completely blocking the way, like a derelict schooner accidentally beached. The house is thirty feet by forty, two stories tall, flat roofed with two big brick chimneys protruding.

The front door was open, and one of Mansell's boys sat on the step grinning. On the roof was John Jellico, a cigarette hanging from his lower lip as he leaned over to grasp an electric wire that stretched over the road at this point. Two tractors held together by a steel cable were hauling the house, which rested on skids so huge that I would have thought they'd have to go to British Columbia to find logs as big as those. But Mansell had found them in his winter wanderings, deep in a gully behind the village.

Nine tenths of the village were on hand. Everyone was yelling, and the tractors suddenly stopped. It was obvious that the chimneys would not pass under the wire. Consternation. Profanity. Much spitting, along with gratuitous advice from below, and John Jellico's bellow from above, "Send some fellers up with me, we'll raise 'er up." Then a grin broke over his face. From his vantage point he could see a figure flying down a back lane. "Hey, there's Everett. We'll be Ok now."

Everett, the electricity expert who had been north on a job, had arrived home at five that morning. Everybody said this was providence. The wires properly loosened, lifted by twenty hands, went tightly and smoothly over the chimneys. Men yelled, the tractors took up the strain, dirt spewed up, and like a giant sled the skids moved, along with the house, inch by inch.

Mildred joined us. "Dunno where me kids is. Anyhow I got a pot of pea soup and a whack of boiled dumplings on the back of the stove." We realized it was dinner time, but nobody stopped to eat: things were going too well. "If that tractor cable parts," Nina said, "someone will be killed." She is from town and not used to our careless attitude to safety. No sooner had she spoken than the steel cable parted with an awesome screech. As God looks after children, no one was hurt. A new cable was hitched to the house and it inched along again.

One man rushed up saying, "Where's Sammy? I can't remember where I left him." We produced the child from a blanket we'd wrapped round him, and father, obviously relieved, took him off muttering, "What would his mother say if she'd known I mislaid him?"

It was really awe inspiring, as the hours went by, to see the way our neighbours used their ingenuity, how the tractor drivers handled the huge machines as if they were toys, manoeuvring them precisely. One trundled down the hill and came up behind the house. One tractor pulled, the other pushed. Men rushed like demented, thrusting more and more logs under the foundation of the house as it turned slowly and finally faced its new home, a hundred yards below the road. Then it canted dangerously. Mildred said, "My Lard, they never even took the dishes out of the cupboard. Just tied the doors together." "That's nothin'," said Grandma Noel. "When they got the house off the foundation and started to haul, someone looked in the kitchen, and there was the cat sound asleep on the rocking chair."

As the house turned and settled into its new home, the sun got low. Tired and dirty and hungry, the men of the village slowed up a bit. They'd given a day's work to their neighbour and soon they would help him straighten the house, and clean up the yard. For tonight, the family would sleep at a twenty-degree list, but the enormous job had been done successfully.

Not long after lobstering was over we had a "time" in the Lodge. All the girls in the village turned out in their finery—they had sent away to Eaton's catalogue and had it come. The boys had haircuts and new ties. Upstairs in the Lodge a spread was set—such food as only village women could produce: homemade bread and butter, hundreds of different kinds of little cakes, pies of many berries from last year's crop and preserved 'til now in bottles, gallons of tea and indifferent coffee. We ate in layers, as Taylor said, and he happened to be in my layer. The ladies of the Lodge hustled in and out the kitchen, breathing down our necks. "More tea, me dear. Now, don't make shy. Make up your supper," and similar encouragements.

While one layer ate, the others sat in rows along the walls of the big room—men on one side, women on the other, except for a few brave hussies who persisted in taking vacant chairs on the men's side. Two local belles, middle-aged but not admitting to it, sallied in just late enough for everyone to notice. One was draped in an old fox skin with the head nestling under her double chin and a black net sprinkled with sequins on her glossy curls. The other wore a tight satin dress of electric blue. Both wore four-inch heels to which they were unaccustomed.

Taylor nudged me, "Now, if you was as smart as them, you wouldn't go round lookin' like a streel."

"Is that what everyone thinks around here? That I don't do them justice by dressing up properly? That's just terrible."

"Hah. I was only making fun. You'll do all right, I daresay. But only t'other day, a feller seen you swimming off the wharf. He tole me he seen someone getting out of the water, and my God, someone was after paintin' her brown. Course I said 'twas only that you went round in the sun with hardly nothing on!"

The music started up downstairs—a fiddle, an accordion and a guitar—and the sets commenced. Now, that was where my two belles shone. They knew every step and they pushed their partners like a coastal boat shoving a dory. Then the modern dancing started. Taylor peered. He shook his head. He couldn't possibly do that, he told Bill. But Bill said, "Oh, dat's easy. Only leppin' broadside."

So Bill and I lepped broadside, jiggled up and down, shuffled our feet and I walked backwards until my toes were trodden to pulp. Taylor thought he'd wait 'til Emmie came to try the new dance, because she'd be easier to "shove round," being as she was half my size.

The dust rose higher, the room got smokier, men got drunker and the laughter rose to the rafters. Em danced a reel with Ned, and leaped a bit with Taylor.

Then she said to me, "Much too good a night to be in here. Let's go."

Down at the wharf was my newly acquired boat—twelve feet long, broad in the beam, good for rowing or sailing. We pushed off, hoisted the sail and went skimming along in the moonlight. The water burned in our wake, lines of light formed round our fingers as we trailed them over the side. A distant gull complained once. Then all was silence except for the lapping of the water at our bow. And we sailed until the stars dimmed and dawn began to break.

By then, the party at the Lodge had broken up, but small groups still lingered here and there. Down by the lighthouse where the circling beams of light spread out over the village street, the drunkest of the old boys were rolling around.

"Best not to go down," Em said, "we'd cramp their style."

"You suppose they can get home by themselves?" I asked.

Just then we heard Bill's deep voice, "Hoist up me leg, b'ys, ah hoist it up—'tis dead."

Grunts. Laughter. Then another voice, "What's you firkin' round fer?"

"Me bottle. Where's me bottle?"

"You drank it. Hey, ever hear tell the story about the feller getting his rum to Deer Lake one winter, before we had the liquor store there and we had to git it by express from Sin John's? Well, he went up on the dog team and 'twas some slippery. He got his bottle of rum and put it in his pants pocket. When he was comin' out of the office, he fell down. He got up then, felt all up and down his leg. Then he looked at his hand and he said, "Thank God, 'tis only blood.""

Gales of laughter rang over the quiet village. Windows opened and banged shut. Then a shrouded figure emerged from the house next door and flitted down toward the lighthouse. The beam of light swung round, and standing before the knot of jolly drunks was the loveliest ghost I've ever seen. And the silence then was broken only by the sound of feet crunching on gravel as one sad drunk swayed homeward along the road in the angry embrace of his ghostly wife!

One Saturday a few weeks later, when I returned to my cottage after my morning's fishing, I saw four women leaning over my fence. They looked well-scrubbed and immaculate in light blue jeans and fancy, expensive-looking jackets. As I walked to my gate, the older woman said, "What a glorious view you have."

Now, I love everyone who loves my view, so I replied, "Really, you ought to drive up into the Gulch. That's something spectacular."

They said that unfortunately they hadn't a car, and before I could think I'd bundled them into my dirty, fish-bespattered car, and off we went. They were enchanted. The younger ones climbed the Pimple, the little green mound off the road, and found exotic plants. They took photographs, while their mother and I sat cosily behind a boulder out of the wind, and talked about fishing and how you get to remote streams and what fun it is to live outdoors. Finally, they said they must go back to pick up some lobsters for dinner. So I dropped them at Bill's store and went on to the cafe to tell Em about my morning's fishing.

Then I met Stewart, who was standing in the middle of the road, arms akimbo, his eyes shining. He looked me up and down and said, "Some class to you."

I laughed. "Sure, some class! But why this morning particularly?"

"Oh, my Lard," he breathed in awe. He peered at me closely and said, "Don't you know what you're after doin'?" He lifted his arm dramatically and pointed to the wharf. "Look."

I looked and there, tied up, was the loveliest, shiniest, richest sailing boat it has ever been my privilege to see.

"When did she get in?"

"Last night. Mean you never seen her this marnin'?"

"No. I went straight to the Gulch. Whose is she?"

"Belongs to them people you had up in the Tablelands in your dirty old car. My maid, them people was the Rocky Fellers."

I don't know why this was so excruciatingly funny to all the village, but all summer long, someone was telling someone else the story, ending with, "And Ella took the Rockefellers up to the Gulch and never asked who they were." You could hear shouts of affectionate laughter clear across the bay, as if to say, "God knows what the old girl'll be doing next!"

Now that August is here, it seems that summer is almost over. It has been a particularly good one as far as weather goes. Lately, I have been engaged in such un-housewifely occupations that I find it hard sometimes to bring my mind back to home and cooking. I have, in short, been sailing my new boat. Mind you, it is a small rowboat and it doesn't sail very fast, but it has been a source of great pleasure.

On the East Coast where I was brought up, we call it a rodney. But out here on the West Coast, they call it a punt, and they aren't very polite about it, either. Here everyone uses a flat-bottomed dory, and they look askance at my round-bottomed craft. On the other hand, I remember that around Lewisporte when I was young, we thought a dory was the most treacherous of boats. One Bonne Bay fisherman predicting dire results, compared my boat with a barrel, claiming that she would tip so easily. But another fisherman dared us to turn her over: he said it couldn't be done, for the bottom was too wide. So, you see, I have been the centre of much interest with my rodney, and I have learned a great deal about boats from people who've practically lived in them.

I hasten to tell you we haven't managed to tip our boat yet, though several times we've been out in a stiff wind. After a bit, the novelty of rowing wore off and we said, "Why don't we put a sail on her? Let's see what she'll do under canvas." So while the boys had a rudder rigged and a mast cut and fitted, I bought some calico, cut and sewed a sail and rigged it with pieces of jigger line. You can imagine what it looked like. Still, I was proud of my handiwork, especially when a fisherman told me I had just the right amount of canvas on her—and another fisherman said it reminded him of when he was a boy, for I had cut and made a "leg-o-mutton sail" like they used years ago. That pleased me, for I thought, "Here we are, doing the same things our ancestors did. Here is my lad, out in the bay, enjoying himself in the same way that his grandparents and great-grandparents did before him." It brought us into the life around us more closely than anything else had done so far.

And I began to think of all the arts and crafts that our grandparents had that we have almost lost. My grandfather, when he was my older son's age, could sail a dory, fish with the men—clean and cure and dry his fish—could saw and cleave wood, mend the roof, and chances are, if driven to it, could build a house—at least, a good strong shed. My sons know about radio and about electricity, but I doubt they could do many things our ancestors did without thinking about them.

The same goes for our girls. Grandma could make bread, cook for a family, sew and clean house and hook mats before she was fourteen. Of course, I'm not saying that we should work our children all day long and make them do all these things. But I do think it would be wonderful if we could pass on some of our craftsmanship to them. For baking a good loaf of bread is as honest and important a craft as anything I can think of. And what could be of more lasting beauty, of more lasting joy and comfort than a well-conceived pattern of delicate colours in a hooked rug?

I wish I could hook a mat the way my grandmother and my mother did. And I wish I had the knack of growing houseplants that the old people had. None of this may have anything to do with keeping a clean home or cooking the proper food to keep the family healthy, but it is part of making a home, part of keeping alive the habits, customs and traditions of our people.

Fortunate are we who have our roots deep in land that belonged to our grandparents and great-grandparents, in land that we care for and build on and develop. You can see it in all the little settlements along our coast—in places where the people have hardly ever moved outside, but where they have learned the ways of the old people, why they did the things they did at any particular time, the why's of the wind and the tides, the days you go fishing and the days it would be useless to try, the days you start picking your berries to bottle against the winter, the recipes you use for your pickles and jams and wines. And you'll hear them tell their children the lore of their ancestors.

The key is as simple as this. I said to my son in his sailboat, "Your great-grandfather once sailed from Exploits to Twillingate in a boat like this, alone on a dark night, to bring a doctor to your grandfather who was then a very sick little boy." That meant something to my son then, but it wouldn't have a week ago before he learned something of our ancient craft and developed a respect for the courage and strength and knowledge needed to handle a craft well in a windy sea.

I think when I am very, very old, I shall enjoy telling my grand-children everything I know about our past, about this most wonderful summer in Woody Point, and all the things I have learned along the way.

If I am any judge of the curiosity of children, I'd say they'll listen with awe.

AUTUMN IN THE BAY

In this story Ella visits the local clinic, where she hears about jannying, the old yuletide tradition of visiting homes in disguise. She witnesses the arrival of herring in the Bay and recounts the story of John Charles Roberts' seed potatoes and their connection with the Scots of Cape Breton.

THE SUMMER days pass all too quickly, and in early autumn I found myself in the position of the little squirrel who frittered away his summer and went hungry when the frost came. I had not bottled fish or greens or berries against winter. It was only the frequent invitation to "tea"—the local evening meal—that kept me from starvation. So one day, when the weekly clinic was in session, I went to the nurse for some vitamin tablets.

The clinic waiting room was narrow, with windows high in the walls. When I arrived it was nearly full: women with small children getting their "three year needle" and babes in arms ready for their first year one; several men, looking sheepish in the preponderance of women, nursed bandaged fingers or stiff legs; young women in all manner of dress and coiffeur, including enormous hair curlers.

I found a seat beside a woman who looked vaguely familiar. "And who be you?" she asked.

I told her, adding, "And who be you?"

"I'm Bill's mother; you knows he. And you're the woman that lives all by yourself up be the graveyard!"

I said I was, indeed.

"My, you must be some brave! Me son was sayin' that when he was fixing our graves the spring, an old feller come by and asked 'en who lived in your house. When Bill tole 'en, he said, 'Wudden you afraid with all them dead people?' Bill told 'en you wudden afraid of the dead people, 'twas the live sons-of-bitches scared you to pieces. Oh my!" she finished, cuddling herself in her two arms, "Me stomach is that bad, it hurts me to laugh."

The door opened and several more people squeezed themselves inside. She whispered, "Who is them?" I didn't know either. Another crowd tried to enter. "Who's them?" I shook my head. After a moment she began to laugh again and, almost in tears before she recovered enough breath, she said, "Just come to me mind, we're like a crowd of jannies, not knowing who anyone is and trying to guess. Only they haven't got false faces." And off she went again in hoots of laughter, bringing hands to her stomach again.

When she had recovered sufficiently, I asked her had she been jannying these late years.[37] "I suppose I have, me maid. I went last Christmas and I'm going again if the Lard spares me. I got dressed up in me poor 'usband's Sunday suit with a piller to fill out me stomach. He was some big, me 'usband, gone this two year." She sighed, then continued brightly.

"I had a false face, too, a real janny face and I made whiskers, just like them hippies, and we went everywhere, even to the Minister's. Course, we never danced in his house, we only said a speech we had all made up for that. And of course, he never knowed who we were. Some of us was dressed up in oil suits, some 'ad their old long skirts. Mrs. Parsons—she was with us—'ad her mother's Sunday 'at, a big one with nasturshums on it. Hardly nobody knowed who we

[37] Jannying, also known as mummering, involves a group of people, disguised in ridiculous attire, who call on local homes during the Christmas season, wearing masks so they will not be recognized by their hosts.

was. Well, anyhow, we went down to Ned's last thing, and of course they asked us would we have a drink of rum. We said we never drinked, and one old feller who wasn't jannying—I knowed him, but of course he didn't know who I was, said, 'Isn't you queer? You don't drink, so I s'pose you don't pee either.' My, wouldn't he be vexed with hisself if he knowed who he was using them words to." Another gust of laughter brought hands to stomach again.

"What is wrong with your stomach?" I asked.

"Dunno, me dear. All I knows is it's bad, been like it all summer and the doctor didn't seem to be able to do nothing wid me. All them pills! Useless, I says, so I'm goin' back to sulphur and molasses next month—maybe that'll fumigate me."

Turning to her neighbour with whom she had obviously more than a nodding acquaintance, she asked, "Blood still poor?"

"Yes, me dear. No better fer all them pills I took. I 'ad t'ree bottles and still they says I got no blood."

"What does she mean," I asked Bill's mother.

"Well," said she, looking me up and down, "take someone like you, now. I daresay you got two-three gallons of blood, but she only got a couple of quarts."

While I was digesting that piece of medical information, a man beside me was explaining how he slipped on the muddy path, hit his back on the bridge steps and believed he'd fractured his kidney. All he hoped was the nurse wouldn't send him over to the hospital at Norris Point, for he'd rather die of a fractured kidney than be frightened to death by "the big, bullying nurse over dere."

The man with the bandaged hand said he'd squat his fingers in the truck door and they went fousty. So he "wropped them up" and carried them to the doctor—like a pound of sausages, I thought—and now they had to be "unwropped to see how they was getting on."

When I finally reached the nurse and collected my vitamins, she, a delightfully pretty and smiling young woman from Manitoba, told me she wouldn't work anywhere else in the world but Bonne Bay. "Where," she asked me, "could you find such a variety of obscure diseases and exotic accidents? They have bad stomachs from drinking boiled tea, eating salt beef and cabbage just before going to bed, swallowing tons of patent medicines. Or they have low blood or high blood, never middling, and they have livers and kidneys in places found in no other human being!"

All ailments aside, our village comes alive slowly this time of year. The rest of the time, the harbour is almost empty—a few sailboats, some dories, the car ferry, a steamer that brings freight every few weeks. But now the seiners come, as they have for many years. They tie up four or five deep at the Government wharf and wait upon weather fit for seining herring. At first the weather was good, but the herring were so close to land that the nets couldn't be put out, lest they rip on the rocks. Then the barometer went down, the wind shifted and we battened down the hatches, afloat and ashore. Outside the Bay it was much too rough to put out nets.

Later, there was a bustle around the herring shed, for the herring had moved off far enough for the seiners to get at them without shredding their nets. Boats from everywhere appeared to share the harvest: every man and boy from the village were in the shed, splitting, gutting, packing, and rolling barrels.

And as suddenly as it commenced, it stopped. One morning a seiner came in early, dejected. No herring anywhere. Only one boat had found herring seventy fathom down and was sitting on the spot waiting for them to rise, but eventually even he came back to port. Maybe this way the herring will live to spawn, and we will have more fishing next year. If you ever saw, as we did, men knee deep in herring spawn, you'd wonder how the species survived this long.

At our local fair in Bonne Bay this fall, I found a display of potatoes with a curious history. The man who grew and displayed them, Mr. John Charles Roberts of Sally's Cove, is almost eighty-seven. He's been married for sixty-three years, and he planted the potatoes the first year of his marriage. He told me he has grown them ever since in the same piece of ground, and he's never had a rotten potato nor a piece of canker this size, measuring off the top joint of his middle finger. While he was explaining this to me, along came another Roberts. Ed looked at the potatoes, picked one up and said, "Well, well, well. I haven't seen them for fifteen years."

"I guess you knowed where they come from" John Charles said, and they smiled at each other. Then he looked at me and said, "'Twas his grandfather, me uncle, who brought them here to the Bay." And this is the story I was told.

Now, Ed's grandfather was Samuel Charles Roberts, son of John Roberts, a Devon man who was one of the very first settlers in Bonne Bay. Like his father, Samuel was a fisherman, who used to catch and cure herring, Scotch style, as well as making dried cod. Sometimes he could sell the herring to American buyers, other times he couldn't. It was a precarious business and besides, too many people shared in the profits. So Samuel, one summer, got the idea that he would go abroad himself and find a market. Where he could go was limited by the size of his schooner. It was only twenty-two tons, and though fishermen had sailed to England in ships not much bigger, it really wasn't to be recommended, if one could find a handier place to market one's catch.

In those days there were a remarkable number of Nova Scotians around these parts, setting up fishing stations and building saw mills. They told Samuel that there were a good many Scotsmen up in Cape Breton, and Samuel thought that if he could find them they might relish a meal or two of his herring. So late in the fall when the wood was cut and stored for the winter's fires, when the cod was dried and packed, and when the herring was all neatly laid, head to tail, in small barrels, Samuel gathered his crew of sharemen, told them what he proposed, and loaded his schooner with all she could carry of their herring and cod.

In December, with the wind tearing down from the Gulch and the spray freezing on the riggings, the little ship bucked her way out of Bonne Bay and set her bow southwest, down through the Gulf toward Cape Breton. Samuel wasn't quite sure where exactly he was bound, but he finally made port inside the entrance to Bras d'Or Lake. They tied up at the wharf, and a few people came down to have a look at the strangers.

They all appeared to be called Mac something or other, so Samuel told his crew they must be Catholics. Now, it's no credit to our ancestors that they were as bigoted a lot as they come, but remember that in those days religions were being fought, albeit on a small scale, not only in Newfoundland but in Cape Breton, too. So Macs, the Irishmen, boded no good for the Protestant son of a Devon man.

Samuel reckoned that they wouldn't get rid of their herring there, so they'd better try somewhere else. But before they could cast off, along came a rather talkative character who set them right about the Macs. "Hell, no;" he said, "There isn't a Catholic within fifty miles of this place. Didn't you see the Orangemen's Lodge on the hill?

Samuel said that he and his crew were Lodgemen too, so the local dignitaries came and invited the Newfoundlanders to a meeting. Then, someone thought to ask what were in the barrels on the ship's deck, and when Samuel showed them the Scotch-packed herring and diffidently said that he hoped to barter them for potatoes and vegetables, they were beside themselves with joy. One said, "The good God looked down on us this summer and favoured us with the best crop of potatoes you ever saw. Don't you worry about potatoes."

Well, next morning, just about daylight, Samuel looked out the porthole and what he saw astonished him. Lines of men coming down the hill to the wharf—with horse and wagon, with wheelbarrow, with sacks on their backs—all converging on the schooner. Samuel knocked the heads out of the barrels and doled out the herring—a dozen to one for carrots, three dozen to someone else for cabbage, a barrel to another who brought a wagon full of vegetables. Samuel said that all the Cape Bretoners went home hugging their herring to their bosoms. And he sailed home to Bonne Bay loaded with the best vegetables he'd ever seen. That was their first trip, but by no means their last, for a very satisfactory and mutually profitable trade went on for many years between the Bonne Bay men and the Bras d'Or Lake men.

Now, out of the potatoes brought home on that first voyage, some were kept for seed. They founded the line that John Charles Roberts had so carefully tended for sixty-three years, in the same piece of ground, without any rotten potatoes, without a bit of canker bigger than the top joint of his middle finger. I've eaten some and I swear, they taste better than any potato I've ever eaten. And if I'm spared—as they say in Bonne Bay—I'm going to plant a bed of John Charles Roberts' Bras d'Or Lake potatoes next spring!

We have had more than our share of rough weather this fall. Northerly wind, lop coming in from the bay, seas breaking on the far shore, normally so calm, and spray driving twenty feet up the cliffs. Gulls like snowflakes rising and dipping over the water, and sure sign of gales outside, the black-back gulls appear. A dirty grey-green sea, whitecaps whipped to foam. Rain beating slantwise, poplars bending stiffly. A driving mist over the sea's face, blotting out the foreshore. The contours of the hills misty black.

One blustery morning as I headed for the mail, I drove along the lower road to have a look at the beach. Murdock came hurtling by as fast as a man can in hip rubbers, shouting, "Got to get me dory." Next thing I saw three men, thigh deep in the swells pulling Murdock's lovely little pink and green boat out of the water. She had broken her mooring and was swamped. Coming in fast right on her tail was what looked like an enormous raft.

"That's part of the government wharf," one shouted against the wind. "Broke off last spring in the ice. God knows where it's been since." And here it was, bearing down on the boys in the boat. "Here," I said, "hitch your painter onto my car and I'll back her up."

"Get outta that. Think you got a ten ton truck? Even you couldn't do that with a VW."

Meantime, the seas were coming in clear over the car, and the storm got worse. All the little draggers moved nervously around the harbour, looking for the best anchorage, or just riding it out. Round and round they went in a stately sarabande.

Finally the wind began to shift a bit and the sky to clear for half an hour, enough to see across the bay where the hills looked like old faded black-and-white photographs of themselves. Up the bay, a heavy mist rose, and a blue smudge showed over the water and the hills, as if they had been washed with old-fashioned blueing. In the well of sky overhead, the sun gleamed and set fire to the edges of the high thin clouds. Up the road came a great chrome-yellow plough, pushing the clean white snow before it.

The aspens are now turning pale gold, the larch still green. And the indescribable colour of the tall grass in the field. Bonne Bay lay black and still, dead calm, fog shrouded. The *Springdale* like a painted ship on a painted ocean. Not a sound, hardly moving. Gad's Harbour light winking in the intense midnight darkness. Little boats scuttled over the calm water. Then, the tone of everything changed, the bay became sullen and sluggish, sky leaden. Later it cleared again, and the sunset was glory, with the cliffs surrounding Gros Morne quite red to purple, the water reflecting close to shore and on this side pink, deep blue, and streaks of gold. A light on Birchy Head reminds me of Whistler's *Nocturne in Blue and Silver*, only silver here is the gold of car lights. A patch of daises gleams in the darkness. The air smells of salt.

Now that November clouds fill the sky, the restless landscape enchants. Sunsets are like tongues of flame coming up behind the hills on the lower side of the Gulch. The almost full silver moon rises long before the sun's light has gone. It shines on the black water, particularly when it catches a tide rip or on a calm spot, and the beams are like millions of glow-worms swarming. Coming up the hill, the moon shining on the frosty snow made diamonds and rubies.

What could be more beautiful than the dim light on the misty-white Tablelands—the wind sighing and shifting the pebbles, stars dim in the haze and the singing brooks! Then, for one magic moment, the haze lifts and Cassiopeia shines from a well of intense blue, Gros Morne is touched by a wisp of mist, with the distant hills black against the lucent sky. Then, a full, full moon, a smooth sea, the pebbles rolling softly, the red and green of Stewart's boat, the utter peace of the black water reflecting the moon and the seaside lights.

How sorry I feel for people huddled in cities, missing the glories of living near the sea in Newfoundland as winter approaches.

WINTER ON THE HILL

With wind and snow most every day, Ella crosses the bay on the ice, prepares for Christmas, and hosts a New Year's Eve party.

WHEN I first moved into my house on the hill, everyone said I wouldn't stay, not after Christmas, not up on that hill alone, only the cemetery above me. To tell the truth I wasn't sure myself, but I had an idea the experience would be worth the trouble.

They warned me that nobody dies here in the winter, so the narrow rock-strewn track to my house, along which I drove in first gear, was never plowed. But they didn't know the "magic monotony" of life perched there between the bay and the low serrated hills, with the sky wide as the ocean, the sameness balanced by the excitement of storms and drifting snow, and the full moon on starry, frosty nights seen through an icicle. Apple-green and indigo-blue shadows on my ski tracks, as black lines of spruce trace arabesques on the white landscape. The air twinkles in the clear, frosty, early morning sun. More than summer was winter beautiful in Bonne Bay, in breathtaking, bone-chilling storms or in cloudless calm when the sun warms us and casts blue shadows over mountains and gorge in an ever-changing panorama. And at night, when the moon was full, I watched the Bay through binoculars. Outside, it looked as if there was a spotlight on the landscape. All shadows black, the snow-covered surface absolutely sparkling and reflecting the moon like a cracked mirror.

Our lives revolved around the barometer and the cloud formation. Each morning we would wait for the verdict of the first one to go outdoors. Was it bitterly cold or "coming on a mild"? No one would dare be quite certain, for wind would spring up in the Gulf without warning and envelope us in drifts thicker than any fog. Caught in such an unexpected storm we would remain where we were until it passed—if outdoors, hunched with backs to the wind and heels dug in; if indoors, unhappy prisoners. Pretty soon, snow fell and my hill became a steep rocky mountain, lovely to contemplate but hell to climb. Fortunately, I had earlier brought up supplies—oil for my stove, kerosene for my lamps and food enough to feed an army.

One clear January night, we had gathered in the community hall for an after-wedding celebration. At midnight, when the older guests went home, the sky was loaded with stars, but at one o'clock we found that we couldn't open the door for drifts, nor could we see two feet beyond the gleam of our lamps.[38] Sixteen of us, including the bride and groom, spent the night in sleepy games of crib and snoozing uncomfortably in wooden chairs. At daylight the villagers shovelled us out.

Later, when I had floundered through the drifts to Emma's house, I heard the story of her neighbour. She was stumbling home alone completely shrouded in drifts, when she was lifted off her feet and deposited on the hood of a slow-moving car, without damages aside from a good fright. Em and her sister, Mab, had gone to the Rectory for a convivial evening with the parson and his wife, and as the house was sheltered by a hill and a grove of spruce, they were completely unaware of the storm. They started home just about the time we discovered we were snowed in, and before they knew it, they were in trouble. Along the road paralleling the seashore, the plow had pushed

[38] According to current weather statistics, the Canadian community with the highest average annual snowfall is Woody Point!

banks of snow ten feet high on each side and into the cut new snow had drifted, soft and impassable. In the pitch dark, they had to climb to the top of the bank and crawl along the frozen mass which dropped steeply into the water. The waves whipped against the seawall and sprayed the top of the bank where one false step would have dumped them into the water. They were soaked to the skin when they arrived home.

Another night I recall, the wind came down a hurricane. The snow fell and drifted and from our frosted windows we could see a light where none should have been. We watched as it grew and glowed like a halo in the snow, and then blackened. A moment later it flared again, then out. "Must be a fire," said Ed. That was a threat any time of year for we had no fire-fighting equipment, but in this wind it would be a terrible calamity in a village of wooden houses built close together.

Ed decided to investigate and if need be rouse the villagers. Grabbing a flashlight, he crawled around the house while we waited, ready to follow if necessary. The full force of the wind hit him and he doubled up clinging to the veranda rail. The gust passed. He moved to the fence. Another lull and he reached the hen house in a direct line between us and the fire. Then he waved and disappeared. Fifteen minutes later we heard him fumbling at the latch, and when Mab opened the door he fell in, exhausted.

"It's all right," he gasped, "only Bill's porch is gone. He put a lantern out in the snow so's he could board up a hole, and that's what we saw." We went to bed to a very uneasy sleep, for the house rocked and creaked like a ship in a full gale.

One afternoon after a big storm, we were watching the ice on the bay. It was four feet thick in the Arm and at least twenty feet thick at the mouth where the drift ice had rafted, and the whole was weighted with tons of snow. "Come here and look," called Jane. "Are my eyes playing tricks or is the shed moving?" Gale-force winds, blowing straight on the coast, had whipped up waves of such strength that they forced themselves under the ice clear into the Arm. As the ice rose and fell, it lifted the piers and pushed the sheds built on them onto the road at drunken angles. It was unbelievable that swells could lift such enormous weights, and yet we could not deny the evidence of our eyes. The excitement of that event we talked about for days.

The next day dawned calm and clear. I thought I would cross the ice to Norris Point to see a friend, but Em warned me I was not to go alone, nor was I to attempt walking for I might stray near the Tickle, which was always open because of the riptides that met as they flowed from opposite arms of the bay. I knew from experience how quickly the wind and drifts could blot out the shore, but still I wanted to go. Em could not, for she had tripped on her skates a few days before and gashed her knee painfully and was now fuming in the house, occupying her hands with a complicated piece of needlework.

Ed came, stamping snow from his boots in the outer porch, and opened the door to shout out that Bill was just harnessing his horse for a trip across the bay and that if I hurried, I might just catch him. The house erupted into frenzied activity as Em brought my parka and boots, Mab my gloves—and everyone asking, did I have a pair of windproof mittens? Was my scarf in my pocket in case I had to tie it over my face against the wind? I concluded they thought I was on my way to the Arctic.

Bill's cumbersome wooden sled attached to a brown mare held only Grandma Holt, bundled in blankets to her eyes but already shivering. She had been laid up with a "wonderful pain" for more than a week and was now going across to the cottage hospital. Most winters, Bill told me, they could take sick people to hospital more comfortably than this, either by boat over open water or in the warmth of a snowmobile over ice. But this winter the weight of the snow had pushed the ice so far down that the salt water oozed up and turned the surface to yellow slush that was impossible for a snowmobile to traverse, except in rare times of well below zero, and then only in very early morning.

So off we started. When we came to the middle of the bay the horse was belly deep in slush and quite unable to drag the heavy sled.

So Bill and I floundered along, sometimes knee deep in snow, sometimes walking over a stretch of frozen crust. The knife-keen wind brought tears to our eyes and made my cheeks ache. I draped the scarf over my face so that only my eyes were visible. Poor Mrs. Holt was almost frozen. In half an hour we were on the other shore and I went my separate way while Bill deposited his passenger at the hospital. I was to meet him at the church for the return journey, but after my visit and a long walk in delirious sunshine, I could not find him. Presently a man with snowshoes slung on his back told me Bill's horse was still outside the hospital door and that he'd be along directly. As I waited, I watched a snowshoed figure whipping over the ice from the other side of the bay, and I thought, "I'll walk anyhow, and Bill will catch me before I'm halfway across the bay."

Of course I remembered the dire warnings, but on such a civil day with snowshoe tracks to follow and Bill close behind, I knew I would be safe. But what I did not know was the incredible difficulty of walking, even with my experience on the way over. I floundered in slush for nearly two miles until I discovered a new rhythm of walking. You must lean forward all the time, half-falling on your face so that your legs come out of the deep holes and forward in one movement. The swift-changing landscape gave me no space for fatigue or fear. I thought instead of the nineteenth-century writer who described the "nervous hysteria of nature," and wondered how he would respond to this.

Wind on the mountains blew snow like smoke down into the valleys. The dark green hills were outlined with a clean black line of trees. Everything gleamed with brilliance that was painful to my eyes, which I could open only for a momentary glance, except when in the dark shadows of gorges and the folds of hills. Where little brooks tore down the mountain sides and cut deep beds, the banks were edged with snow overhangs like scalloped lace.

When I came into the house Em said, "My God. Your face! It's like an old boot. And your eyelashes are white with frost."

"I walked," I told her.

"You idiot."

Then, recovering from her surprise, she asked "If you didn't intend to go on the sled, why didn't you take your skis with you?"

"Skis? On ice?"

"Why not? Use the things the way God and the Norwegians meant them to be used—for travelling. You'd get across the bay in half the time with a tenth of the work." It hadn't occurred to me to use skis for anything but running downhill, but from then on I used them on unplowed roads, over ice and through woods, and so came to the proper enjoyment of skiing.

Much later that day Bill returned, rather concerned for my safety and with a note from Mrs. Holt for her daughter who was, at that moment, in Mab's kitchen having a mug-up. Grandma Holt had lived her entire life in a small cove, remote and isolated, where her grandparents' Devon speech had lived in her and her children, though a little corrupted. She called wet, clinging snow "clitty," and described a smooth hillside cleared of trees and gently sloping as "suant." She closed her back door with a "hapse" and her shed door with a wooden bar called a "toggle." She never went visiting but "cruised around." When I visited her in hospital and she confided that she would love a "nightingale" to keep her shoulders out of the draft, we ransacked the village for a woollen shawl to drape over her.

About this time, the village was nearing a crisis. The previous summer had been rainy, and although the grass grew high, much of it had rotted before it dried to hay. Now, people with horses, sheep and cows were obliged to cut down on animal rations and to scrape shed floors for wisps. The horses with their ribs showing looked pitiful; the sheep wandered the roads picking up scraps, and the cows looked disconsolate where they stood, knee deep in the snow-covered fields. And worse was that village merchants had reached the end of their supplies not only of hay, but also of oats. Even in the large towns animal feed was scarce, since the ice on the Gulf and the snow on the railway line had brought freight hauling to a trickle.

Then one memorable morning, a three-ton truck appeared,

loaded with bales of hay that disappeared like frost before a July sun. Millions of sparrows flew in for the leavings and, according to Steve, "made an awful charm" with their twittering. Ed's cow was so happy with the new, sweet hay that she gave enormous quantities of milk. But another crisis was building up. Nobody had stored away enough coal for the stoves and furnaces. This severe winter made such inroads into the coal that we were now down to a few lumps, aided and stretched by birch billets that we hated burning, since it meant endless trips to the shed for stoking the stove. Why the merchants didn't put enough coal in their vast sheds to tide the village over and, incidentally, to make a few dollars by charging extra in March for coal stowed in November was hard to understand.

Ed's neighbour, pushing eighty-two, was in a bad plight, for he had run out of coal. However, the hay truck had made a trip to the woodlot six miles away and had returned with a load of birch sawed into short junks with a power saw. These the driver had dumped at the old man's front gate on a snow pile. Next morning, bright and frosty, the old man was out with his axe, splitting the wood. He stopped long enough to greet us and to say, "If any of them fellers in St. John's who burn birch in their fireplaces saw this, they'd die. They never ever saw a birch bigger than a starrigan," holding up the smallest stick he could find to demonstrate.

After helping him to move the splits, we went to dinner, glowing with hunger and a sense of accomplishment. We had homemade pea soup, roast pork with baked potatoes, string beans and spinach from Mab's cellar, apple pie with clotted cream, dark fruitcake and coffee—not to mention great mounds of homemade bread and yellow "real" butter.

Then there was Christmas. In my childhood in Lewisporte, a sure sign was the appearance of a small barrel of grapes from Spain packed in sawdust. To whet our appetite for the next day's feast, the traditional Christmas Eve supper was boiled—salt herring and potatoes. Only then would we decorate the tree and put our gifts underneath. With the glow of coloured lights and candles in the window, we would sit by the tree and sing carols. Us older children would bundle up in woollens, gather outside a friend's house and set off to sing for invalids and shut-ins. We would walk quietly on the frosty, crunchy snow, up the lane from the road to a house set in a field and sing, ragged but lustily, "Oh Come All Ye Faithful," then on to other houses 'til we could go no farther. Returning home for a warm-up and a hot drink, we'd get into our best caps and coats with a little corsage of pine cones and a red ribbon on the collar, and head off to t   h   e midnight service at church. Walking home, the Northern Lights would sometimes swirl across the sky and hang curtains of subtle green and yellow and turquoise all over the sky—and the mystery of Christmas would strike us afresh.

In Bonne Bay, Christmas season started around the first of November. Every afternoon I would drop in on friends on my way to fetch the mail, and I would find them all, dinner dishes washed, sitting at the table with the stove roaring hot, pouring over the catalogs. It was always, "Have a cup of tea...you're in no hurry, there's plenty of time" and "Now, tell me which one of these you'd get for Bill—or Wanda or Mary," or whoever, and I would be asked for advice on everything from hair ribbons to snow boots. Then together we'd make out the order—Lord, how complicated we thought the forms—and trudge through the mud in the late afternoon to the post office.

Accompanying all this activity were smells the like of which don't exist anymore, I swear. The number of back doors I went through to be greeted with shouts of delight, as cookies, cakes, and all sorts of goodies came from the ovens in perfect shape and were offered to me, for sampling of course. Far more food than any self-respecting middle-aged woman should eat in a twelve-month.

On Christmas Eve most of the villagers went to the church, which smelled of fir boughs and candles, and we'd sing old carols. That year outside the church there was something grand and new and marvelous—an outdoor tree decorated with hundreds of coloured lights. As this was our first Christmas with electricity, we went whole hog. A tree in front of the church, one on the highest hill above the village, decorated by the village council, and two small trees lit with blue lights on the verandah of one of the merchant's houses. The children gasped in wonder, and so did we.

The next morning the sun rose over the far hills on a white world, and the frosty air glittered and danced, as if it were folded in Christmas paper and tied with silver ribbon. Empty the village road was, but not lonely, for I knew that in every house the children were opening and gloating over their presents. Nothing moved outside, but the hovering gulls and the clouds. No sound broke the stillness until the church bells rang out, and people appeared from everywhere in their Christmas finery. Then I went feasting with my friends, who knew that my sons were thousands of miles away. What love and friendship they gave me on that Christmas day.

For the next few days all was quiet and slow, a time for visiting the old and housebound with some of our best baking, and a jar of jam or some grapes. Then the fun began. I recall, though it hardly seems possible now. We had five parties in a row, none of which broke up before the early morning, and some that went on 'til after breakfast. Somehow, we would find time to sleep and wash dishes and prepare food for the next spree. And what wonderful finery turned up. The prettiest girls I've ever seen, looking like fashion pictures from the catalogues, the latest in jewellery, hairdos six inches high. The latest dances, too, which led to the apex of the evening when one of the girls would pull Grandpa—rather the worse for dipping into the punch bowl—onto the floor to teach him to jive.

I had a party, too—open house on New Year's Eve. I honestly never knew before the pleasure of being hostess to an entire village. In the afternoon, tea and cakes and wine for the elderly, who came uphill on horse and sled. Then from eight in the evening to four in the morning with a break for the watch-night service, friends poured in. Pea soup simmered on the stove in a great vat. The music never stopped.

The next morning the sun was a creamy misty disc. A triangle of shiny silver shone on the water. Snow drifted downward, infinitely slowly. Patches of blue over the hill behind the house. Windows a forest of palms, flowers like morning glories on the pane.

Several weeks later, I dropped a pencil on the floor and it rolled swiftly to the other end of the house. I found that I'd tilted about five degrees, thanks to the combined weight of my guests stomping out the rhythm of the "Squid Jiggin' Ground." I had to have the sills jacked up to straighten the floor, but it was worth it.

I would not be surprised if my New Year's Eve party has now gone down in the folk history of Bonne Bay.

FRIENDS AND NEIGHBOURS

THE WONDERFUL EMMA TAPPER

Emma Tapper, who appears in many of Ella's stories, was one of her closest friends in Bonne Bay. She guided for Ella during the Killdevil days. Here is the story of how they first met, and something of Em's upbringing.

I FIRST met Em when her brother Harry answered my appeals for help in my new Killdevil venture with, "I daresay my sister, Emma, would come for the summer, although I don't think she'd like working indoors much. She knows all about boats and engines and could certainly tell you all about the river."

"Sounds promising. Ask her to come and see me soon, will you?" We were walking down the country road as we talked.

"There she is now," he said, pointing to a lithe figure in khaki slacks and shirt coming toward us. She was small with ash-blonde hair and a beautiful mobile face, and she walked gracefully. A warm smile lit her face as she said, "I was coming to see you soon. I used to love your place when the Simpsons lived there, and I'd like to see it now that it is lived in and cared for after all these empty years."

"Do you suppose you could guide for my guests?" I asked her.

She hesitated a moment. "Yes, I'm sure I could and I'd love to. But did you ever hear of a woman guide? How do you think your guests would feel about it?"

"I don't think they'd mind much if you were good at it. Why not take a chance?"

And so she became indispensable guide, advisor and my right-hand at Killdevil. She knows every rock and ripple, every resting place for salmon and trout in the twelve-mile stretch of the Lomond River. She knows the trees that overhang its banks, where the wild orchids grow, and where you can find the delicately scented, white lily-of-the-valley. She can take an ailing outboard motor apart and put it together again as good as new. It was something to see Em tail a big salmon with her bare hands and safely land him. She would grasp the salmon firmly with lightening swift wrist movement, just above the tail and then lift him out of the water where he would hang from her fist, paralyzed.

Speaking of her childhood when her father worked for the St. Lawrence Lumber Company in Stanleyville and then Lomond, Em told me that, "When we lived in a big house, the brook ran down a few steps from our back door. We had a little boat called *Baby Tapper*, just big enough to get around three-foot-deep pools. The first fishing I ever did was by our back door with a bent pin and a line for tiny little trout. We weren't allowed to keep them, so we'd flip them into a pail of water. They'd fall off the pin without our touching them. Each kid had his own pail, and at the end of the day we'd see who had the most fish before we put them back in the brook.

"In the winter when I was a child, we would ski in the woods. I had to go out to Woody Point to my grandmother's to go to school. Doctor Green was in East Arm then too, so in the winter his boy, Tom, would ski out to Woody Point with me every Sunday night and home again on Friday. I wouldn't do it now, but in those days it was nothing."

She told me that her father, an ardent fisherman, had given her a fly rod on her twelfth birthday and taught her how to use it. "He used to take me with him when he and Uncle Bryant and Doc Green and George Simpson, the company manager, went fishing, and he would show me where the salmon lay and explain why they were there. I practically lived on the Lomond River, and I guess I know every rock in it. Tom and I used to walk on Saturday mornings to the river and fish all day. Many's the time we came home when we couldn't see a hand before us. I wish you could have known the river then—salmon behind every rock."

Boats and fishing, gardening and berry picking came naturally into her activities. In no time at all, she was also included in the hunt for moose and caribou, and learned about the wild backcountry and the skills necessary to survive, as well as making her an excellent marksman.

After her mother's early death, Em learned to help her older sisters keep house for her father and younger siblings. She did all the traditional women's work: knitting, sewing, bottling, tending the garden, keeping cows and hens. And she was always ready to drop everything for a few hours jigging in the bay. A neighbour once told me, "I often heard her say, 'Well, nothing for Father's supper. I suppose I'd better go jig him a fish.' Then she'd go off in her boat across the bay to the foot of Killdevil, and soon she'd be back with a cod or two. Em never waited around for someone to bring her what she needed."

Once she told me, "You know, I went and bought a piece of land up on the hill by the cemetery in Woody Point.[39] There's six acres in all, and some day if I ever get the money, I'm going to build a house there. And you know what I'm going to do? I'm going to look after old people—old men and women—and I'm going to let them do whatever they like. If one wants to go jigging, I'll get hold of a dory and I'll buy his fish. If one wants to plant potatoes, I'll give him a piece of land and I'll buy his crop. If the women want to, they can knit all day, every day, and I'll sell their socks and mitts. Whatever they want to do, I'll let them, even if it kills them in the end. I think it's a sin the way old people get shoved aside. Better they should die fishing or cutting wood—that's as good a way as any, and meantime they're happy."

---

[39] There is a story around that some of Em's land she won from a neighbour in a card game.

Years later, having settled in Woody Point, Emma helped run a family restaurant and tourist cabins, and made both high-water marks in cleanliness and good taste. When the Seaside Restaurant closed on the death of her sister, while others would have sat back and fiddled away their days, she cast round for something else to do. She investigated pottery making, and enrolled in classes at the Corner Brook vocational school. She returned home to set up a studio to make attractive pottery which was sold in the Bonne Bay Crafts shop, now long gone. She still found time to learn weaving, run the tourist cabins, look after a large house and cultivate a big garden.

When fall comes, the freezer is full of homegrown food and the cellar shelves loaded with jams, jellies and pickles. Not only that, but she tars the shed roof, mends the plumbing, keeps up the fences and gives advice on all these skills to anyone who asks. And when one is lucky enough to go fishing with her, one sees that her skill and her knowledge, as well as her delight in being outdoors, is as great as it was thirty years ago.

Em is one of those rare friends with whom regular communication is unnecessary. There might be between us years apart, never writing. Then, one day I could appear in her cafe or on her porch, and her face would light up. Once after a long absence, I arrived in Woody Point by coastal steamer at daybreak. A robin sang and a cow lowed as I went through the gate of Em's garden and up to her door. She was sleeping on the porch with the full light of the sun on her small thin face. When she saw me, she smiled and said, "Oh good. You're here," as if I made a habit of appearing unexpectedly at sunrise. "We'll go fishing later on, but now you get into the bed upstairs—you look sleepy. I'll call you if you're not up when I'm ready." When I woke, the sun was pouring in through the window, reflecting on the walls and ceiling the dancing water of the bay outside. It was hot and brilliant, with the clarity of the northland on its rare days of cloudless, windless weather, the clarity of sun-flavoured wine, so hot that I walked barefoot down the path and across the road to a late breakfast at Em's cafe.

She agreed to be written about only because she has a strong conviction which she wants to share that to live in the country and survive, one must know something about everything connected with daily living. She regrets that the children growing up around her are deprived of many ways of living an interesting life by not being taught about every skill the community possesses. She believes that life should be built on self-sufficiency and the willingness to help one's neighbours. As someone once said of her, "She's the finest woman salt-water ever wet, and she could, if she felt like it, run a motor boat upside down!"

HUGH MCKENZIE'S GRANDDAUGHTER

The McKenzies of Glenburnie were among the early settlers in Bonne Bay. Ella visits a lady from the third generation of this family and learns about home-life of long ago.

ONE DAY I was invited to take tea with a joyful old lady in Glenburnie. She had coal-black hair and pink cheeks, and she made me welcome in her kitchen, being one of the few women who did not insist on visitors coming into the parlour. And no wonder, for the kitchen had just been painted a shining white, with a dado of pale blue all around and cupboard doors to match. On an ancient wooden rocker was a woollen afghan, subtle blue and purples and violets, which she had just finished crocheting. The cloth she laid on the table was purest white with blue and pink forget-me-nots embroidered at the corner.

"Blue is my favourite colour," she said when I complimented her, "I fair hates all that green and yellow people mixes together."

She poured water into the teapot and laughed: "Puts me in mind of my sister. She knit some socks for her husband, always using up bits, she was, and she knit them yellow and green stripes going round his legs. He had to wear 'em, but he told me he had to keep his eyes shut when he put them on, because they made him want to throw up. Finally he dropped them, by accident like, in the washing tub in boiling hot water, and you should see how they came out—colour of pig mash."

By the time we were seated at the table, a crowd of children had entered quietly and were sitting on the edges of their chairs, staring at me with wide eyes. "Now then, what are you all doing inside this lovely day? Wants a cookie, eh? Or to have a look at the woman? Now, out with you all and don't let me see you round here for another hour."

She swept them off gently, took her chair and sighed, "Them children. You'd think nobody could cook like their grandma. In and out all day long, and that's not half of them."

I complimented her on their good manners and healthy looks and she said, "Yes, my dear, they're all McKenzies. All looks alike—like me."

"And were you a McKenzie? I've heard about them. You must be a granddaughter of the original Mac then."

"Yes, and a good bit I minds about me grandfather Hugh and me great-uncles." And this is what she told me.

In the mid-1800s, the first McKenzies would sail out of Scotland each spring with their families and supplies and would return in the late fall with dry cod, smoked salmon and timber. They came to Bonne Bay in the 1870s and settled in the bottom of the bay to fish and farm, cutting lumber to build their solid houses. They kept sheep and spun their own wool, out of which they wove cloth and knit sweaters, socks and underwear. They made their boots from the hide of their cattle. And, as anyone will tell you, they were the best craftsmen in the entire area of the northwest coast. Acres of land they took in on government grants. Then they died and left the land to their large families.

"Why, I can mind," she said, "when I was only twelve, I hooked mats and spun wool, and I even made skin boots from the sealskins me father got. A dollar a pair and find me own materials, that's what I got for them. Now I s'pose you'd pay five dollars for them."

"More like forty," I said, and her eyes widened with surprise.

"There now! What is the world coming to, at all? Forty dollars!

Why that was as much, almost, as I could earn in a year when I was young. I minds when I went out in service first time at the merchants, I got four dollars a month. For that I'd get up in the morning fore sun-up, and I'd make the fire, bring water from the brook and put on to boil. And I'd have the washin' done and on the line by the time the men came in from fishing. Then 'twas off to the flakes. Of course, the men used to prong up the fish out of the boats, but we'd have to clean them and put them in the shed in salt. Ones we salted the week before, we'd have to take out and put on the flakes to dry. By then t'would be dinner time. Then off again, turning the fish, cleaning the splittin' tables, and so forth. And before you went to bed, you'd have to mix bread so's it could rise overnight."

"What would you do in winter when there was no fishing?"

"Oh, we all had our mat frames, and in the fall we'd get in some brin bags and we'd cut up our rags. I guarantee you, 'twas more than your life was worth to leave any clothes around—they'd go into the mat, for sure. So every afternoon, when dinner was done, we'd get out our mats and hook away 'til tea time. Then we had to knit—we knitted all the time—to keep the men in mitts and socks where they was cutting wood all day. And sweaters—hundreds of them, it seems to me. Course, we were always carding and spinning—even the tiny ones, for they had to pick the wool and help us twist it."

"No fun, ever?"

"Oh my, yes. Twelve days of Christmas, my they were times! We couldn't do one tap of work them twelve days, I tell you, or we'd get a lickin'. And that meant we had to cook and bake and mix bread for a month beforehand. But we'd forget all that when the time came. Everyone went dancing and jannying, night after night. And we'd have a Christmas concert and a tree and all the children got presents—old people too. 'Twas some funny watchin' an old man stumpin up through the hall to get his presents from Santa Claus, and Santa asking him if he'd been good all year."

She laughed and wiped her eyes with the corner of her starched apron and poured another tea for us.

"What did you eat at Christmas time?" I asked.

"We always had goose in our house, killed it ourselves. Of course, Christmas Eve we always had boiled herring and potatoes, to get our stomachs to rights for Christmas dinner. Then we'd have a bit of moose or caribou in case someone came for tea. Caribou used to come right down to the beach, them times, but we don't see them anymore. Oh yes, and we had pork—always had a leg or shoulder of pork hanging up in the storeroom, and you never ate pork like it."

"Was it a special breed of pig, or what?"

"Not special to start out with, but soon as September was out, we would start fattening them and would rub them with pot liquor every day to stretch their skins. Pot liquor? You knows—where you boils spareribs and salt beef with cabbage and potatoes and peas pudding. We used to have it two, three times a week, and the water in the pot is what we'd bathe the pigs in, nice and greasy. Nothin' better for stretching skins and you knows an animal can get only so big as his skin will hold."

"Pies and puddings? Did you have old recipes from your mother and grandmothers?"

"Now, hold on my dear. Wait 'til I tells you!"

But by this time the bus had gone, and I was just as happy to walk home in the fading twilight, that long, infinitely lovely period of our northern spring day. I walked uphill and down, past tiny houses with their yellow lamps, past black outlines of the mountains against the darkening sky and the silver sheen of the wind-riffled bay. Orion was travelling south with Sirius in his wake; the pole star shone faintly. I saw the moon rise twice in my walk—once from a hilltop under Pickatenny Reef and again by the beach in Hell Cove.

That was a night I wouldn't call the King my uncle!

CANTANKEROUS UNCLE GEORGE

Many an argumentative old man has made life difficult for his family by insisting on doing what he wants and not what he should. This story is about one such character, well-known and respected in Woody Point many years ago.

ONE SUMMER morning, I woke early. Not a wisp of smoke from the village chimneys, not a person stirring. The bay was like a mirror, and it was hard to tell where Uncle George's dory ended and its reflection began. Even Uncle George himself was still, oars poised in midair. Then he spied me coming down the path to the wharf, and he dipped the oars with a mighty pull, sliding to the wharf and tossing me the painter. He hopped across the stage head, arms loaded with half-dry cod. Hopped back in the stage and out again with three delicious purple plums in his wizened little hand. He gave them to me, calling me "Sir."

"Beautiful morning, Uncle George."

"What's left of it," he growled.

I could see that he was put out about something, for all his showing off. He didn't even glance at me.

"Get a lot of fish this morning?" I asked.

"Look for yourself—hardly none at all," though the dory was writhing with cod and mackerel.

"Never got up 'til half-past four this marnin'. Overslept meself, that's what I done, and that Fred, he wouldn't wake me if the governor hisself was coming."

He sat on the thwart seat, his gnarled hands between bony knees, his rheumy eyes now turned to me, "That Fred," he mumbled, almost savagely.

Fred was the old man's son with whom he lived down in the Cove. We liked him, but the old man said he was lazy, and he was afraid of the old man's wrath.

"Lazy enough to sleep 'til six o'clock every marnin. And you know what he done last week?" Uncle George grumbled on, "that day we had the sou'easter? Come out after me in the power-boat." He spat in disgust.

"Well, you did break your promise. You said you wouldn't go outside the point. It was a living gale in here and we were worried about you, out there alone."

I could have told Uncle George that I was one of those who urged Fred, much against his better judgement, to launch the big dory with the seven horsepower engine that Uncle George called "the power boat" and fetch the old man home. I could have told him, but I didn't, for I would lean over to the point of falling on the back of my head to keep in the old man's good books.

Uncle George snorted, "Living gale, me eye! I seen worse weather than that many's the time. 'Sides, it's me own business if I wants to get drowned. I guess I'm old enough to know me own mind."

"If I had reached my nineties, like you, I'd want to die in my bed," I argued.

"I'll die when and wherever I feels like it," he retorted, and with a sly look he added, "I got something to tell you, only you got to promise you won't blab to Fred nor nobody. I wants to tell him, meself, when I gets round to it."

Whatever it is, I thought, it's sure to be something to put Fred out of sorts. I promised to hold my tongue, and Uncle George, all ninety pounds of him, scrambled up over the slimy logs as nimble as a ten year old and sat beside me, his sticks of legs dangling over the wharf.

"Well, that day of the sou'easter, I wasn't fishing!" He peered to see the effect this announcement had on me, and satisfied with my startled expression, he continued.

"No sir, leastwise not for cod. I was catching pulp logs."

I gulped, took a deep breath and said, "Do you mean to tell me you were out there alone in that gale in your small dory, hauling those great, wet logs into your boat?"

"'Twas too good a chance to miss. See, I figgered out the night before when I went to bed that the wind was coming up, and I knowed the Bowater tug was hauling downshore with a boom. I knowed the seas would drive them logs over the boom and float them inshore. So I just got up before anyone else and I picked up, oh, must'a been a cord—and stacked them all behind a big rock on the beach down below the Point. Wait 'til Fred sees 'em. He'll be fit to bust."

"Uncle George, you are absolutely crazy! Anyhow, I don't believe it—you couldn't pick up that much waterlogged wood, slimy and all as it is, and then stack it on shore."

"All right for you then if you don't believe me. I'll never tell you nuttin, no more," he said gloomily.

"But listen to me a minute," I begged, "if anything happened to you when you were out there alone, we'd never forgive ourselves. Think how bad we'd feel if you got drowned."

"Wouldn't bother me none how you'd feel, if I was drowned," he said and lowered himself with a swift motion into his boat. He tossed to my feet a small cod and said, "Go on home now, and cook that for breakfast. I got to stay here 'til eight o'clock, 'til Ned and them gits up. Can't have them breaking the law on account of me."

That was Uncle George—you never knew what was coming next. First the pulp logs, now the law. Later that day, I asked "Ned and them," as Uncle George called the family who ran the restaurant on the waterfront, "What's this about him and you and the law?"

Ned laughed, "It's just a small lie we made up so's the old man wouldn't get us out of bed before sunrise to buy his fish. We didn't want to hurt his feelings—and you know how it is with us, working 'til midnight—so we told him there was a new law out saying we couldn't buy or sell anything until eight o'clock in the morning."

"He believed you?"

"Oh, yes! I daresay it's hard on him, having to sit round for an hour or more, but it's the only time of day he does sit, so a spell won't hurt him."

That was true enough; at ninety-three and a few months, Uncle George spent every waking hour on the move. I had never seen him walk, only propel himself with a peculiar half-run, half-hop that covered a lot of ground without visibly tiring him. "I goes to bed every night, eight o'clock sharp."

Fred once remarked, "He wouldn't care if the Queen of England came to visit him, he'd just say excuse me, good night, and off to bed he'd go."

Occasionally, after his work was done and before his bedtime, Uncle George would turn up at the restaurant where every evening we would congregate for a beer and a chat. He would hop in and sit at the nearest table, and if he were in the proper mood, he would talk.

One evening when he was in a good mood, we were talking about Sally's Cove, and I had just remarked that nobody had ever told me about the food floating ashore—the grub that Henry had said, "Come ashore all down the coast back in the war."

"You remember that, Uncle George," Ned said.

"Just guess I do. Got a good bit of it, meself."

During the Second World War, when liberty ships, loaded to the gunwales, were carrying food from North America to Europe, they often went through the Straits of Belle Isle that separates the island of Newfoundland from Labrador. One night in a bad storm, a liberty ship broke in two pieces on the rocks and spilled her cargo into the sea.

"She broke right abroad in the middle, the way I heard it," said Uncle George, "and then the wind veered round and blew straight in on the coast. Well sir, she was loaded with all manner of stuff and we got the most of it—oranges, apples, hams, flour—oh, and great big tubs of dried powder."

"My Lard, that marmalade," someone interrupted. "See, we didn't know 'twas marmalade then, so we didn't know what to do with it, and we...."

"Stop interruptin'," said Uncle George, "Let me tell it me own way. After all, 'twas me who found it."

We quietened down.

"I wuz out jiggin' that marnin'," continued Uncle George, "when all of a sudden I sees this stuff floating down on me. I just sat there and gaped. I never seen nothin' so queer. Well, by-n-by I seen 'twas oranges, so I out with the dip net and in with the stuff 'til I could hardly move me arms, and I had nowhere to put me feet, the dory was so full. And still 'twas coming," he paused for a swallow of beer, wiped his mouth and looked around.

We were still quiet.

"Well, then, I come ashore and told all hands. So we all went out, remember? We hauled in oranges, then apples—wonderful sweet and soft, they was—and when we'd get a boatload, we'd go ashore and stow it, and off we'd go again. We got a tub of lard and a few hams, and I got a barrel of flour, all by meself."

"Surely that was no good?" I asked.

"And why not? Once you got to the dry part inside, 'twas wonderful nice flour. Course, outside round the barr'l staves, 'twas proper barm." That was the common word for a fermented mixture used to rise dough.

And all this time, Uncle George said, people down the shore were walking on oranges and apples, nowhere else to put their feet. They, too, stowed as much food as they could find room for.

"And what about the marmalade?" I enquired.

"Oh yes, the marmalade. Well, we cooked that stuff every which way. Mind you, we didn't know what it was then. And when 'twas cooked, 'twudden fit to eat, we gave it to the pigs. That's the Fall you should have been here—our pork was as sweet as figgy-duff. Anyhow, we ended up soaking the stuff in tubs and tubs of water. It swole up something wonderful, so we cooked it and 'twas perfect."

"Dehydrated marmalade!" I exclaimed.

"Sure, and the most of us lived a good part of that winter on what we sove out of that wreck."

After Uncle George had gone home, a friend who was visiting me said to nobody in particular, "Too bad that old man has to work so hard. I thought he had a son. Can't he support the old boy?"

"Oh, Fred can," said Ned, "but he isn't able, because the old man won't let him."

The truth was that we thought "poor Fred," not "poor old Uncle George." He was prevented from doing a duty which every Newfoundlander is brought up to believe his by Divine Right, that of expiating for all the wrongs we had done our parents by supporting them in their old age. Fred was truly in a dilemma. All he could do was attempt to circumvent the old man's wilder projects and look to us for sympathy and understanding.

"Stop the old man from fishin', and he'd shrivel up like a dry worm."

But stop him from going into the woods alone, from climbing onto roofs and from rowing alone in a gale, Fred could and generally did. Until the day he came to us and said, "Me father is bound and determined to tar the roof tomorrow. He's got the tar-pot ready. What am I goin' to do, in the Name of the World?"

"One thing," said Ned after a pause, "you could hide the ladder. He wouldn't have the nerve to borrow one, because he'd have to tell what he wanted it for. And you know that nobody would lend him one for that."

"But where'll I hide it so's he won't ferret it out?"

"Chuck it up on the barn roof. He'll never find it there."

A few days later while Uncle George was waiting in his dory, "So's not to break the law," he told me, "Hah, fooled Fred this time. Thought I wouldn't find the ladder, did he? But I did—on the barn roof. Fullish feller, Fred." He paused. "Had an awful time getting the ladder down though, I had to climb in the hayloft, crawl through the window and hook the ladder down with a gaff-hook." Tough as nails, Uncle George had climbed onto the cottage roof and tarred it from stem to stern.

Then, one evening in early autumn when the sea birds were coming in-shore and everyone was planning a trip out birding, Uncle George hopped into the restaurant, his beady eyes glittering. He pulled up a chair, ordered a beer, looked around the room and said, "I s'pose you heard what Fred done today?"

Nobody spoke as Uncle George peered at us, suspecting deceit.

"Mean to say you haven't heard? Well, I s'pose I might as well tell you," and he took his jolly good time at it.

"Seems Fred and the Fisher boys went out birdin' in their dory this marnin'. They went out past the Point and got a few, and then they decided to row further out the bay. 'Stead of emptying their guns, they just shoved them under the thwarts. One of the triggers caught in a piece of danglin' rope and shot Fred clear through the knee. He's over to the cottage hospital now with a great lump of cement on his leg. Dried as hard as the foundations of Ned's house. And that's the way Fred is going to bide for the next three months." He leaned back in his chair with an air of triumph.

"I bet he's some glad I got me dory and me jigger, 'cause now he's got somebody to fish for him and earn a dollar. Too old to go fishing, says you. Well, I might be ninety-three, I still got me two arms and me two legs, and I got a lot of go in me yet." And taking a large swig of beer, he said, "I'm not fullish enough to shoot me own leg."

Sadly, one night that June, my dear cantankerous old Uncle George died, without pain, with only a day's illness, having the day before been chopping wood. His coffin was taken to the graveyard in his old dory, because that is what Fred thought he would like.

JIM SHEARS
OF ROCKY HARBOUR

The Shears family was among the first settlers in Rocky Harbour. Ella here tells something of the background and amazing ingenuity of one branch of this prominent Bonne Bay family.

THE VERY first thing I remember about Jim Shears was his telling me, "When my grandfather came here a hundred years ago, he landed ten hogsheads of salt right on the beach where you're standing. There were only two families in Rocky Harbour then and they said, 'What are you going to do with all that salt?' Grandfather said, 'Salt me fish. If I can't catch that much here, I won't bide.' 'You'll never do it,' they said." Fishing is poor in the shallow bay, crawling with surf, peppered with rocks and the wind straight in from the Gulf of St. Lawrence. But the old man used the salt and bided, with his wife and four children. And his grandson Jim, said, "Come on up and see my family."

On a rise in a clearing stood a big house. Behind it a brook, a waterfall and a long weather-beaten shed—Jim's sawmill. The house was full of youth and laughter—a big family and dozens of friends. Here was the home of a man who performed no miracles of courage, who talked no fine words of wisdom, but who lived each day for what he believed to be the ultimate good, who created around his family a wall of security, belonging and sharing, and who was light-hearted and full of the love of little things. A man tall, lean, with faded blue eyes in a thin, square-jawed face.

"Want to see our mill?" he invited. "The boys and meself built it. Cross-handed, though, because we built the house the same time, and they weren't very big then."

Towering over us was a twelve-foot, ponderous wheel of wood. Jim pulled a string and the water from the falls was diverted into a trough. It poured over the wheel and it turned creakingly, but without drag or pull. The little trout in the pool below hustled for safety in the overhanging banks. "Now, come inside," said Jim, and there, wherever you looked were canvas belts slapping round. Band-saws, circular saws, drills, lathes—everything whirling, driven by Jim's water wheel.

"Now I'll show you something else." He pulled a switch, and presto! Electric lights. "Got my house all wired too," he said proudly. "The boys and me made the machine last winter. Works good, too." Brains and hands they had, but no money. So with their phenomenal ability with mechanical things and their profound belief in their ability to improvise, they made what they needed.

Jim grew up under the influence of his other grandfather, who is said to have deserted a British man-of-war, and with an assumed name lived uneasily, never knowing whether English or French lorded it over his bit of ground. Both were his enemies. Once when Jim's father was a child, a warship anchored outside the harbour and sent ashore a boatload of sailors. One of them called the old man by a name the child had never heard, and then he said, "So this's where you got to. Don't you fear. I won't tell I saw you." As Jim commented, "I guess that's the way the best of us come here, if the truth was known."

His father believed in letting the boys alone, so when young Jim said, "I want that piece of land on the hill," his father said, "All right. Go ahead and clear it." Jim did, and from the wood he built a twenty foot motorboat, as good as ever seen—and all before he was sixteen.

Then an older brother, home for a visit from the States, took Jim back with him. Fascinated by the big concrete bridges then being built everywhere, Jim got a job making the wooden forms into which concrete is poured. Then something happened, as they were working on a giant bridge. When a sixty-ton crane began to settle into the mud just below the dam, consternation turned to pandemonium. The pumps couldn't clear the water as fast as it seeped in from the leaks in the dam. While others tried frantically to block the flow, Jim looked around for something to make do. "Here, pass me that sack of charcoal," he said quietly. Taking a shovel, he sprinkled fine coke over the water. It sifted down slowly, water pressure swirled it into the holes, and soon the dam was tight. The crane came out undamaged, and that was when Jim's career really began.

He prospered enough to write to his girl, "Come on down and we'll get married." They did, the first thing when she arrived, though Jim laughingly tells how they searched all night for a preacher. But bridge building goes on in queer places, and each of Jim's four older children was born in a different part of the country. "Guess we'd have had one in every state," chuckled Jim, "if the Depression hadn't come."

And that gave Jim time to think. He began to remember that clearing in Rocky Harbour, and he knew he couldn't live much longer without the land and the sea that was deep in his bones. Jim's wife confessed she'd always thought Rocky Harbour a much better place to bring up a crowd of children. It was a hard time, but they put together the mill and sawed lumber to build a home.

Well, with the house built, the mill bringing in a few dollars, and the boys and girls growing up, they had long discussions about what they'd work at next. Then one stormy fall night, a great barge beat in on the rocks, and the forty-ton loading crane on it was given up for lost. Jim and his boys thought otherwise. With only two light chain blocks, their brains and hands and their knowledge of the sea, they made a runway from barge to a scow, using logs they cut and peeled on the spot. Between heaving seas, over jagged rocks they rolled and pried the crane over with poles and rescued it. The crane was restored to the grateful barge owners who told Jim he could have what was left.

One son said, "Must be a lot of iron in that barge, Pop. Let's get it. It might come in handy." So they burned the wreck and collected ·every last link of iron. While the boys built a lean-to near the mill, Jim made moulds in the shape of anchors. The oldest boy wrought the iron and sold enough anchors to buy a tractor. Up to now they'd been sawing in the woods with an old car engine. It wasn't that they despised modern methods. They just hadn't the cash to buy expensive machinery. Now they set up operations in a cove across the bay from Lomond.

"Come over and see our new camp," Jim said. "It's a dandy fit-out." I think they made that tractor do everything but the cooking. It took them to the woodlot, ran the saw, planed the lumber, took them back to the camp and dragged the dressed lumber out to the scow for loading. They worked together, Jim and his four boys, from dawn to dark.

Occasionally Jim would knock off for a spell. He'd ease himself down on a log beside me and say, "Did I ever tell you about the pool back of Gros Morne? It's full of salmon. Let's go in sometime and see if we can catch one." He liked sharing with friends the things he loved best. His boys knew that, too. They knew he was just and full of affection and that he—quite rightly too—thought his sons as good as any man, and better than most.

When they made money with the tractor, Jim said, "Now boys, we'll share out." But the boys decided, "We'll keep in partnership. You take the money, Pop. We know where it is when we want it."

And just as Jim could rely on his children, so he could on his wife. I shall always regret her sudden death before I had the chance to know her well. I do know that with a house full of children and not much in the way of labour-saving devices, she was calm and full of affection. Her girls and boys all have the same quality. Once I saw them helping her to feed a crowd of unexpected guests. They turned out twenty-five meals without a single unnecessary movement. And what food! Home-processed moose meat and salmon. Homemade bread, fresh butter and jam with thick, yellow cream, and tea as black as your boot.

John Fox's oil-drilling operations at St. Paul's needed a new scow—a big one forty feet long, twenty feet wide, and weighing about twenty tons. Would Jim build it? Of course. Up the valley they went with the tractor, cut the trees, sawed the lumber and hauled it to the beach. Now a scow must be built bottom up, and how will you turn it over especially when you haven't much to make do with. Well, Jim got empty oil drums and lashed them to the scow to float her on the tide. The tide came in, the scow floated. But still bottom up! So the boys and he put their wits to work.

On the right side of the scow they built a wall of rough timber. Against it they piled as much sand as they could load on the scow bottom. They tied a hawser clear round the middle of the scow and attached the end to their motor dory. Then they anchored each corner of the loaded side firmly with anchors and long chains. As the tide rose, the scow began to tilt, so they put the motor boat full speed ahead. The anchor chains tightened, and suddenly the great clumsy thing shot skyward, turned slowly and landed right side up. The whole twenty tons! They sat on the beach and laughed.

Once I heard Jim say, "The fellow I worked with in the States has made a fortune now." He didn't say it enviously, though, for I think Jim knows he has made a good life—a pattern I could wish for all mankind. I think if there were more like him, we could really believe in the dignity and rights of man. He and his family always make me think of the poet's line "Bless mine hands and fill mine eyes, and bring my soul to Paradise."[40]

[40] From Hilaire Belloc's poem "The Birds." *Verses*. New York: Laurence J. Gomme, 1916.

NAN HARDING REMEMBERS

Here Ella visits a grand old lady in Norris Point who supplied visiting Royal Navy ships with fresh bread in the late nineteenth century and who tells of her early life working with the well-known Reverend Joseph Curling and his wife.

I HADN'T been long in Woody Point when Em said, "I must take you to see Nan Harding, Uncle Bryant's mother. She's one for yarning, so we'll have to take a whole day off." We did that, crossing to Norris Point by the morning ferry and walking up the lane to a big, square white house with a glassed-in veranda across the front.

Nan was then nearly ninety years old. All day she would sit enthroned in a rocking chair on the sun porch that overlooked the cove and the rock-lined entrance to East Arm. Directly in front of the house was a garden such as one rarely sees in our climate, with a birdbath, a goldfish bowl rimmed with symmetrical smooth stones gathered from the beach around Sally's Cove, and sweet rockets, sunflowers, dahlias and roses. Nan loved colour and variety. She loved company, too, and had plenty, for everyone who passed through the village came to visit. At any hour of the day, she would call for cups of tea and plates of cake for her guests. These would be brought on a silver tray covered with a linen cloth, and Nan would dispense hospitality with the air of a dowager duchess.

She had a phenomenal memory, except the matter of her second marriage. This she had obliterated from her mind the moment she decided it was impossible, and that was not long after she had contracted it. Her first husband, who died young, was Bryant's father, and she had returned to her son's house to live out her life as John Harding's widow.

Em had warned me, "Don't ask questions. She'll take the helm, but where she will sail, God only knows."

Indeed, Nan covered vast distances that day as we sat with her on the sun porch, while she finished a piece of "fancywork," her hands as busy as her tongue.

"My, that's a pretty ring," she said, admiring my labradorite stone. "I minds I had a beautiful one once—diamond it was that John brought me from Halifax. I lost it—dear me, wasn't I put out about that. I even cried. Handsome man, John was, and generous too. Course, I deserved the ring, considering I got him started in business, so to speak." She smoothed the silk of her dress with a long thin hand, and a little smile crept to her lips and her fine, grey eyes.

"We were doing just fair with the fish and lobsters that time, certainly not getting rich. That was when the British men-o'-war used to come in to water and get whatever supplies they could. One day, the rear admiral's flagship came in, and I mind I was in a hurry because I wanted to dress up and go on board with John. Well, I was in the kitchen taking the bread out of the oven, when who should come in but the admiral's steward. He was some taken with that bread I can tell you, said it smelled just like Heaven. He asked me if I could spare a loaf for the admiral's supper, so I wrapped a bun in a cloth and gave it to him.

"Well, next morning, who should come to my door but the rear admiral himself. My, he was pleased with my bread, and said it was the best he ever ate. He said he wanted to ask me something, so I invited him in."

What he wanted to ask, to Nan's utter astonishment, was would she undertake to supply the fleet with bread during the summer cruises? Nan said she couldn't do that, never in the world. For one thing, her oven was too small, and for another, how on earth could she mix such enormous batches of dough? The admiral swept aside her objections. They sat at the dining-room table and he drew plans for an oven to be built in the backyard, such as, he said, the women of Quebec used. They discussed making wooden troughs for mixing and made mathematical calculations of the ingredients. Then, while John built the ovens and fashioned the mixing troughs, Nan collected her materials.

"The first two batches were hard as rocks," she recalled, "and the third was so soft it wouldn't rise. But we got the hang of it finally and began supplying the ships with good, homemade bread."

Then the admiral said to them, "Why don't you supply us with fresh meat as well?" So John travelled the coast, by boat and on foot, bargaining for animals on the hoof to be collected when needed. Later, when the business increased so that he was supplying not only the West Coast fleet but that in the East as well, he imported cattle from Canada and grazed them on the fields behind St. John's.

"So we worked up a good business out of loaves of bread, didn't we?" Nan concluded.

While she slept after lunch, Em and I wandered by the beach. "Fantastic woman," I said. "Was she brought up here?"

"Oh no. She came here with Parson Curling when she was a youngster. She used to help Mrs. Curling with the children and the cooking. She met John here—says he was the first person she saw when she landed off the schooner, and that he started courting her right away."

Now at that moment, I was far more interested in the Reverend Joseph Curling than John Harding. "Does she remember much about the Curlings?" I asked, for in the late 1800s, Joseph Curling was well-known along the coast. He built schools and churches, started a lending library in Woody Point, and attended to many medical emergencies.

"My dear, she remembers everything. She can repeat word for word any number of conversations. Of course, she may have made them up, but if she did, she has told them so many times that now they are truth to her. Anyhow, they're the most interesting conversations you ever heard." So we managed that afternoon to steer her to the Curling family and her life with them.

"Reverend Curling was a kind of tall man, thin, with a nice face. He talked strange, though. Sort of bit off his words, just like Englishmen do now on the radio, but we got used to it. The first thing he did when he came, in the middle of summer it was, was to call a meeting, and we all went down to the church to hear what he had to say. He wanted us to build a parsonage and to fix up the church, which was p   r   e   t   t   y dilapidated I must admit. He had plans all drawn up for building, so that the men said he must be a good carpenter. He said they could start in the fall getting out logs and sawing the lumber, and that would give them something to do when they couldn't go fishing. And they thought that was a good idea.

"He had us pretty excited, I can tell you, and when he sailed away with Bishop Feild, we promised we would do everything he wanted. We didn't see him for a good spell after that. He went down the coast in the *Lavrock*[41] to visit places that hadn't seen a clergyman for years and then he went back to St. John's to be ordained.

"It was November before he got back here and we had the parsonage started—two rooms finished and the roof on—and we couldn't wait to see how pleased he would be with us. I can't tell you how it made you feel when he looked you straight in the face and told you what he wanted done, because you knew that he was thinking all the time of your good, not his. Anyhow, when he came he brought two teachers, two helpers and a man who went around with him to all the places he visited. I think he must have been a missionary, too. And you should have seen the stuff they brought: books and papers and pencils for the schools, and nails and glass and doors and window sashes for the buildings. It was like someone coming

[41] The ship Curling, who came from a well-to-do family, gave to the Church for its coastal missions.

down from Heaven.

"He was pleased with the work and he settled down in the parsonage for the winter. Soon he called another meeting. I'll never forget that one. He gave it to us, I can tell you, about how dirty the place was. That was true, of course, but we'd got so used to it that we didn't give it a second thought. He told us the first thing we had to stop was throwing refuse and dirty water out the back doors, and the next thing was we had to fix up the lanes and paths so that we wouldn't be up to our knees in mud half the year. Then he told us what he was going to do for us: schools with everyone learning to read and write; churches with proper baptism and marriages; sick visits. Oh, it was going to be wonderful. But the Parson said he wanted us to help him do all this with the help of God. He was a saintly man, I can tell you, but he didn't expect God to do it all. Fact is, he did a good bit himself, what with buying the nails and tools and window sashes out of his own money, and paying the school teachers, too.

"Well, that winter he was with us nearly all the time, only once going away by schooner to take one of the schoolmasters down and to visit the sick. That's when we found out he was as good a seaman as a Christian. Some of the old men said they never did see such a good hand with the sail—such a calm, coolheaded man in a gale. And he was as good a hand walking on snowshoes, once he got the hang of it. He used to walk for miles on them to visit somebody sick or to hold prayers in some little cove where there was only a family or two."

Nan paused in her narrative. Then she leaned forward toward me and said with stark intensity, "Now that I'm older and know more about the world, I wonder how he stood it! How could he have lived among us, so happy and so good, he used to comfort and fine living, so far away from his own kind?"

His parishioners were pleased when he married Emmie Robinson of St. John's. He brought her back to the Bay of Islands by way of the Strait of Bell Isle, making visitations along the way and so taking six weeks for the voyage, a strange honeymoon, surely. Beautiful, gentle, well-educated—Mrs. Curling came to the village like a burst of summer sunshine. This, by the way, was Birchy Cove, later renamed Curling in their honour.

Nan said, "How well I remember her. I went to live with the Curlings as soon as she came and didn't leave them 'til I went to my own house with John. We fixed up the parsonage with curtains and flowers. We taught the women how to cook lots of new dishes, and Mrs. Curling went to visit the sick people every single day, carrying good food to them and always ready to help with their families. Pretty soon, every house in the place had curtains to the windows and flowers in pots on the sills."

Wherever they went, they were needed either for spiritual or physical help. The distances they travelled were long, often in extreme cold. On their first trip to Bonne Bay, in winter over the hills and marshes by dog team, they passed a stormy night in a lean-to which they made in a snow-cleared space with trees woven into a shelter. Next day, when they reached the settlement, the hungry dogs took chase after a stray pig and unceremoniously dumped the parson and his wife in a snowbank. On another trip, in midwinter, they came upon a man whose hand was badly mangled in a shooting accident, and him they treated with the contents of Mrs. Curling's sewing kit— white silk thread, a needle and a pair of nail scissors.

"Before he went away for good," Nan told us, "they did have a few years of peace and quiet, and they had one friend of their own kind, anyhow. I remember that it was around 1880 that the Government sent the first Magistrate to Bay of Islands—a retired Navy man—and he lived with the Curlings a good part of the time.[42] But they lost him, too, and that was a very sad thing. It happened in February of a wonderful bad winter—snow drifts and bitter cold, when Parson Curling was down here in Bonne Bay. It was on a Sunday and we had three services that day, the church packed every time, and Parson Curling was tired. Just as the last service was done,

[42] Commander William Howorth was appointed in 1877 and died in 1881.

a message came that the magistrate was terribly sick and wanted his friend. So Curling with two other men started to walk back to Bay of Islands in the dark. They walked all night and most of the next day until the evening, when they knew they were lost. They made camp in the woods, and I minds Parson Curling telling afterwards how they only had one match and they never in the world thought they'd get a fire going with the soggy wood. But they did. Anyhow, when they reached the Magistrate's house the next morning, he was dead. I don't believe Curling ever got over that.

"Many's the death bed he had reached in time to give comfort, and now his best friend had died without him. Shocking thing, wasn't it? He went back to England soon after that for a trip and when he came back, he only stayed a few years before he left for good. John and I used to hear from them sometimes, but we never felt they were gone. Everywhere we looked we saw things to remind us of them, and hardly a day would pass without somebody mentioning them."

In the evening when we were seated at the elegant mahogany table with its heavy old silver and English china, Nan said, "I wouldn't have been me, nor John the man he was without the Curlings. Come to that, there wouldn't have been this house with all its comforts, either. We couldn't want what we didn't know was in the world, but the Curlings showed us that there was a better life than the fishermen then lived, and more to it than just food and shelter."

In the place that still bears his name, Curling built a beautiful church. Simple and white, it nestled in a grove of spruce trees that divided it from the churchyard. It was furnished with oak pews, lamps and hangings of brass, and simple but lovely stained-glass windows— all of which Curling gave to the people. I remember the church well—how the sunlight filtered through the windows and filled the air with amber, how the building sat on the earth as if it had grown there, until it caught fire one night and burned to the ground.

Only once did I see Nan after this visit. She died at ninety-two during a winter when I was far from home, and I still miss her. Bryant is dead, too, and the rambling old house overlooking the hills

MORE OF MY
FAVOURITE UNCLES

Vignettes about some of the wondrous old men in and around Bonne Bay, whom Ella grew to admire and love.

UNCLE STEVE said, "I'm well over ninety, but I don't suppose you'd believe it. I can hear as well as you can and see a good sight better'n you, seeing as you wears glasses.

"Yes, times have been tough here in Crolly Cove, what they calls Curzon Village nowadays, but we got it good now. With this old-age pension, 'tis wonderful. You can go and live where you like, and pay your board. You don't have to put up with nobody you don't like, just because they're related and got to look after you when you stops working. We got it nice here with me son, and four generations under one roof. Not many can say that. And now we can drive to Corner Brook and be back the same day. I minds when I first went there. I couldn't get used to no cow manure on the roads.

"We got our own sitting room, and when there's a racket on we can shut the door and be quiet. We bought a television once, but we sent it back because all we could get on Sundays was dogs yelping, and youngsters dancing and screechin'. Never no nice singing or services. But radio now, yesterday we had a wonderful church service on that.

"Winters we used to keep the Twelve Days of Christmas, and

you'd get some lickin' if you worked in them days. We had dances and parties and cruised around, wherever there was an acordeen. One time we were having a set, going the length of our house, and one feller came down hard and went right through the kitchen floor. The old Waterloo stove broke abroad, and the oven went in the hole after 'en. Nobody got mad, though, 'cause 'twas Christmas."

And here is how Uncle Steve invented a paid job to ward off hunger. "Once I minds, we weren't long married, and come fall we didn't have much in the house to eat, and there was no work. Feller next door, he didn't have anything to eat nor drink, and he had a big family. Times were real bad and I was getting desperate. So you know what I done? I went up in the hills, there in the Gulch, one pitch dark night, black as the devil's boot. I drove ten big horses over the old wooden bridge. Of course, I almost lost me life when the bridge collapsed under us. But me and the man next door, we got enough work out of fixing the bridge to feed us all winter.

"Yes, I daresay I'll go out and set a few rabbit snares by and by, when me hand gets better from strainin' of it helping a feller dig his potatoes the other day."

That was Uncle Steve, as fine a man as any.

UNCLE JIM has a feeling of responsibility toward his family of twenty or so cats. "When I gets out around one of them days, I'll call them to me and name all the new ones. Now—there's Peck, always in trouble, and Baby Blue Eyes—just look at he. And Fluff, and old Tom, father of them all. Me woman said if I died before she did she was going to kill all me twenty cats and put them in me coffin. Wonderful fright St. Peter would get."

Jim was born in L'Anse au Loup, and was taken to Forteau as a baby. He has not been back there for thirty years. Had he stayed in Labrador, Jim would have had a place of dignity and importance, with his family house full of furniture and his fish store full of gear, but he came to live in his wife's village, where he had nothing, not even friends. And although he had been a successful fisherman and lighthouse keeper on the rock of Belle Isle in the Straits, he now had to keep his family going by doing odd jobs for neighbours, between jigging, gardening and cutting firewood. Once he complained to an insistent employer, "I wish it would come to snow and fill 'er in from Gros Morne to Pickatenny Reef and then my Lard, you wouldn't be able to get at me."

Jim can make snowshoes and fashion elegant sealskin boots, and lately his skills have been in demand from people rediscovering the joy of snowshoeing and the glorious comfort of skin boots. How much this means to him can be seen by the briskness of his stride as he goes through the village, greeting everyone. Too deaf for the burden of casual talk, Jim says, "If I didn't have me cats to talk to, I'd go out of me mind." He is too old to walk the hills and too tired to roam the mountains for ptarmigan and rabbit, so he finds warmth, love and a reason for living in the animal world.

The man who sang at the Newport Folk Festival, ARTHUR NICOLLE, told me, "My father was a Jerseyman. He came out here to settle, and we've been here ever since. There was five brothers of us and we all worked together, fishing and cutting wood and tending on the gardens, though mostly the women did that.

"I daresay I can mind all the songs I ever heard sung. Oh, the time we had when we went to the States, Mrs. Walters and me, to that place where they do all the singing, Newport. All kinds of people were there, and me and she got right up on the platform and sung to them all. I can't sing as well now, of course, as I could then, but I daresay I'll sing you about the wreck of the *Ethie*, down 'long shore. You ever heard tell of that?

"I heard lots of songs when I was fishing with me father on the Labrador, and I can remember them all. People used to come from all parts of the Island and when we were done fishing or the day was bad, we'd go to work and sing to each other. That's how the songs got round.

"None of me other brothers can sing a song, only me, and often we goes down to Mrs. Walter's for a singsong. She learned lots of hers on the Labrador, too. Them times, girls used to go along with their fathers to do the cooking for the crew, and sometimes they'd come and sing with us when their work was done. Mrs. Walter's mother was a wonderful fine singer, and I've heard tell that when she was alone with the children and her husband in the lumber woods, she used to keep them awake all hours for company and she'd sing to them. Of course, they'd have naps in the day to make up for that. But when she'd sing them sad songs, she'd have the youngsters cryin' and bawlin', then she'd have to sing a funny one, though come to think of it, there aren't many of those."

UNCLE WILLIAM, well into his eighties, has just visited me. He was on his way home to Trout River and dropped in for a cup of tea. "I'm some pleased to see you, Uncle Willy," I told him;. "Yes, my d   e   a   r   . Had to be sure you was snug and warm, you a lone woman all be yourself way up here. What you doing' wid your time?"

"I'm writing down where we all came from. Your family is from Devon, I know."

"Yes, all 'cept me grandmother." And off he went. "Me grandmother, oh she was a handsome lovely woman and everyone loved her. When me grandfather came out first, he went to Bay of Islands with Baird, the man he was buying salmon for, and they went ashore to a house of people belonging to our crowd from Devon. Anyhow, there was a baby in the cradle, and grandfather rocked her and sang to her. Next time he went back, many years later, he married her! Isn't that a wonderful good story? They come down to Trout River and that's where we bided. When Father grew up, he got some land and he settled down and reared all of us, eight or nine of us home to one time.

"We had wonderful beasts them times. Once we had twenty-nine horned cattle and two oxen. They was all of 900 pounds, I'm sure.

One time we were taking them up over them cliffs to pasture, and one of the young fellers drove me finest beast over the cliff and killed her. Well, I was that mortified I cried. Anyhow, I went home and got me boat and went round to get the carcass, and 'twas some starmy. Time I was finished, I was nearly drowned. Next day I had the shivers, but I went out on the beach to mend me net. Then I got it. I shivered and shook and couldn't get warm anyhow. Me brother went up to get the doctor, he fifteen miles away, and when he heard 'twas me was sick, he come right on. And there I was under all the quilts we had, nearly shivering meself to pieces.

"Well, he told me sister he thought I was gone, but seein 'twas me, he had to do everything in the world for me. So they wrapped me in hot bread poultices all over and I lay in that bread I dunno how long. By and by I got better, though me skin was burned through with them poultices. 'Twas six months before I done a tap, but I been good ever since."

There aren't many jobs TAYLOR PARSONS, the kingpin of Trout River, who built my house on the hill, can't turn his hand to, but the job he likes best is one that takes him into the mountains. "Once a mining crowd come out here, wanting to go up the Gregory Plateau. They asked me the way, but I told them 'I won't let you go up there alone. Suppose a fog come in, you could get lost in no time.' So I went with them, and sure enough a fog come in. But I knew that country like the back of me hand, so I was going along, up the brook, feeling my way, when one man behind me called me to stop. He said an older feller was way behind, and we ought to wait. So we did, and by and by up he comes, puffing and blowing, and he said to me, 'When you're over forty, you won't find this walking so easy.' And I said, 'Well, sir, I'm fifty-nine me next birthday.'"

· Taylor could do an ordinary days work, then walk in to the plateau or, if it was winter, snowshoe, make a fire in the cabin for his employers, cook a meal, bed them down and put everything to rights before he slept. He has forgotten nothing that he heard from prospectors, mining engineers and promoters. He is sure there is "millions of copper" deep in the Gregory Plateau, but he doesn't expect to live long enough to see it mined. Just as well, for Taylor ambles through the unspoiled woods, looking for signs of caribou and moose, occasionally bagging a ptarmigan.

And telling yarns. "Many's the time I've seen the steamer come in the middle of the night, anchor off the cove and send the mail ashore in a life boat—seas beatin' in, rain coming down and maybe high winds. And I'd have to put on me clothes and haul the mail sack into the house, 'cause we ran the post office then. Then the wife and me would put on the kitchen fire and dry out the letters in the oven. The wife used to get that anxious, 'specially when the old-age pension cheques came—every three months or so and about $25 each—in case the salt water would wash off the names.

"'Twas awful sometimes, women coming home from hospital— and babies too—and we'd have to get them ashore somehow. On our backs, if they weren't too big, and seas coming in over our long rubbers and running down our legs. No wonder that when we finally got the road in, we all went crazy buying chrome tables and dining-room suites and all that kind of stuff. Some different from luggin' stuff in on your back from the life boats. But you know, I went over to the East Coast once and I didn't like it one bit. All closed in, like, and you couldn't see the water, not like here, where I can sit in me kitchen and watch the breakers roll in."

UNCLE ALBERT was a great talker. He had the most stunning combinations of profane and sacred words it has ever been my privilege to hear. Nobody else had the imagination and wit to think them up. I remember one day when we passed a less than handsome specimen of humanity, and Uncle Albert said, "My, isn't he hugly? I wouldn't want to walk over his face with me bare feet."

Another time he solemnly told us that he had a gun so powerful that one night he took a shot at the moon and knocked a "Goddamn great spawl off it."

"Don't you youngsters swim off my wharf," he would bellow. "I don't want you all chewed up by sharks."

"But there aren't any sharks round here," one child shouted back.

"Who told you that?" he barked.

"Me father," came the answer, and when Uncle Albert saw it was the Minister's daughter who spoke, he paused, then yelled, "Well, the cod out there is as big as sharks and just as dangerous."

When I told him that I was going to get my own boat soon, Uncle Al said, "That minds me of something I got to tell you. Whenever I hear about a woman gittin' a boat I thinks about that Scotch woman we had here t'other year. She was determined she was goin' to find work for all the poor fishermen who couldn't make a living. So one day she comes up to me and says, 'Do you know anyone around here who could make a tin dory?'

"You must be making a mistake, Ma'am," says I, "because you couldn't make no tin dory you could stand up in, much less go fishin in."

"Oh no," she said. "A tin dory. Maybe you people haven't heard about the latest things down here."

"I couldn't see the point of tin when we got wood, so I said, 'Maybe we're not up-to-date, and who told you about them tin dories?'

"Well," she said, it was one of them politicians she goes around with.

"Oh well," says I. "Politicians, they'll tell you anything, 'specially if they's the Liberal kind."

"Oh no," she said. "He was serious, and he said if we could make tin dories down here next winter we could sell them to the fellers in Corner Brook."

I knowed enough not to argue with her no more, but the next time I saw that politician I asked him, "Can you sell tin dories in Corner Brook?" And he said, "Oh my, yes, you could even sell twelve!"

Then there was the time Albert was down to Lomond with a full load of lumber on his truck headed for Deer Lake, and I had lost the clutch out of my car. "Now Albert," I said, "how about you towing me to Deer Lake?"

"No, my dear," he replied, "I can't tow you with this full load of lumber, but I can push you up the hills, and you go so far as you can on your own."

"Albert," I said, "you're crazy."

But I got in my car and ran down Barter's Hill and so far up the other side as I could. Then he'd push me up the rest. When we got to the garage in Deer Lake, the water was pouring off my face.

"Why," he asked, "are you too hot?"

"No, just scared to death!"

"But we made it, didn't we? I'm not too stunned, I suppose."

"No, Uncle Albert, you're not stunned at all."

Everyone's friend, UNCLE SAM, died suddenly of a heart attack. It feels as if some of the cement holding us together as a village has gone. Sam sitting in the cool September sun, on a lobster crate behind John Jellicoe's shed. Quiet voice, his big forefinger shaking at me in emphasis. Once I asked him why he was so happy and singing as he worked. "Sure this is the first time I've seen this day," he replied.

When they were taking him to the hospital, his wife jammed his old cap on his head. He said, "Oh my, what will St. Peter say when he sees me coming in this cap?" Later, lying on the stretcher being carried down the lane, he looked at the sky at one bright star and said, "That's where I'll be soon, up there looking down." And within the hour he was dead.

VICTOR CAMPBELL:
EXPLORER, SAILOR, FARMER

In this story, Ella Manuel tells of a remarkable Englishman who patrolled the West Coast with the Royal Navy at the end of the nineteenth century. Later he led a party exploring the Antarctic, was a naval captain in the First World War and afterwards, and eventually retired to a farm in Black Duck.

I FIRST met the extraordinary Victor Campbell in Corner Brook where he and his Norwegian wife, Marit, had settled in the 1950s. He had been in the Antarctic with the last expedition of Robert Falcon Scott, and had led the Northern Party, which survived the long polar winter thanks to his strong leadership. In another time, Victor would have been good company with great English explorers of the past, like Drake and Raleigh. He would have been an elegant figure with his beauty and grace, his cultivated mind, and commitment to adventure. In his homespun tweeds, walking his fields, he was the handsomest man I have ever seen, with a strong masculine face, beautifully sculptured and softened by his famous smile. "The smile of an angel with the heart of a hornet," Cherry-Garrard wrote of him in *The Worst Journey in the World*. And Lady Scott, in her memoirs, related that at her wedding, where Victor in navy whites was groomsman, she whispered to Robert, her bridegroom, "Couldn't I marry Victor Campbell instead? He is so handsome."

Campbell's family had been Royal Navy people since King George III. Victor was fond of saying that he went to sea at the age of two weeks, when his father, a naval captain, was posted with his wife to Halifax. He stayed on shore until he was three when, on the death of his mother, he was sent to his grandmother, who lived in Hampton Court Palace in a wing reserved for Royal Navy widows. At the age of sixteen, he tried to join the Royal Navy, but was rejected on grounds of health, so he promptly enrolled in the Merchant Navy. After four times around the Horn in windjammers, he was promoted to bosun at the age of nineteen. It was then that the Navy did accept him and soon took him as a junior officer aboard the frigate, HMS *Cordelia*, to patrol the west coast of Newfoundland to keep an eye on the French presence.

That was in the summer of 1896, when his cousin Jock Campbell was in command of another frigate. The two met on a salmon-fishing trip to Harry's River in Bay St. George, staying at a log hut that Jock had built on a little piece of land nearby. "It was," said Victor, "the most beautiful place I had ever seen, and I was determined to go back there, someday."

That time did not come for almost twenty-five years. During that period, Victor sailed into ports from Jamaica to Hong Kong, quite happy with his lot until the day he heard of Robert Falcon Scott's plans to explore the Antarctic. "Why did you want to go?" I once asked him, and with that fascinating smile he replied enigmatically, "To get away from women." I had to be satisfied with that. He regarded his Antarctic adventure as an interesting but small part of his life, and not until near the end would he talk of the eight months he lived with five companions in a hole dug in the snow. To hear his story was to live vicariously that incredible time.[43]

---

[43] The saga of Campbell's Northern Party has been described in many books, most recently in *The Wicked Mate: The Antarctic Diary of Victor Campbell*. Edited by HGR King (Erskine Press, 1988), and two books with the same main title, *The Longest Winter*, one by Meredith Hooper (John Murray, 2010) and the other by Katherine Lambert (Smithsonian, 2004).

Victor joined Scott's ship, the *Terra Nova*, a Newfoundland square rigger converted to steam, which took the Expedition of 1910-13 to its Antarctic base. Because of his experience in surveying and mapping, and because Scott early recognized in him the qualities of a leader, Victor was put in charge of what became known as the Northern Party. Their first task was to carry out prospecting, mapping, other scientific observations, and to make sledding journeys from Cape Adare, nearly 600 miles north of the expedition's base camp. This they did without more excitement and discomfort than was usual with any party completely cut off from the world and dependent on their own meagre resources. Then just twenty days short of a year later, on January 8, 1912, they were landed in Terra Nova Bay with only light provisions and summer equipment. They were due to be taken off in about six weeks and returned to base camp some 250 miles further to the south.

"You have to remember," Victor told me, "that once away from base camp, we were quite on our own. We could not communicate with the others, nor they with us—no radio or planes in those days. A good part of the time we were marooned, you might say, by the sea, which was neither open nor frozen hard enough to sled over. Overland it would have taken us weeks to reach base camp, through country completely unsurveyed, full of glacier tongues, crevasses, and mountains. However, that was part of the game. We accepted it, thought no more about it, and got on with our work."

When their work was over, they came to the seashore to wait for the *Terra Nova*, due on February 18th. "One week went by," Victor said, "then another. And one day we realized the *Terra Nova* was not coming for us. We thought she must have foundered in a gale." Actually, she was barred from reaching them by ice and adverse winds, and after many abortive attempts, she sailed off to New Zealand for desperately needed supplies, including coal for her engines.

"You must have had an anxious time of it," I commented.

"No. Not once we'd made up our minds that we had to stay where we were 'til the sea froze solid. But we were anxious about the ship, and would have given anything to know what had happened. As for ourselves, we knew it was a matter of months before we could move, so we made the best of it."

This was their situation. With the polar winter approaching, the six men had skeleton rations for a few more weeks, summer sledding clothes, thin canvas tents, lightweight sleeping bags, and nothing else. They were on a shelf of beach on what was later named Inexpressible Island, strewn with boulders where the wind blew with such force that Victor said one always had to lean into it when walking, and that if it suddenly abated one fell headlong.

"Food was our first concern," Victor told me. "We kept strict watch for seals, though in the beginning there were quite a number around. We killed as many as we could before they disappeared for the winter."

They took thought for shelter, too, knowing that the thin tents would not long stand up against blizzards. They dug into a snow drift to make a cave, twelve feet by nine feet and a little more than five feet high, and shored it up with what timbers they could spare from packing cases and sledges. There the six men settled down to live through the Antarctic winter.

"I wonder you didn't all go mad, cooped up like that," I said.

"We got used to it gradually. Actually, all we had to do was live from day to day, eke out our rations and try to keep warm. If today was bad, perhaps tomorrow would be better."

The cave, or "igloo" as Victor always called it, was dark and damp. Their only light came from a lamp of seal oil with a piece of frayed rope for a wick. Their food came from a fire burning in a piece of tin which was fed by suspending seal blubber over it to melt, drip on bones, and burn with enough heat to cook their meals. Their most difficult task each day was to chop enough meat from frozen seal carcasses to feed themselves and keep the fire alight.

"We ate so much seal meat, I rather think we smelled like them," Victor laughed, "and we did strange things to provide variety. I remember one night when it occurred to me that a little mustard for seasoning would be interesting. So I went to the medicine cabinet, but unfortunately what I took in the dark wasn't a mustard plaster but a linseed poultice. We didn't discover this until we began our meal, and then we had to eat it, because we couldn't afford to throw anything away." Once while cleaning a seal carcass, they found a fish in its stomach. "Not quite digested" Victor said, "so it made a wonderful dinner."

Apart from seal and penguin, they had a daily ration of one biscuit, one piece of sugar and one cup of cocoa made with water. "Almost anything was a welcome change, even a seal flipper, for we always kept one for scouring the pot. One night when I was the washer-up, I must have forgotten to remove it when I cleaned. Next day after a particularly nauseating meal, we found the dirty dish mop in the bottom of the pot. How we laughed."

How could they have laughed, I asked him, holed up in a cave without room to stand up, or stretch full length in sleep, while outside there were only interminable darkness and unabating blizzards?

"Oh, we played games and read and lectured each other on our experiences. I gave a course in History. Priestly gave a series of talks on geology. Levick kept us fit with drill—he was the doctor. And we had four books to read, including *David Copperfield*."[44] They had prayers every day, sang hymns and did Swedish drill exercises. The worst part of the day, Victor recalled, was when they had to go outside, when the howling wind would shred their tattered clothing, and the seal meat they carried would drip cold blubber on them and their belongings. Then sometimes the stove would smoke and blind and choke them.

Once they almost smothered. A match struck to light the fire went out immediately. Another was lit and burned with a sputter before it too went out. Victor seized the nearest thing at hand and broke a hole through the roof to let the air in. Several times during the following months the same thing happened, usually when a snowstorm had choked up the chimney they built, and they finally set a watch over it

[44] This later turned up in New Zealand, tattered and stained with black oily finger-prints, having been given by Campbell to a member of the expedition. Eventually it found its way to the Dickens House in London where it remains.

whenever snow fell or the wind blew, for they did not want to die of asphyxiation. Towards the end of their incarceration, they came down with dysentery. Victor said that nearly broke their spirits. They were too ill to drag themselves outside, so the cave daily became filthier.

"Did you never lose hope?" I asked him.

Victor sounded genuinely surprised. "Of course not. After all, the worst thing we had to endure was not knowing what had happened to the others. We would have given anything to know if the *Terra Nova*'s crew was safe, and if Scott had reached the Pole." That was, after all, the real goal of the expedition.

This was the time, Victor recalled, when all of them began having dreams, unbearably vivid dreams of hot water, open fires, and huge meals. It was also the time when their food supply went so low that it was either starvation or possible death on the ice. When the decision to move or to stay became imminent, a miracle happened. Out of nowhere, at a time when it should have been impossible, a seal appeared. Abbott, the seaman of the party, killed it with a rusty pocket knife. He lost the use of three fingers in capturing the seal, but he saved the party from starvation.

Finally, on September 30th, Victor judged the ice was safe to drag their sledges over. The six men now began the long trek south to Base. He said that when they started out, "We couldn't stand upright. We'd been doubled over so long in the igloo that it was agony to straighten our backs and lift our heads."

They climbed barriers, crawled over hummocks, traversed glaciers for ten days, before they spotted Mt. Erebus, the volcano smoking on the horizon above the Base and knew they were safe. But they were still a hundred and fifty miles away, and one of the six was so ill that it became necessary to leave him behind with Levick. Either they had to increase their daily ration for the sick man and trust to luck that they would be rescued before they were utterly starved, or the rest would have to go for help. They chose the latter course, and in a few days came upon a cairn in which quantities of food had been cached.

"We fell on it, burrowing like dogs and scratching away the snow with our bare hands," Victor recalled. "Then we sat down and feasted. We each had a tin of lard. I remember I saved some of mine and put it inside my shirt. That night I woke with the strangest sensation. I felt as if something wonderful had happened, I couldn't remember what, at first. Then I sat up in my sleeping bag, fetched out my lard and ate it. I don't remember ever being happier."

On November 25, 1912, ten months from the day they first burrowed into the cave on Inexpressible Island, they walked into base camp, every man alive and well. "I couldn't have done it with ordinary men," Victor said, making light of his achievement as leader. But Evans, captain of the *Terra Nova*, on revisiting the cave and finding Victor's notes, wrote, "Here is a tale of altruism and grit, so simply told, so full of disappointment and privation, all of which they accepted with fortitude and never a complaint. I had to stop reading, as it brought tears to my eyes."

In 1913, Victor brought the *Terra Nova* back from Antarctica to London. He told me, "It was a sad time. We had failed, for Amundsen had reached the South Pole first, and Scott, Wilson, Bowers, Oates and others were dead. All I could think of was to get far away."

He volunteered then for two years' survey work in Arctic waters, but two months later war broke out in Europe. After Gallipoli and winning the DSO, he commanded the Royal Navy monitor HMS *M24* in the North Sea Battle of Jutland. He won further recognition in an incident that never ceased to amuse him in the telling.

"It was a rough day, and we were pitching badly, when I caught sight of a German U-boat. My gunners couldn't get a sight on her, so I steamed full speed and managed to ram her before she could submerge. I was most surprised when I got home to find a piece of her hull neatly wrapped around the *M24*'s bow."

After that came the *Warwick*, another Royal Navy destroyer, which was under Victor's command when she was the flagship in the Zeebrugge raid of 1918.

After the Armistice, Victor took part in an attempt by Britain and other nations to intervene in the Russian civil war on the side of the anti-communist White Russians. He returned to England when the British withdrew in April 1919. In London, Campbell stayed only long enough to settle his most pressing affairs before sailing for Newfoundland and the log cabin on Harry's River. Soon he returned to England. "I felt I should go home once more to say my goodbyes properly," Victor told me, "and that was my undoing."

He smiled that angelic smile at his wife. "You see, one day walking through the hall I met a friend who insisted that I come to dinner with him. He was short a man and thought I might amuse the Norwegian Royal party who were visiting London at the time. I went, met Marit, and proposed to her before the night was out."

"And did you accept him right away," I asked her.

"Well," she replied, "what would you have done?"

"Snapped him up before he could change his mind," I told her.

Beautiful, dark-eyed Marit was Lady-in-Waiting to Norway's Queen Maude, and as soon as she could be relieved of her duties, she married Victor, and they came to Black Duck, not far from Stephenville, where they built a new home and filled it with treasures from Marit's Norwegian valley and Victor's adventures. Many a visitor came by, and many a grand party was held there.[45]

After he died in 1956, Victor was buried in the old United Church cemetery in Corner Brook. Marit returned to her beloved Norway to live out her days in the mountains and valleys she loved. On their wall at Black Duck there hung an oak slab on which was carved in Gothic relief: *Sleep after toil, port after stormy seas, / Ease after war, death after life, does greatly please.*[46]

---

[45] Alas, the house was destroyed long ago by ice from the flooding river nearby.

[46] From Edmund Spenser's *The Faerie Queen* (1596) book one, canto nine.

BEYOND
BONNE BAY

DOWN TO SALLY'S COVE

As the road north from Rocky Harbour was being built in 1953, Ella walked the old coastal trail north from Baker's Brook. In Sally's Cove she met three old Roberts brothers, all born in Bonne Bay in the late nineteenth century. Here is the scene as she picked her way north.

IT WAS late October that I drove through the Humber Valley and along the road to Bonne Bay. It was clear all the way down to the water's edge at Woody Point. But crossing the bay on the car ferry, the sky darkened, and the wind rose. Late in the evening, I arrived at Rocky Harbour, the surf pounding on the ledges, the lighthouse stabbing the gloom. But never is it dark or damp in Rocky Harbour for me. There is always warmth in the Shears' home. Their house is back in the woods by a stream, which tumbles over the homemade water wheel that runs their sawmill. It is idle now, for the men are working on the road, poking slowly along the coast, linking homes once isolated.

"I'm going up that road," I told them. "Down," they corrected in automatic chorus. "Down," I echoed obediently, though North is always up the map to me. Then one man added, "'Tis pretty rugged along there and going to snow soon. But you can ride to Baker's Brook with us tomorrow when we go to work, and you can get a truck from there." When I announced my intention to walk, they were amazed, but at least polite about it.

That night I slept to the melody of the brook, with a full moon at my window. At 5 a.m. it was cold and black, but a breakfast of moose steak, homemade bread and coffee you could put a fork across and not dent—now that was some good. From my place of honour in the truck's cab, I could hear the sleepy men grunting as they heaved sacks into the back, and heaved themselves after. We drove on down the road, picking up workmen along the way. There was no talking, as we rattled over rocks as big as your head, then lurched drunkenly along the beach, for the road through the woods was impassable, and we had to detour.

We passed the lighthouse at Lobster Cove Head, a few weather-beaten houses, more rocks and stumps, and we were at Baker's Brook. The sea roared unceasingly, and I could only stand by leaning against the wind. In a landscape empty of houses and fields, filled with the roar of wind and sea, it was startling to come upon trucks, bulldozers, graders, and dozens of men hurrying to start their work.

But that was not for me. I crossed the bridge, high over the rushing brook, which anywhere else would be called a river, walked back down to the beach and soon was out of sight. I hitched my pack higher on my shoulders, and began my walk to Sally's Cove. I'd wanted to do this for a long time, because I think you cannot know a country intimately unless you walk through it. And I did want the memory of Sally's Cove as it was, and as it would not be for long, once the road went through.

So I walked that morning in a world that, for all I saw of birds, beasts or men, might have held only me. I thought of the original Sally that morning. One story goes that Sally Short and her children were heading for Woody Point in flight from her husband. Darkness came on them, the wind rose, and they were shipwrecked. They put ashore in the uninhabited little cove and sheltered in a puncheon found lying on the beach. There they slept and the next day, the wind having abated, continued their journey down the coast. Another story held that a woman by that name had left Bay of Islands in a punt, rowing

184 NO PLACE FOR A WOMAN

cross-handed northward along the coast until she was shipwrecked here, and took shelter in the cove.

It was a dark day, the sea tortured by the wind. Green combers rolled over the shoals, rattling the pebbles, and pushing the brown spume which piled up on the shore. Then the wind took the froth and hurled small bales of it upon the beach. The stunted trees creaked and groaned. Driftwood was piled high at the waterline, along with bits of wreckage, and an old boat hull. The rocks were green, blue, red, mauve—sprinkled with gleaming quartz. Every step was a fascination. A wonder I ever got anywhere, that morning of driving mist and howling wind. But at Green Point I found shelter where the noise was lessened. Here I rested on an old winch, near two battered huts with boards weathered to grey velvet, and lobster pots piled alongside.

My eyes followed the long, slow roll of the sea, my mind remembering the fury around the point, and there came to me a luminous, elemental truth. In a flash, I knew what a sailor meant when he said, "The sea is never cruel. It is kind." I knew, because I saw that the wind torments the water, drives it, and whips it without mercy. It is the wind that is inimical. The sea is its victim. Rather would the water caress the land than pound and smack it with giant waves, but the wind drives it to frenzy. That is why a sailor feels a tenderness for the sea, a pity, for it is subjected to such punishment.

Past Green Point, the track wound inland through mesh and tuckamore, and petered out aimlessly. I went knee deep in mud. I backtracked. I detoured, and I became afraid, physically and spiritually. Really scared in that empty, bleak landscape. Then suddenly a bird sang, clear and sweet, and I went on, singing myself, until I came to the track again. Now, it skirted the cliff tops, the wind raved through the dead branches, and the rain began to fall. I was wet, cold and tired when I walked into Sally's Cove.

At the first house I came to, where children looked from the window,

I knocked at the door. It was opened by a smiling woman. "I'm look-ing for Aunt Polly Roberts," I told her. "Her granddaughter lives with me in Corner Brook."

"Oh, you must be Ella," said Mrs. Decker warmly. She took me into her cheerful kitchen, fed me a succulent dinner and gave me good talk. Meanwhile, Aunt Polly heard I was around, and came bustling in to fetch me. A wisp of a woman, perhaps seventy-five years old, she moved with the speed and grace of a bird. She took me to her spot-less little house, to meet her husband, John Charles Roberts, whose English is something beautiful to hear, and whose huge bulk in the blue fisherman's jersey was topped by a face of such serenity. It was he who insisted I sample his raspberry cordial while he told me about Sally's Cove.

Then we came to his brother Mark's house, full of children and young people and old. Mark, slim and straight, a softly weathered beautiful face with blue eyes, was encircled by his lovely grandchil-dren running around. Everyone talking! One said, "You know the Brandies out there—that long reef—" and a new story was given me.

Years ago, an English man-of-war, the *Pegasus* I think her name was, went aground on the Brandies. The commander put ashore, filled with wrath, demanding to know why the reef was there when it wasn't on the chart. "Well," said Mark's father dryly, "I don't know about the chart. But the Brandies have been there since I can mind. And now you're there too!"

Could the local men give aid to the ship? Well, they supposed they might try to pull her off with their dories, but by the time they got to rights and rowed out, the British seamen were already hard at it. John Charles said you never saw anything like what they did. There were 300 men on board. They all ran like hell to the starboard rail, then across the deck to the port rail, back and forth, and rolled the vessel right off the reef!

I was taken to meet Eli, the oldest of the Roberts brothers, just as hearty and friendly and lovable as the rest. It was he who countered a visitor's comment, "What, no telegraph, no radio—why you've no idea what goes on in New York or London" with "No worse off than them people. They don't know what's going on in Sally's Cove."

What hospitality that afternoon! But now the day was over, and Aunt Polly bidding me goodbye said, "When you came into the kitchen, 'twas just like you was one of my own." With a load of fresh lobsters, bakeapples tinned by Mark, and inside me more raspberry cordial, do you wonder that I left Sally's Cove feeling that immeasurable wealth had been showered on me? To be counted one of them— those gentle people with the natural manners of a true culture. As long as I live, they will be my friends.

Of that wondrous journey, there is much more to tell, but time runs out. Memory is strong. When it fades and the going is rough, I shall hold in my hand a pebble from the seacoast, round and smooth like a medallion. I shall savour its texture and remember the essence of my people, my land, my heritage.

THE NEW ROAD NORTHWARD

Not long after Ella walked to Sally's Cove, the dirt road reached St. Anthony. In a CBC broadcast in 1964, she described the opening up of the Northern Peninsula, and some of the changes the new road brought to coastal people.

WHEN MY friend phoned me from Portland Creek and said, "The river is just right; come down for an evening's fishing," I felt as if someone had called from Mars inviting me to dinner. A few years ago, to visit Portland Creek would have been a major expedition of uncertain duration by boat, since the wrong wind or too much would have marooned me for a week or exposed me to the risk of ship-wreck. Now I am fifty-five miles from my friend, on a dirt road that meanders along the finger of the northwest coast of Newfoundland, reaches the top and swings east to St. Anthony where, for the moment, it ends. It is known as "the road down north."

"Pushing that road down the coast is like opening a Christmas parcel—you never know what you're going to find," said a friend. Each mile finished reveals surprises to the people outside and opens a new life for the villages along the road.

Ever since the coast was settled, the people have been isolated, especially because of our lack of harbours and the uncertain weather. Then last year, the last link of road was closed, and ten thousand people suddenly found themselves within reach of the world, a large part of which seems to have been beating a path to their doors ever since. A sociologist could make what might well become a classic study of the people on this coast and the effects of sudden access to the rest of the world, including their inundation by strangers. I can only report what I have seen happen to my friends.

It used to be said that along the northwest coast were only poverty and rampikes—the skeletons of dead trees. There are plenty of those still, but there is also a landscape that would take your breath away—majestic, empty, haunting. Now, I am afraid my friends will never be left alone long enough to enjoy it, for the "forces of civilization" are bearing down on them.

When I first travelled the coast, walking part way on headland trails, cadging rides in motor-boats from one cove to another, I would be fed and given a bed by people I'd never even seen before. All I had to do was knock on a door and, believe me, that hospitality was not repaid in money. The good breeding of the people always made me feel humble; they had time to be courteous, and their courtesy was born of a genuine concern for others.

Now they are much too busy. Already bombarded by the talk of hundreds of irresponsible salesmen, they are flinging away their hard-earned money on the conventional symbols of modern prosperity. Con bought a deep freeze and a jukebox last week. He filled the deep freeze with ice cream, cokes and hot dogs and set up in business, trusting the jukebox to lure customers. The jukebox wouldn't work, not even when Con lifted it, shook it vigorously and dropped it with a resounding bang. It still didn't work.

A respected local businessman of seventy-odd, returning from his first trip to the city of Corner Brook, told me, "I bought a car and a truck. Then I bought two coffins—one for the wife, one for meself, and then I went to the liquor store and bought nine bottles of rum."

The progress of the road is marked by what they describe as bath fit-outs—tubs, basins and lavatories—fuel oil stoves with hot-water tanks, and plastic pipe to bring water into the houses. All of which is gratifying, for it is high time the people on the coast had some comforts. No longer do women have to bring turns of water for laundry; nor do the men have to spend freezing weeks in the forest, cutting and hauling fire wood, for now the road means the oil trucks can deliver fuel frequently.

The rhythm of life has indeed changed, particularly in the traditional occupations of fishing and pulp-wood cutting. A fisherman in Sally's Cove told me that halibut had been "eating the rocks" all summer, but when the fishermen had caught enough to eat, there was no way to get their fish to market. Up in Cook's Harbour, for instance, at the end of fishing season when cod had to be salted and dried, men carried it on their backs or in handcarts to the barrens to lay it in the sun. Now trucks whiz along over the rocks, dropping their bundles of wet fish, picking up the dry, and it's easier to cure a thousand quintals than it used to be to dry a hundred. That means real money, with dry cod as much as twenty dollars a quintal.

The woodsman used to pack his gear and grub and go into camp for several months. Now a company bus fetches and delivers him every day. For the woman, too, this is a kind of revolution. No longer does she carry the burden of running the house and bringing up the children all alone. And the road means a lifeline to the doctor and the hospital. One nurse reminded me of the last time she saw me, down in Norris Point, sixty miles from her home. She had come fourteen hours in a motor dory in the wake of a hurricane with a pregnant woman, who just reached hospital in time to have her life and that of her baby saved. The same nurse had just come back from the same hospital to which she had set out six hours before with a child in convulsions. Tears ran down her cheeks when she said, "My dear, you'll never know what that road means to us on this coast, with no doctor and no hospital 'til Norris Point."

The trouble is that the people on the coast are having creature comforts thrust on them, some of which are turning out to be expensive and not so comforting. The telephone men, for example, went hurtling north in the wake of road builders, stringing wires as they went. Suddenly everyone wanted a telephone. One woman, on acquiring hers, sat all day with the receiver to her ear in case someone wanted to talk to her. Which reminds me of Lawrence Durrell's definition, "The telephone is a modern symbol of communication that never takes place."

And mail trucks deliver every day to villages that once received mail every two weeks. The trucks disgorge catalogues of goods, some of which nobody needs; ads for everything under the sun, incomprehensible forms to cover expanding bureaucracy, and a few personal letters. Other trucks bring intriguing foods within reach of everyone, and naturally everyone is happy to relieve the monotony of fresh fish and potatoes and garden greens, wild berries and wild meat in season. But now they have to cope with empty milk tins, soup tins, fruit tins, and the problem now is what to do with the mounting piles. You can tell how long the road through any village has been laid by the height of the tin can mountain.

In one of the more northerly villages, a man who feeds his six children on fresh milk and homemade butter and fresh beef in fall gave me a new view of the road when he said, "I 'lows I'll have to get rid of me cattle. I can't afford to have trucks and cars kill them one by one."

At the moment, youngsters down north from eight to eighteen spend much of their time in small shacks, eating hot dogs and chips and listening to the jukeboxes the road has brought them. But they also climb on big yellow buses that take them to wonderfully attractive new regional schools where, for the first time, they can receive more than the most elementary education. Teachers do not shudder at the thought of isolation. They can get out on weekends, and there are more of them together in villages where the regional schools are built. Students attending Memorial University can now get home by road rather than by the fortnightly coastal boat. Corner Brook, with all its services and facilities, is somehow nearer.

And for me, the end of isolation is the one great, shining, hopeful thing the road down north has brought to our coastal people.

CENTENNIAL ON
THE UPPER HUMBER

In the summer of 1967, Ella spends a few peaceful days on the river celebrating Canada's 100th birthday, and looks ahead to the world her grandchildren will inherit.

WITH MY first grandchild now born, I imagine how his children and grandchildren would celebrate the end of Canada's second century. I wonder how they would take my leaving a memento for them—an account of my celebration of the first centennial, on good rag paper, of course, so as to preserve the document. They would all then marvel at the old days when one woman could own half an acre of earth and a house on it. So, I'm going to write it all down, for they will know none of the wonders I have told.

In July 1967, as Canada celebrated its one hundredth birthday, I drove with two friends through the heart of the Great Northern Peninsula. We travelled over high hills, around hairpin bends with not another vehicle in sight, for this was a private road of the Bowater Company leading to the upper reaches of the Humber River. Down this floats pulpwood for a hundred miles or more to the paper mill in Corner Brook.

On the hillsides, the spruce and fir grew tall. This was second-growth timber, for this part of the country had been logged when Canada was less than fifty years old. The road was lined with aspen, birch and maple. The sun blazed down and we reached the road's end. A chain at the entrance to a bridge over the dam was lifted by the caretaker and, as I stepped out of the car, he said, "Shush," and pointed upstream where a giant bull moose was dipping his nose into the water. He drank, lifted his magnificently antlered head with water streaming off his muzzle and ambled slowly up the bank. "He comes down every evening for a drink," the caretaker said, "and he's as tame as a puppy."

He talked about the river—no salmon yet, but plenty of trout— and about the people who came to fish. There would be hardly anyone yet, so we wouldn't be disturbed. The caretaker helped us load food and gear into a big dory, attached the outboard motor and chugged us up river. We threaded our way through the rocky channel, the water ahead all purple and gold, the wake behind tinged with pink. Half an hour or so upstream, we came to an island on which stood one of the last remaining aboriginal pines, all spread out on top like an umbrella. We drew up at a neat little wharf, and unloaded before a lovely house, the like of which you wouldn't believe on a little island in the midst of a remote river. It stood on a rise surrounded by fruit trees and flowering shrubs, all brown logs and blue trim and enormous windows.

Inside, it was even more astonishing. Electric lights, carpets, old furniture and deep armchairs, a fieldstone fireplace and in the bedrooms linen sheets and fluffy wool blankets, for this house had been built for the director of the paper company as his very own fishing lodge, no expense spared. Now that he was dead, and since the new director apparently cared little for isolation or fishing, company executives used it frequently for holidays, and we were guests of one of them.

We stowed our gear, ate, and putting up our rods sat on the little wharf talking quietly and dabbling dry flies on the surface. We almost fell overboard laughing at the minute trout who hurled themselves out of the water after our flies. We had a game lifting the flies higher and higher over the bland surface to see who could bring a trout farthest out of water, and watching them streak away, marked by the white edges of their fins.

As the sun set and the spruces on the far bank traced black lines in the red sky, one isolated group of tall trees far away from us looked like an enormous billboard in the sky. Another moose appeared, a young one, and had his evening drink not a hundred yards from us. A beaver swam out into the river, dived when he saw us and reappeared just over a bed of reeds. There he stopped for supper, upending himself and diving in water so clear that we could see him completely below the surface as he tore at the roots and gobbled them up. He'd had a busy day, had our beaver, and he was hungry. Off in the distance a robin called. We heard a loon. Darkness fell and gigantic mosquitoes drove us indoors, and so the day ended in quiet sleep.

The next day began for me by a persistent knocking outside, as if someone was tapping on my window with a pebble. I looked out, but could see nobody. I opened my door softly and found no one stirring in the house. The noise went on and as abruptly as it started, it stopped. The mystery was solved when I stepped out on the lawn, just in time to see a woodpecker fly back to the tin stove pipe and begin his tattoo. Apparently he did this every morning, at least every one when people were there. I should have been warned, but then I wouldn't have been out at daybreak, nor seen the rabbits playing about.

All that day was sheer magic. I borrowed an old dory and rowed across the river towards the mouth of Taylor's Brook, following it up and up, around bends, under blow-downs, wading and pulling the boat where I couldn't row. I saw many wonderful things. A bittern sitting on a dead tree branch, all hunched up and glaring at me. The young moose again, breaking out of the bushes and drinking at the flowing stream, so close I could have walloped him with my oar. Millions of little trout circled my dory, playing about and enjoying themselves. And I saw a mother duck and four young ones, learning to swim I presume, and not the least put off by my presence. I picked strange wildflowers, collected a few mushrooms and allowed my boat to float with the current, back for lunch in the kitchen with window frames, shelves, cupboards and floor painted in a soft red. Then I dozed in the sunshine under a cliff lined with flowering crab, lupins, asters and raspberry canes, and later ambled along the trails through the woods, finding strange beauty at every step.

My host and I floated down the Humber in the dory, hardly making a ripple until we came to an old boom on the bank. We tied up there and cast our lines over the water. So many trout besieged us that we filed the barbs off our hooks, teased the little trout and were amused more than ever at their antics. Until one huge one leaped, missed the fly, leaped again and swallowed it. Then another and another, until we had enough for supper.

As we were making for home, the watchman came from the boom with a bottle opener he thought we would need and a few bottles to go with it. He told us, "I took the 'General' down to the lower boom this morning" —the General was a Corner Brook doctor who haunted the river— "and did he ever get some trout! I thought I'd have to kill him to get him out of it."

As evening came, the sky grew pink, its reflection in the still water perfection. The sun went down in a heat haze with one cloud streaked across it, slowly down, three-quarters showing, then a half, then a quarter, until finally only the tip of the golden ball. The birds stopped singing. The beaver returned to fill his stomach and give us a show. A flotilla of ducks crossed the river led by mother like a full-rigged schooner. The loon let out one lunatic giggle, and a late thrush began her exquisite song. The mosquitoes settled down on us, and we went inside to eat our birthday dinner. It was July 1, Canada's Day.

What a feast it was. The fresh trout elegantly cooked. Lobster as well, and fresh tomatoes and blueberry pie made from last year's picking outside the house. And to make it a real feast, a bottle of good wine that tasted of sunshine. Then we settled before the huge fireplace, and set the birch logs ablaze against the chill. We just sat and stretched and sighed, replete with happiness, not speaking as we drank our coffee. With these friends, we did not have to chatter to break an uncomfortable quiet, for they valued silence as much as I.

When we'd had enough silence, we turned on our old radio, tuned to the BBC and heard the most magnificent concert of Beethoven coming clear and gloriously melodious across the Atlantic to us in our remote little room on the Upper Humber. Rarely did we hear music so undistorted as we did that night. What luck, I thought, to be with friends on such a night in so peaceful a place.

Then, I reminded myself that we ought not to think only of ourselves, but also of the well-being of our environment and all it contains: earth, air, water, animals, birds, plants, trees. We have only the loan of them for our lifetime—a sort of ninety-nine-year lease— and as decent tenants we should turn the property over to the next tenants in as good a state of repair as we found it. Then, maybe in 2067, Canadians will still have something to celebrate and somewhere in which to celebrate it.

CHASING THE HERRING

As the Second World War ended, and life began to return to normal, Ella wanted to see for herself something of the commercial herring fishery, so she joined a purse seiner cruising Port au Port Bay.

HERRING ABOUNDED in the Bay of Islands during World War II. Local fishermen were busy in catching and packing herring, and the fish merchants were spending large sums in building processing plants and a dehydrating factory. Then for some unaccountable reason the herring moved farther south, appearing in Port au Port Bay, more than fifty miles by sea from Bay of Islands. Fishermen with only motorboats and power dories could not follow the herring this far. Moreover, there were few fishermen around the shores of Port au Port Bay, since men here were occupied in far more lucrative pursuits at the nearby United States airplane base at Stephenville.

In order to get sufficient raw material to keep the Bay of Islands fish plants operating, their owners introduced purse seiners—large diesel-driven boats about seventy feet long that with a crew of six to ten men could range over long distances for several months without having to refuel or replenish supplies. They were attended by small schooners called "packers" which brought the seiners' catches to the factories, and it was on the packer *Susan*, that I shipped out of Bay of Islands for a fishing trip four o'clock of a pitch black morning at the end of November.

"I'm a brave man to take you on this voyage," said my cousin, owner of the purse seiner *Western Star* that we were headed for, "and you are a foolish woman to go. You'll be good and seasick and scared to death, and you'll wish you'd stayed home." All of which was perfectly true, except for the last, for I'd go again tomorrow to watch them hunting for the herring that should now have been well inshore. We were to cruise around Port au Port Bay to search with echo sounders for the elusive little fish that meant for so many of my people the difference between hunger and plenty.

I went aboard the *Susan* at Curling, the centre of the herring fishery in the Bay of Islands, where the fish are unloaded, cleaned, cured and packed and shipped all over the world. The houses here line the shore, the little coves and harbours now crowded with the over-

f   l   o   w

of workers from the industrial town of Corner Brook, but Curling still retains its authentic flavour. When the herring run is on, excitement catches your throat, life stirs and bustles, even the children work in the sheds, cutting, cleaning and packing—and well paid too.

But now the waterfront was deserted. The only sound the damp wind slapping against the rocks and the tide sucking it out with an eerie swish. The straps of my packsack dug into my shoulders as I clambered over empty barrels and piles of lumber, peering into the darkness for the *Susan*. Her skipper had said on the phone, "We don't wait a minute after four. What wharf? I don't know. You'll find us somehow." Find them I did by the sparkle of the galley stovepipe, and I jumped the rail precisely as the *Susan*'s hawser left the bollard.

"Thought you weren't coming," the skipper said.

"Hoped, you mean."

But he had the courtesy to settle me comfortably in the wheel-house.

As we watched the crew make ready for sailing, my cousin said to me, "You know, Newfoundlanders are people with one idea, and that idea is fish. We might pretend that we are becoming industrialized, but we are still convinced that fishing is the only *real* occupation, the only real wealth. And the curious thing is that although we are avid for mechanization in everything else, most of us believe in our secret hearts that the best way to fish is the way our grandfathers did it. I think that the fisherman believes that you can't improve on that, or he is afraid that big boats and seines and long liners will take away his living."

"But," I argued, "if you had to depend on the local fishermen, you'd have to close up your herring processing plant."

"That's why I've got these purse seiners with echo sounders and the ability to range long distances. I can't depend on the Bay of Islands herring, and the fishermen can't go where we're going now. But, when we first brought the purse seiners into the bay, the fishermen threatened to finish us."

"No?" I said—in delight, I must admit, for I love a rousing tale.

"Oh yes. You don't remember because you were away then. They came down to the plant in a body, and one big fellow, the ringleader threatened to heave me over the wharf if I didn't take the seiner out of the bay. I bluffed a bit and told him if I went overboard, he'd go too. And I could swim! I held them for a time, but I must confess whenever I went over to the plant, I was a bit scared."

"You know," he continued, "we've been fighting over seiners for a hundred years. Not the purse seines, of course—they're comparatively new—but about seine nets, those vertical nets that surround, trap, and then haul in schools of small fish. Why, as far back as 1878 an American ship put in Fortune Bay on the South Coast and dropped a seine net. There was a proper riot, and the local fishermen tore up the net, smashed the dories and drove the Americans out. That went on for two years, and in the end the Americans presented England with a bill for fifteen thousand pounds sterling for damages we Newfoundlanders had done to their herring fishing. And England made us pay a quarter of it, just to punish us. Our great-grandfather—yours and mine—was herring fishing then, and he made a fair living at it."

Just then the captain appeared on the bridge, and we were off. The cook brought us steaming coffee from the galley, and we hugged our parkas round us against the gale coming in the bay right towards the *Susan*. She didn't mind, as she moved away from the pier, past the shelter of a big freighter. Out we steamed, bobbing and tossing, slowly forward through snow scuds that hid the shore, over grey water that seemed to stretch forever. We rounded the point at the mouth of the bay into a tide rip that gave me uncomfortable moments. Then we settled to an even heave and dip with which my stomach could adequately cope.

Our radar, that blessed friend of sailors on our bleak coast, linked us with the hidden land and guided us toward Port au Port Bay. Past high cliffs, when we could see them, past the Serpentine River, its sullen mouth giving no hint of its lovely salmon pools and the trout-filled, tree-sheltered inlets. We passed Fox Island, two miles off shore, with its greasy slopes reaching up to clumps of spruce on one shore, cliffs and shingle beach on another, while from the rocky shores many shelving ledges reach out, hidden by high water. On one of them clearly visible in civil weather, there lay for years what looked like the wreck of a steamer. Finally we reached Port au Port Bay, sheltered only in a southwest wind, venomously dangerous in a northerly gale, offering no shelter against a storm. And the wind sprang up with appalling vigor, stirring up the waves in the shallow water.

The *Susan*'s skipper said, "In a wind we generally anchor under the cliffs off Fox Island and pray our anchor'll hold. If the wind shifts we shift too, like in a merry-go-round. And I guarantees you that if the wind is fifteen miles an hour anywhere else it's fifty here." He pointed out the white hull of the *Western Star*, the seiner I was to join. "She's not making a set now. See, her net is hanging against the boom, so we'll put you aboard while we can."

The *Star* was a Nova Scotian-built ship on the lines of a Pacific seiner with bridge, superstructure and living quarters forward in the blunt, rather ugly bow. Aft in the low, squat stern there is a clutter of machinery. The main boom carries a derrick for the seine which lies coiled in a huge box-affair on a turntable. The yardarms carry smaller dip nets or brailers on ten-foot handles lashed to the mast, and everywhere ropes, winches and dories. The ship carries radar, an echo sounder and a ship-to-shore telephone, which makes the bridge a very efficient place.

Our captain was a grizzled middle-aged man with wrinkled eyes and a soft voice. For years he's been following the herring, spring and fall, up and down the coast. Usually the seiners go out for days, weeks on end, fishing, filling the insatiable maw of the smaller boats that move in to load the herring and sail back to port again. They have a good night's sleep, while the seiner's crew toss and fight the wind and fish and fish. They are cold and wet much of the time and always in danger. The captain only sleeps when bleary-eyed, and drunk with fatigue, he naps on his feet.

In the galley where the stove blasted out heat, we sat down to a meal of fresh cod boiled with potatoes, onions and scruncheons of fatback pork. We consisted of the skipper, my cousin, the cook, and seven fishermen with wind-burned faces and crinkled webs of wrinkles round their sailing eyes. Though their hands surreptitiously brushed tousled head and several caps were quietly removed to acknowledge the presence of a woman, they greeted me warmly, plied my plate with food and drew me into their conversation. In the midst of it came a tremendous whistle blast. It brought me to my feet, but not as quickly as it did the others. The skipper darted up the companionway, the crew went in ten different directions at once. The cook dropped a pan of newly baked buns on the table and shouted at me "Herring!" adding, "Get up on the bridge if you want to see the fun."

There the skipper scanning the echo sounder gestured widely with his arm. "That's a pretty good school," he said quietly, "We'll go round them." Then to me, "Now you'll see something. Keep your eyes open and yourself out of the way. If we have what I think we have, nobody will pay much attention to you for the next few hours."

A curtain of half-mist, half-snow shut out the world except for a few miles of dirty grey water. The men worked urgently to lower away the small boat, and a burly sailor moving like a great bear in his sheath of woolens and oilskins climbed in and took the end of the seine. Fastening the oars in the locks he rowed off, sometimes lost for minutes in the swell. The *Star* at slow speed ambled off in the opposite direction, paying out the net from the starboard beam, everyone anxiously helping so as not to snag the precious net. Our ship swept round in a circle, as the little boat bobbed alone, small and vulnerable on the grey sweep of water, until we turned back toward it. Soon we were alongside and we picked up her end of the net, which now lay in a wide circle, bobbing corks on the water's surface, dragging lead weights below. Then we began to pull the leads together, making the purse strings shorter to close the bottom of the net and catching the herring fast. The water's surface seethed and boiled, losing its greasy amorphousness in an iridescent shimmer of herring. I never would have believed so many fish could live in such a small space.

The winch groaned and squeaked. The wind howled, snow and water soaking mittens and trickling up sleeves. The eternal tossing made standing erect a painful task. The brailers, small ropes ready to tip the fish aboard, flapped loosely from their lashings, and the sailors stood ready to start loading as the net came on board. Then they stopped, looked at each other with consternation, and alone on the bridge I felt a constriction of fear. My cousin climbed heavily up the ladder and entering the shelter threw his cap on the table with a gesture of frustration. "We broke the net," he said slowly.

"What! After all that work, that's terrible," I said.

"Could be worse," he said. "Once we searched for three weeks, and the first school we sighted was so big on the sounder that we didn't dare put out the net. It would have been in shreds. Oh well, we'll get over it."

The winch had now lifted the great wet net thirty feet into the air. It hung under the powerful derrick light, a grey-black triangle. Behind it and through, I saw in the clearing sky the shimmering dancing colours of the aurora. At the base of the triangle, on the glistening deck, stood six men with arms uplifted to the net, their oilskins shining ebony. For one perfect moment, beauty static— the beauty of dancers frozen in motion, in the night's black frame. Then the broken net dropped and folded on the deck. And the skipper declared, "There's nothing for it except back to Curling."

So back we went. Though chastened by their bad luck, the crew, like all fishermen, would be venturing out again before long.

BACK TO EXPLOITS

As a girl, Ella often visited this lovely island where her father grew up. Many years later she returned, sharing a boat ride with Gail and Gerry Squires, who had made a seasonal home there. It was here that Gerry began to develop his artistic vision of Newfoundland landscape and spiritual heritage. In this story, Ella also tells of three old brothers who once lived on Exploits.

OUT IN Notre Dame Bay, about an hour's ride by motorboat from Little Burnt Bay on the mainland, is the island of Exploits, where my ancestors settled over two hundred years ago, and where some of them lived until it was abandoned. As a child I thought the island Paradise, full of friends and relations, some of whom lived in a big house with bay windows and carpets and curtains and furniture such as I'd never seen before, and I thought Buckingham Palace must look like this. And memories of sitting on the beach and sucking lobster claws we swiped from great-uncle's lobster store, of jam and cream and homemade bread that my first, second and third cousins fed me.

Exploits is properly two islands separated by a narrow gut. Empty houses face this gut, protected from ocean winds by the high h   i   l   l   s encircling them. The once beautiful gardens have now gone to nettles, fences blown down, wharves rotted—you'd think it was a cheerless place. We found that far from being so, it was sheer beauty and solitude, and for me a curious dialogue with the past. The four cemeteries are full of the graves of Butts, Wells, Sceviours, Lillys, and Manuels—all of them intermarried until you're never quite sure who your cousins are. The headstones yield tragic stories such as that of Great-Uncle Tommie and Great-Aunt Priscilla, who lost six little children within two months. And history too, for here in one cemetery is buried John Peyton, with whom for a few years lived as a servant Shanawdithit, the last Beothuk woman.

Some of the houses are new and well-built, some are old and some are veritable mansions. One is a rambling English-style house, painted red, set among shade trees, with a rolling lawn around. My cousin's house, where I stayed, is cuddled in a rock cleft, fifty feet f   r   o   m the water and the stage-head with its dories. A stream runs from the hillside down a gully and straight under her house into a huge well which you reach by opening a door off the kitchen. And the delicious taste of that water. When it rains, you can lie in bed and hear the stream run under the kitchen, with an unworldly gurgle.

The main road is grass-grown, and it is like walking on a carpet, one of the few places where you can walk barefoot for miles without stepping on broken glass. It is a magic place. It reminds me of what Freya Stark said about deserts. Here one can look on our universe from a detachment of loneliness, weigh our values at leisure, and judge them anew in the presence of the almost eternal.

One man whose family has been there as long as mine does not think Exploits cheerless. He knows and loves every rock, every tree, and more about the history of the place than almost anyone else. He stayed as week by week, more and more families left. The post office was removed, as were the small general store, the lighthouse keeper's and the pilot station from which men went out to guide cargo boats through the intricacies of the hundreds of islands in the Bay of Exploits. But Richard stayed, and he was there when we returned in summer for one last look at Exploits, and the shell of the once-grand home of my great-uncle, Josiah Manuel.

Richard always said people would return. Gerry Squires was one, having spent childhood days here when his parents were the resident Salvation Army officers. Lately, he and Gail and their two little girls came by, and were enchanted. So they moved into an abandoned house and set up housekeeping. They found beautiful wooded hills through which you can walk all day in perfect quiet. They found grassy coves with lovely clean beaches, wild sweet berries, flowers in great pastures, and fish swimming around abandoned wharves. On the northern side of the islands are gaunt cliffs where the sea beats in straight from Greenland and creates such excitement that you couldn't possibly miss TV or newspapers. They found that though they spent half the day cleaning lamps, fetching water, chopping wood and preparing food, it was worth it, for outside the weather was doing exciting things in a dazzling procession of days.

Eventually they found a house to buy with a view over the bay, circled by little islands that turn a heavenly violet blue in the sunlight. They borrowed or bought the absolute necessities from friends who'd left furniture behind. The longer they stayed, the surer were they that they had done the right thing moving from Toronto, to which they dashed off every once in a while to earn enough for another six months of paradise and painting.

Now with a few more congenial people around, they could buy a boat to link them with the mainland for necessities and mail, and in case of emergency. They can live here on next to nothing—firewood outside the door, land to grow vegetables, good grazing for sheep and cattle, and wild fruit for the picking. A line from near the kitchen window will produce a fish almost anytime. Even in the winter, with supplies in the earth cellar and plenty of wood, it is exciting—storms, calms, and the challenge of isolation. So they plan to spend the winter there and foresee no great problems. The worst they've encountered so far is that the men smoked their way through the tobacco supply. After ten days of smoking leaves and tea, they put out in their dory and rowed to the mainland, five hours there and five back. Which is no more than my grandfather did many times.

I am reminded of three old brothers who lived here years ago, in a little frame house which had sheltered four generations. They had sonorous Biblical names—Aaron, Luke and Jonathan. Aaron was short and plump, with a bushy moustache and a wicked grin that popped out at me when he asked, "I s'pose you haven't got any bad books with you? I fair loves bad books." His pocket always bulged with something to read, and he could be often seen furtively pulling it out and sticking his nose into it. I never did discover what the books were about or what constituted in Aaron's mind a bad book. But I'm sure his hair would have curled even more than naturally if I had loaned him any of my very bad, modern novels.

Luke was of middle height and very slim. He had the face of an El Greco angel and was quiet and gentle. Jonathan was well over six feet, broad as a house, with snowy white hair falling over a handsome florid face. He loved cribbage even more than Aaron loved bad books.

Jonathan's wife, Alice, was a tiny bent-over woman who bustled about like a sparrow. And she had to, for she kept house for her husband and his two widowed brothers. "They are always up to something," she said, "and when they're not, they're messing up my kitchen with brew and bottles."

Alice had everyone's interest at heart—and why not? She was related to most everyone within a hundred miles around. She told me her grandfather had settled on Exploits years ago. "He was a kind of a doctor from the old country. He came out to St. John's but he didn't like the crowds of people, so he mooched along the coast until he found this place, the first person to bide here." She showed me his great shoe buckles, silver hammered over prongs of iron to hold the buckles' weight on the ribbons of his shoes. "I bet he was a dandy in his young days," she said. "Yes," said her husband Jonathan, "and he was some tough. He was alive when I was courting Alice here— some bonny maid she was, too. The old man wouldn't let her marry me 'cause I had nere boat of me own to go fishin in. So I had to play crib for a whole week straight before I won a skiff off a feller down the shore."

Obviously neither Alice nor Jonathan regretted the trouble, for they made you believe all the love stories that were ever written. And Alice, having outlived her two sisters-in-law, now looked after three of the most fascinating old men I've ever had the luck to meet.

"I dunno how many times I nearly lost the lot of them," Alice told me. "I minds the time when Aaron and Luke went out lobstering, just off the cove. And the wind came up and they were gone so long that we just about gave them up for lost. We decided to launch the motor boat and go after them. It was some windy. You could hardly stand up, with the gale right in on the land and the breakers up over the cliff. Just as we got the boat off, I seen something black bobbing up and down way outside. I near died of fright. You know what it was? 'Twas Aaron and Luke hanging on to the bottom of the dory and it upside down, and they riding in on the breakers, just like they was in a sailboat.

Aaron took up the story. "We were log-loaded with lobsters and gear. 'Twas our last trip for the season. All of a sudden a big wave washed in over us and we went under. Everything tipped out and sank, except the dory and she rode bottom up. Neither one of us could swim. So I yelled to Luke to hold on while I got off me guernsey and hove it over the bottom of the boat. Then he tied the sleeve to his arm, and I tied the other sleeve to my arm and we hung on, comfortable like, 'til the wind drove us toward the shore. Good thing the guernsey was from me own sheep's wool or it would have tore apart."

The wind was more than five hours about its job driving them ashore, but Aaron and Luke survived with nothing worse than sniffles. "The worst off was Alice," Aaron said. "She was in bed three days with fright."

The brothers had a reputation on the coast for what they euphemistically called "cordial," though they well knew the wallop it packed. "Don't give him any more," Alice would beg her men when they plied a visitor over-generously. "He won't have the sense to get home if you do. Course, if he was staying the night, I wouldn't care. Then all I'd have to do would be to pick him up and heave him

on the bed, and I'd know he was safe for the night." That would set
the three big men and their visitor doubling over with laughter. "Why,
tiny little Alice, she couldn't heave anything bigger than a tomcod!"

They were quiet for a space, savouring the calm of the evening.
We drank our bitter brew of tea, the men smoked peacefully, and
I made quick notes for the story I would one day write of this day.
But now, in case I precipitate a rush for Exploits and the simple
life, I hasten to tell you there are many abandoned villages around
Newfoundland. Why don't you go and rescue one?[47]

---

[47] When Ella wrote this account, not long after the vigorous resettlement program
of the 1950s and 1960s that emptied many outports of people, there were others
that might have been rescued by those with money and foresight. A few still remain today.

AMONG THE SCOTS
OF THE CODROY

Though much has since been written—and recorded—about the music and the history of the Codroy Valley, Ella's first-hand impressions add a fresh view for those unfamiliar with the Scottish settlers of this part of Newfoundland.

THE FIRST time I journeyed south beyond the Port au Port Peninsula to the valley called Codroy, it was 1945, just as the War was ending. I had to go by train, for the road had not yet been built. The valley is drained by two rivers. The Grand Codroy flows to the sea through a narrow gut where banks of sand and gravel continuously shift and make the entrance dangerous, but inside there is shelter from all winds. The Little Codroy flows into the sea about four miles south of the Grand. Between them are thousands of acres of rich land covered, especially on the valley sides, with birch, fir, spruce, and tamarack. Years ago, the Grand Codroy was navigable to large fishing vessels, and the harbour was well-known to fishermen from Nova Scotia and other foreign parts. A visitor from Cape Breton in the 1870s wrote, "The land is scarcely surpassed by any of the Lower provinces for its fertility. I took a survey of the vast and magnificent valley, unbroken by barrens and rocks, until the sight was lost amid the dark and gloomy forest which, robed in its sombre green, seemed to mourn the neglect in which the vale below was left."

I arrived at a gloomy little place called Doyles, hardly more than a whistle stop, with a clutch of houses surrounded by a thicket of stunted, twisted evergreen trees which dripped sadly in the mist. In the gathering darkness of a late September evening, so inimical was the landscape that I felt a cold fear in my bones, a sense of being alien and rejected, a feeling that increased as the brightly lit train disappeared, and I was alone on a little wooden platform.

Presently a vintage Ford, its headlights comforting in the dusk, pulled up and a deep voice said, "You for Walter's? He said to bring you. Jump in."

The car was already full, but the men somehow diminished their bulk, loaded me and my luggage and set off, bumping over the rutted road toward the river. Even in the growing dark I could see the hills rising above the broad, slow-moving river in the middle of which were reedy islets. Yellow lamplight flickered from windows of cottages set back from the road, patches of light across the black ploughed earth. This was farming country and my fellow passengers smelled of cow and hay.

Our driver said, "Sandy seen a big bear this morning down by the Block. I hope my youngsters don't hear about it 'til after they get the cows home." And the man next to him added, "'Twouldn't make any difference to my young'uns. There's not a bear in the world big enough to frighten them young savages: I wish there was."

The car stopped. The driver said, "Here's Walter's house, up there on the hill. Through that white gate you'll find the path," and put me down. As the noise of the car receded, I heard the wail of bagpipes. Never before had I *really* heard them—not from a distance, out of doors. Nor had I ever been farther north in Scotland than Loch Katrine, but in this moment I was transported to the Hebrides, as tales of them, heard and read, floated to the surface of my mind. Again, I felt this alien sense, as if I did not belong to the landscape or it to me.

The music stopped. Walter's voice rang out, "Hold on, there. I'm coming," and he raced down the path and swooped up my luggage. "Just trying out my pipes. Gave them a drink of cold tea this morning." I laughed, being ignorant of the care and feeding of bagpipes. And never far away was laughter that long, gorgeous week that I spent with the Scots of Codroy.

Walter's wife, Mary, and their two boys and two girls aged ten to two, were waiting on the porch to usher me into the largest, most littered kitchen I have ever seen. Here, under the lamplight at one of the tables were bottles of ink, saucers of paint and stacks of scallop shells. On another were loaves of newly baked bread, and a half-plucked fowl. In all the years since, I've never seen Mary's kitchen less cluttered. True, scallop shells have given way to modeling clay, clay given way to mat-rags, mat-rags to manuscript paper in quires and reams, and always Mary in the midst, creating.

She is a Scot with a long, proud ancestry. Of medium height, she is buxom and dark with a smooth complexion and bright brown eyes. Her mouth is thin, belying the warmth of her spirit, and her wit is a byword among people whose every phrase is a barb. Currently she was being addressed as "Mrs. Pratie," because of a letter she had written the newspaper, deriding the quality of potatoes from beyond the Valley.[48] Mary had bought a sack of imported spuds, only to discover that "somebody had a grudge against them because their heads and tails were beat off." When she cooked them, "They came out a pretty shade of green." Her speech may have been pedestrian, but give her a pen and she would flay pretension, bigotry and dishonesty.

All this I learned later. When I first saw Mary, she struck me as a harried housewife, whose husband in an excess of hospitality had wished a strange woman on her for a whole week. But with the children asleep and the fowl plucked, Mary thawed.

"I have it all planned for you," she said, "but I don't know how it will turn out, seeing that you're the first one who ever came to the Valley to hear our music, and the boys are terribly shy. I asked

[48] In the mid-1950s, Mary McIsaac, as Mrs. Pratie, wrote a series of humourous stories for the *Western Star*.

them for tomorrow night, about ten of them," and she repeated a litany of names that go back into Scottish history as far as the memory can reach.

"Tomorrow being Walter's day off, I planned for him to take you fishing to Overfall Pool. That will give me time to get ready for the party."

Walter McIsaac was manager of the local co-operative society and an ardent fisherman. I wanted nothing more than to cast for a salmon in the Overfall, except perhaps to hear the fiddles and bagpipes and Gaelic songs that Walter had promised me when I met him in the radio station a month before. That meeting was no accident. My earlier remark in a broadcast that Newfoundlanders sadly neglected their folklore and songs, had so incensed Walter that he came to contradict me. To prove his contention, he had invited me to the Valley.

The next day's fishing was memorable. Walter's family had provided for at least fifty years the most memorable guides in the Valley, and Walter proved no less efficient. The river was low, the season late and the main run had long since passed upstream. "Still, we might hook the odd straggler if we're lucky," Walter remarked, "and in any case, you'll be able to say you fished the Grand River at last."

The Grand Codroy River was really grand. At Overfall, it flowed swiftly over a razor-sharp ledge directly into deep, black pools. Walter, tall, loose-limbed and sure-footed, dragged me across a frightening stretch to a riffle, at the far end of which was a boulder, three feet or so out of water.

"This is where I come every opening day," he said. "Fact is, I came the night before, and I sat on the rock until daylight so's nobody would beat me to it." That's the kind of fisherman Walter is, and unselfish too, for he gave me the best pool and all the benefit of his knowledge of the river. I landed a salmon eventually, and in my attempt to reach shore, tumbled into the deepest pool and was conveyed home on a railway speeder, every stitch of clothing dripping wet. Mary said later that it was the fly bites, the dirt and the wet on me that endeared me to her friends, who were sitting a-bulge in the kitchen when Walter and I arrived. I was evidently not a city slicker come to laugh.

After greetings, they assembled their instruments and shyly at first, then with enthusiasm and enjoyment, they began to play. Young Angus had a fiddle he'd made from a cigar box. Sandy had the oldest pipes in the country. Hughie had a butter-smooth voice. "I couldn't put the cat out in English 'til I was sixteen," he told me, "because we had only the Gaelic in our house." And then there sounded a wild Highland lament. The cozy Codroy sitting-room gave way to the dark, forbidding valley of Glencoe, echoing to the call of battle, and its wailing and sadness. That was the magic of drone and chanter. There was magic, too, in their fiddles that set feet twitching to tunes like "Miss Drummond of Perth," "Bonnie Lass o' Bon Accord," and "Road to the Isles."

Mary asked them to play "Flowers of the Forest," which was her favourite, but they weren't quite sure of the tune. Since I was the only one who could read music, they begged me to play it on the organ from an old song book. They hummed and listened until Albert tucked his fiddle under his chin and tentatively bowed a note here and there until the pattern was firmly in his mind. Then the bagpipes took it up, and away they went, the melody sure and true.

Old Hughie, tall, spare and white-haired, danced an ancient sword dance. Nine-year-old Eddie slipped behind him and imitated the steps with tremendous concentration until he could perform them alone. Then Hughie and Sandy—he with the round red face, as plump as Hughie was lean—took between them a handkerchief and sang a milling song, the while performing the actions.

Before I left the Valley on that visit, Mary and Walter agreed with me that we simply had to find some way to bring the wealth of this music and dance out of the Valley so everybody could enjoy it. So we arranged a concert, a *ceilidh*, in Corner Brook. Those who could leave cattle and field came in to perform, and we filled the Parish Hall for two nights and a third in Deer Lake. The music was good, and their

pleasure in making it so evident that one forgot they were not sea-
soned stage performers.

"Where did all this Scottish culture come from?" I asked my new
friends.

"From the Highlands of Scotland via Cape Breton," they told
me. And gradually I pieced the story together, going from one old Scot
to another, prodding them to greater depths of memory by questions,
hints and, above all, accounts of what their neighbours had told
me. Of course, one would contradict another, each trying to uphold
the honour of his family, each remembering only what redounded
to the credit of his clan, so that some of the stories could never be
reconciled to others. Still, it made a fascinating pattern, full of colour
and movement and beauty. My friend Mary's passion for family
history was unique in a country where nobody cared much for where
he came from as long as he knew where he was going. She gave me
the following story.

In 1801, on a ship called the *Dove of Aberdeen*, there arrived in
Nova Scotia a Scot named Donald "Oban" Gillis and his wife, Ann,
"a robust, vigorous woman." They settled on a farm in Cape Breton
near a place called Big Brook and reared five sons and six daughters.
Donald's grandfather, also named Donald, had fought with the
clans in support of Bonnie Prince Charlie, including at the Battle on
Culloden Moor. Of Donald Oban's many children, one, again named
Donald, married Margaret McNeill, and in the mid-1800s, the two
came to the Codroy Valley, the first Scottish settlers. Neither the move
nor the destination was without reason.

The ninety-year-old granddaughter of Donald, the first settler,
told me that her grandfather had left because they didn't want to
stay when Cape Breton rejoined Nova Scotia. They had left Scotland
in the first place to get away from persecution and poverty, and they
didn't want it again. They thought, for sure, that life would be pretty
hard for Roman Catholics when they joined up with Nova Scotia.
Such an attitude came in part from the oath then administered in

Nova Scotia to members of the Legislative Council there. They were required to swear, "I do believe that the Invocation or adoration of the Virgin Mary or any other Saint, and the sacrifice of the Mass as they are now performed in the Church of Rome are superstitious and idolatrous." You could hardly expect staunch Highland Catholics to welcome that sort of thing.

Incidentally, when Confederation with Canada was the burning issue in 1948, an old Scot in the Valley thundered out at a public meeting, "Donald Oban led your fathers out from slavery. Let you not lose what he gained for you." Despite the warning, the Valley voted solidly for union with Canada.

Now the first Donald, being a fisherman as well as a farmer, must often have fished along the coast of Newfoundland, and he must often have been driven to the sheltered lower reaches of the Codroy River. No doubt he ventured farther up the river on one of his visits and found a country very like his grandfather's homeland. The valley, broad and lush, is beautiful always, but on a misty evening when the mountains loom and the crevices blacken, you can see the pass of Glencoe and Loch Lomond rolled into one. So having left Cape Breton with his wife and young children, he sailed up the river until he came to the gently sloping banks of its middle reaches. There he paced off a hundred acres or so of rich land and claimed it for the Gillis homestead. He was alone in the valley for the first year, except for a band of Mi'kmaq and one English family, but soon his Scots neighbours joined him, and the Valley was peopled with McIsaacs, Bruces, and MacDonalds. Hugh McLean came too, and helped himself and his five boys to "two miles of land between two brooks."

All this was told to me by Mrs. MacDonald in her lilting voice, sitting in her rocking chair, hands folded, supremely contented. "I remember my Grandfather well," she said. "Six feet tall he was, and a giant of a man, dark and handsome too. He taught us our catechism in Gaelic, and every Sunday and Lent day he would get out his big Gaelic prayer book and read to us. He never spoke English that I recall, though we children learned it when we got a schoolmaster here. I can remember too how happy my grandmother was when they commenced to build a church and a Priest came to visit. Grand-father told us that when his first two babies were born in the Valley, Grandmother cried because they could not be baptized. So when the second was old enough, he bundled the lot of them into a schooner and went over to Cape Breton to a priest. One of the babies was my father."

Mrs. MacDonald married Joseph, a carpenter, and had sixteen children. Not satisfied with that number, she adopted two more. "I was used to large families when I was growing up," she told me. "There was a big crowd of us, and then there were my uncles and aunts, some of them not much older than we children. How I remember my Uncle John—wasn't he the lad! He grew to be bigger than Father and Grandfather, and when he was a young man his favourite pastime was jumping out of one puncheon into another without touching. You try that some time."

The best tales about John, the "Lad," came not from Mrs. MacDonald but from Mr. Bruce, older by two years than she. Hughie, on his day off from road mending, offered to take me to visit him. As we walked up the long lane to the Bruce house, Hughie said, pointing to the roof, "Will you just look at him! All of ninety-two, and him up mending the roof. Well now, I'll be off when I've introduced you; he'll talk better without me around."

Mr. Bruce swung down the ladder and smiled to show as fine a set of natural teeth as you'd find anywhere. He could hear a pin drop and could see near and far without spectacles. He acknowledged the introduction and led me into his house. Before my feet were over the doorstep he began.

"The first thing I have to tell you is that we are Scots, though I'm sure there are some who told you we are not." There was more than a trace of French in his speech. "Some will say our true name is Brucard, or some such, and that we changed it to get into the Valley. But I will tell you why we spoke the French and not the Gaelic. There was a Bruce man who fought with his clan beside the Bonnie

Prince. He fought well, and at the end of the wars he had to go away from Scotland because his life was in danger. He crossed to France, to St. Malo, and there married a French woman. So, of course, he must speak French and so must his children. But that didn't make him a Frenchman! When his children grew up, one of them came to the Grand Banks to fish for cod. Now, you know about St. Pierre, down off the south coast. French, it's been, right from the start. Well, that's where this Bruce man went."

Mr. Bruce filled his pipe, watching me from the corner of his eye to see how I was taking all this. Then he went on. "This French-speaking Bruce came over to Codroy Island one summer, for Codroy Island was then always French, no matter who owned the shore; they could fight all they liked about that. Well, on this island Bruce met a fine, handsome woman from Quebec who had come over on her father's schooner. So he married her, and settled down back in St. Pierre. His son, John, it was who first came up into the Valley, and he married a McLean woman. They were my father and mother, and we're just as Scottish as the Gillises or anyone else. And another thing, all this about leaving Cape Breton because of religion and freedom and all that. Haven't you stopped to think about free land?"

"Well, I just heard the story yesterday," I told him, "and really haven't had time to think about it at all."

"You should. Not, mind you, that I'm saying they did not want freedom, but just remember the state of this country then. The French didn't own it, nor did the English, if you make a fine point of it, but everyone knew the English finally would. Meantime there was all this good land belonging to nobody. No grants asked for, none given, so a man could be sure that if he took a hundred acres or so, cleared and planted them, when the time came for grants, he wouldn't be turned away. Some of the first settlers finally paid thirty cents an acre for their land, others got it for nothing."

After a cup of tea, and before I left, I asked if I might come back another day to hear more about the early days in the Valley. "Certainly," he replied, "as long as I'm not in the middle of an important job."

So, when one day rain and high winds kept him indoors and away from "an important job," I visited Mr. Bruce once more. His kitchen this time was overflowing with life and activity. His granddaughter washed sheets in a huge galvanized tub. His great-grandchildren played at trains on the floor with saucepan lids, and his grandson worked with hammer and nails on a battered chest. Bruce took me to the "inside room" furnished with a new sofa and matching chairs of red with threads of sparkling gold.

"Handsome, isn't it?" he asked with obvious pride. "I bought it out of the catalogue. No duty either! My, that's some comfort to get things from Canada now without paying duty. Seems to me that business was half what was wrong with our country—duty on everything, even food. And for such a long time, too. You take John Gillis now, the man you were asking about. If he didn't have a terrible time with smuggling when he was made the first customs officer here in the Valley." I asked Mr. Bruce if he himself had figured large in one of John Gillis's big cases, as I had been told.

"Oh, yes. The story of the schooner from St. Pierre. I was only a boy then, but I remember it well. It was shortly after the Newfoundland Government put a duty on spirits. Before that time I don't think they even knew they had a West Coast. Anyhow they made John a customs officer, and when this three-master put into Codroy harbour, he decided she was carrying rum. So he impounded her."

"How on earth do you impound a schooner?" I asked.

"Easy. You take her sails, hide them away, and then she's helpless. We thought for sure this one was, because John locked the sails in his store loft. That night I didn't sleep very well—had a toothache. So I got up and looked out the window. The moon was just coming up and there was a light breeze. What should I see then, but some men skulking along the road carrying a big bundle of canvas. They went down on the wharf and got aboard the schooner. So I hauled on my clothes and run up the road as fast as I could go. I banged and banged on John Gillis's door, and by and by he opened it. I was that out of breath that all I could say was, 'The Frenchman got the sails. The Frenchman got the sails.' Then John let out a roar of rage, and frightened the dog so much he leaped out the window. Well, by the time John got down to the landwash, the last sail was going up and the schooner was under way. He raced back up the road, banging on doors and shouting. Four men, all as big as John and just as mad, jumped in the dory with him and took after the vessel."

That must have been an epic race. A three-master in a light breeze with a half-hour's start on a dory manned by four oarsmen. But they won and as they came alongside the schooner, they threw a grapnel over her rail and clambered aboard. They fought with fists, oars and boathooks, overcame the Frenchmen and brought the schooner back to Codroy.

"That was the night Sandy Joe discovered his head was softer than an ash oar," said Mr. Bruce, "and Andrew Gillis had his lip split from nose to chin. I was there when they came back—forgot all about my toothache, I did. And still they were not sure what she had in her hold. Since the French skipper would not take the tarpaulins off the hatches, John decided then and there to remove the covers himself. By this time the moon was well up, and it was light enough to read by. The boys went down in the forward hold and came up with a big barrel. They rolled it down the gangway, and up the hill right up to the schoolhouse door. John called his four friends by name to come inside, and the rest of us went home." The next day the story went out that the "jury" sat round the stove and sipped. One glass. Silence. Another glass. No verdict. After the third large swig, John smacked his lips and pronounced solemnly, "Dom good rum!" And they all went home feeling very righteous.

"You couldn't have been a very peaceable lot," I suggested.

"Peaceable! My dear woman, they were the worst lot of fighters you ever heard tell of. Down by Codroy, out at the end of the Valley, there was an open field where they used to have fights regularly. I can remember one when Alan McArthur's grandfather fought Louis Collier—he was an Englishman from Codroy village—over something that happened at a dance. They fought all day, practically naked they were, until Collier won the fight, but not before McArthur ripped all the skin off Collier's ribs with his knuckles. They fought with the

English, with strangers, and sometimes with each other."

"You take that bonfire night business. Of course, I know that most everyone now has forgotten why they have it, but in my day there wasn't a Catholic didn't remember about Guy Fawkes, nor a Protestant who didn't remember what the Catholics almost did. Feelings ran pretty high, I can tell you. Once I went with five boat-loads of Catholics and cleaned up on twelve families of Protestants down shore. I won't tell you where, because I'm ashamed of it now, and I'm only telling you so's you can know what times were like then."

"Do you mind my asking you about those times," I asked.

"No. For sure I don't. I think it's a good thing for someone to dig into our old minds. The days we knew when we were young were hard ones, but they were good, too, in many ways. We were contented, and we had plenty of fun. I dare say we did some wicked things too, but I don't suppose that will be held against us too much at the Day of Judgement. And when you get to be as old as me, you do a lot of dreaming and remembering. You begin to see how all that happened to you and those that went before goes into your children. And if they don't know their history, how can they know themselves? So I thank you for all your questions."

"And now," said the old man, "you being a radio person, would you write these stories down for to put in our family Bible?" Aware of the great value the Codroy people place on their proud past, I said I would. And now I've done so.

THE ZEPPELIN
OVER FAMISH GUT

Ella learns the brief history of the zeppelin that lost its way.

A VISITOR to Woody Point, Mr. Anstey, told me this lovely story.

"I minds the time after the First War when I was down in Famish Gut, what they call Fair Haven nowadays. One marnin' after me breakfast, I went down the road, and there were big crowds of people out. The women were pulling their hair and cryin', and the men was running around everywhere. And there, coming down on us was this big balloon thing. It come in me mind then, that before I left St. John's I read in a paper that an English zeppelin airship was coming over, and I knowed right away that was it. The next thing I thought was I better go to every house and tell them, 'cause I knowed they never saw a newspaper.

"Well, as I was runnin' along, I seen an old man with a gurt big sealin' gun. 'I'm goin' to shoot dat ting,' he said, 'and with me three-quarter shot, I can hit it too.'"

"Oh moi," I said, "Don't do dat! Dat's a British zeppelin."

"The old man lowered his gun 'British is she? Then I'll leave her bide.'"

"So, I ran on 'til I was out of breath. I got to the last home in the cove, and there in the kitchen, such an uproar. Dirty dishes and cups on the table and everyone sittin' mournful, crying and praying. I

222 NO PLACE FOR A WOMAN

asked them what was going on. The old man at the head of the table told me they was sitting there having their breakfast when the oldest girl looked out the window and hollered out, 'Oh moi. The world's to an end. Here comes the Blessed Lard.' 'Then she fainted, and we can't get her to, so we lef 'er lay where Jaysus flang her.' And there she was, face white as a tombstone, straight out on the floor lookin' dead."

Not quite believing the story, but relishing every word, I asked Mr. Anstey what on earth a zeppelin was doing in Famish Gut.

"Oh, she lost her way and she was trying to pick up the rail tracks and follow them to St. John's."

And did she, I asked?

"Oh yes, indeed she did, and she come down in Quidi Vidi pond. But before they could throw out the anchor, she bounced up, and she kept bouncing up and down. They say the last feller out jumped twenty feet, before she bounced the last time and went out over the water and was never seen no more."

So now you know about the zeppelin that lost its way over Famish Gut.

MISSIONARIES, MEDICS, AND MILITARY MEN

MCCREA IN
"FISH-AND-FOG LAND"

Throughout the long and complex history of relations with the United States, there came a time when an American invasion was thought to be imminent. Ella retells here how an officer sent from England to defend Newfoundland discovers the ups and downs of life in St. John's and recounts one of the last duels fought there.

THE YEAR was 1861, the time, late afternoon of a dull December evening. Lieutenant Colonel Robert McCrea had finished a hard day cleaning up the garden of his newly acquired villa. Having spent a good part of his life in the outposts of the Empire, he now looked forward to a long holiday with his wife, peaceful and safe as the English countryside surrounding him. Not an hour later came a knock, and a letter from a military comrade was delivered to his hand. "My dear Sir, the Colonel has just come from the Horse Guards. A great deal more shine about the *Trent* job than we thought. We are all ordered off to Canada. You are told off for Newfoundland and sail next Saturday on the Liverpool packet. Thought you would like to know."

The *Trent* job, about which there was more "shine" than they thought, was an incident during the just-commenced American Civil War. Two gentlemen from the southern States were returning to Paris and London where they represented their government. They succeeded in running the blockade that the northern navy had flung round the southern coast, and managed to reach Cuba. There they boarded the *Trent*, a British mail steamer bound for England. On her passage home she was stopped by the Northerners, boarded and relieved of the company of the two southern gentlemen, who were placed under arrest. This was rather irregular. The *Trent* could, of course, be boarded in order to examine despatches, and she could, in fact, have been escorted to an American port for adjudication. But nobody had authority to take two of her passengers prisoner.

To quote official documents, "The British government could not allow such an affront to the national honour to pass without due reparation." So they sent an ultimatum to the American government, backed up by troops sent to Canada and Newfoundland. It almost precipitated a war, and it did precipitate our hero McCrea into the most chaotic fifty hours of his life, as he packed his belongings and scurried around to see what he could discover about his destination, Newfoundland, about which he knew very little.

"Newfoundland?" said one of his friends. "To be sure. Know all about it. Fish, you know—tremendous place for salt fish."

"Newfoundland?" said another, "Oh yes, certainly. Know it very well. Banks, you know. Tremendous banks of mud and awful fogs. Take care of yourself. Cold, coughs, bronchitis, eh?"

A third friend said, "Newfoundland? Never heard anything of it, except they cook everything in cod liver oil. Rather not go there myself."

Finally, McCrea went to a well-known chart and map shop. "Newfoundland," said the shop man. "Certainly, Sir. American, I think. Northern or Southern? Oh, British colony is it?" And as he searched around, all he could find was an old Admiralty chart of the Grand Banks, but no information about McCrea's destination. Finally in despair, McCrea remembered an officer's widow, a lady of mature years, who he dimly recalled had spoken of Newfoundland. He beetled off to see her. She laughed at his pronunciation. "Oh 'Newfunlan', why yes, I remember. I was there several years. I liked it very much and was very happy there."

"What did you do there?"

"Do? Well, I don't think we did anything."

"I mean, how did you amuse yourself?"

"Oh, there were no amusements. It's quite out of that sort of thing, except letters which arrived every six weeks or so."

"What about roads?"

"Scarcely any. But in winter you can go everywhere in the sleighs. The food was not bad. Beef was fair, bread was good. Summer was too short for vegetables, except cabbages which grew in the ditch of the old fort. But there was plenty of salt fish, pork, wild duck, and Irish Papists. Oh, I remember now, it was an awful place for wind. It blows terribly, always blowing. We were often obliged to walk out tied two and two together."

So, with a stout heart, McCrea embarked from Liverpool for Queen and Country, ready to defend with his life the garrison of St. John's against all enemies, especially American. I needn't tell you that he found it a far different place than it was when the officer's widow of mature years resided there. Indeed, out of his two years in what he affectionately called "fish-and-fog land," McCrea fashioned a fine tale, replete with hilarious scenes.

What a time he had getting to St. John's. The packet first put in at Halifax to land the soldiers who were detailed for the fort there. As they were to lie all day at anchor, McCrea joined other passengers and got off to stretch his legs and admire the fine town. Meanwhile, an English naval frigate happened in, and her captain, said to be rather fierce and difficult to deal with, seeing the idle packet, immediately ordered her to sea. Consequently, a number of passengers were left behind, none more anxious than McCrea, who was told he might catch up with his ship in Sydney, nearly 250 miles distant, when she put in to refuel.

Off he went by sleigh headed for Cape Breton in the dead of winter, with the passengers snuggled under buffalo robes. The going was good until snow on the track dwindled to nothing, and the horse could not pull the sleigh over the bare ground. Out they got, walking to warm up their feet until they came to a trestle bridge covered with slippery ice. The horses made it across, but McCrea and another man were immediately down on their backs, unable to stand or move. Picture the scene then as the two supine passengers were towed and dragged across the ice "bumping, sliding, laughing," by those with "sparables" on their boots.[49] More than half frozen, they eventually reached Sydney where McCrea rejoined his ship, and two days later arrived in St. John's.

The harbour was all frozen over, dull-looking and opaque, save where round the ship it cracked like a frozen mirror. There was no sign of movement on the frozen land, except for one man on the wharf, who beat his arms over his chest for warmth and looked with complete disinterest at the Liverpool packet. At last the noon gun boomed, and a little iron-sheathed vessel bustled out to pick up Mc-Crea and the other soldiers. There was now quite a crowd of "big-limbed loafers and apple-cheeked damsels" gathered around to see the new soldiers come ashore, and to watch as each man made a jump onto the pier, slip, slide, stagger, and then go heels up, helpless on the icy ground.

And so it was all the way up to the garrison, until bruised and weary they reached the building full of bare, empty, cold rooms. The wind rose and whirled snow around corners, and the daylight faded as McCrea followed his servant to the room assigned him— "a dome-like chamber with a vaulted ceiling dimly lit by a candle, upon whose miserable combustion the riotous breezes entered freely by many holes and chinks." His servant, tugging at the frozen cords of a valise, paused to say, "I can't make head nor tail of this here stove, Sir, it's awful."

Now this stove was a Yankee contrivance called a "Franklin," in front of which they were alternately roasted and frozen. The smell of sulphur and heated iron was beyond endurance, and when the blower was off, out went the fire in ten minutes. When the blower was on, the

[49] Short nails or cleats hammered into the soles of one's boots to prevent slipping.

furnace exhausted their fuel at a terrible rate. Fussing with the stove until he was as black as tar, McCrea went round the room and chinked up all the cracks he could find, with paper, dirty linen and a cement of mutton lard. It was not a very edifying introduction to life in New-foundland, and while feeling sorry for himself he was visited by an old friend with whom he'd once served on the other side of the world.

"H'm," said he, "these quarters are not in very good order, I can see. I should be most happy to repair, but the money's the thing. They've screwed and tightened things down to the very last turn. They are afraid to ask Parliament for money for the Colonies."

Then, whisking the suffering Lieutenant Colonel off to his own house, a much better picture emerged, as McCrea related. "A pleasant bright hall with a staircase running spirally round to meet a gallery upstairs, while down the stairs came little girls in white muslin dresses, bare necks, and golden curls. In the living room, creamy white walls, pictures, flowers in blossom, stands in odd corners spangled with goblets and knickknacks."

And what do you think they had for dinner in this country where nothing was edible but codfish? Palestine soup made of rich cream and Jerusalem artichokes, a pair of roasted fowls, plump and tender, and a chop smoked to a succulent flavour. Then followed a boiled leg of mutton, French beans, mashed potatoes, and grouse-pie with kidneys and mushrooms. Wrote McCrea, "Ye Gods, what a perfume rose to the nostrils of a hungry man, when the lid of the pie was lifted." Rounding off the meal, gooseberry tart with clotted cream, fig pudding, jelly, tropical fruit from Puerto Rico, Cuba, and Spain and tipsy-cake—sponge cake soaked in sherry and brandy.

Then, a stroll in the cold along Water Street. On one side, McCrea notes, are the better sorts of shops, which sell "an *omnium gatherum* of most of the necessaries and rubbish of civilized life, where one might purchase a crape-bonnet, a chimney pot, a wedding ring, and a bottle of Radway's Ready Relief." On the other side of the street the shops "dispose of but six articles: old crockery, apples, lucifers, herrings, stale buns, and rum, the greatest of these." On one side mercantile emporia, on the other "speaking generally, grog-shops."

McCrea relates at length the last duel fought in St. John's, in 1826. He calls it the last, so there must have been others. However, though I have found accounts of disgraceful quarrels between hot-tempered politicians around the island, quarrels that properly could have been settled at sword point, so grievous were they, I have been able to find no tale so fine as McCrea's.

In those days, "before steam rapidly shuffled mankind together and rubbed off the sharp edges of our human vices," card playing was much more of a business than pastime. Men played cards from early morning to early next morning, winter and summer, spring and fall, and only big stakes could keep up excitement for that long. Players would stake seal pelts and a quintal of cod on a rubber, and many a good ship with its costly cargo changed hands nightly on the turn of a card. At the first whist party he attended, McCrea met a man who had landed from Ireland in an old pair of corduroys with half a crown in his pocket, and carved his fortune out of pure luck. He won at three-card loo a lot of cask staves, and set up as a cooper. Then, he won several tons of seal oil to fill the casks. His next prize was a schooner which he sent to the seal fishery, and she brought back a thumping load. "Well, Sir," McCrea was told, "he staked that against a building yard, won it and played again for a parcel of oil vats and won these. And he kept on 'til he made a hundred thousand pounds, and all the loose cash in the colony. Now he has filled the highest posts in the government with great credit."

So you see, card playing was something of a serious occupation in St. John's in the good old days when men staggering home half slewed with rum, dressed in the coarsest home-spuns that you wouldn't give away, were worth a hundred thousand pounds, but couldn't sign their names. And add in the lust of gambling, love, hate and jealousy, and you have a pretty fair background for the tale McCrea told of the duel long ago.

Just where a little stream flowed into Quidi Vidi, by a rustic bridge was a small cottage, where the daughter of the house was particularly pretty, shy and gentle. Two young soldiers, one a captain, the other a lieutenant, had both fallen abysmally in love with her. Whether from lack of opportunity or from indecision, the girl seems not to have favoured one over the other, and a fierce jealousy developed between the once bosom friends. One spring evening they met with others for a game of cards. A cheerful fire burned in the grate, and in front of it was drawn a large table, covered with an old red cloth, on which scattered the greasy cards played so many times before.

Flinging down their silver, the party got down to old Irish loo, which when played by gentlemen was the safest, liveliest and most sociable game in existence. At first, they all enjoyed themselves, but then the young lieutenant got so quarrelsome and awkward that most of the others dropped out. Since the captain was dealer, by the rules he had to stay in. Cards were drawn and the captain won. As he was about to take the pool, the lieutenant said, "I'm not looed. He cheated. Yes he did. He took the King from the bottom of the pack. I saw it." And he grabbed up the pool. Then seizing his glass, he hurled the hot contents into the captain's face. Quietly, the captain wiped his face, reached for his hat and left the room. As he did so, the lieutenant dashed toward him and completely beside himself with anger, aimed a kick at the captain.

In those days an apology was a rare thing to offer or accept, yet the captain for all his provocation told his friends that he would be satisfied with an apology, for thinking of the girl they both loved he wanted no publicity. "Oh well," said one friend, "you do as you please, but when a man insults you, then kicks you, isn't it a bit too late for apologies?" There was nothing for it then, but to send a challenge, arrange seconds and meet in combat.

About a mile from the hill on which the Cathedral so proudly stood was a deep and sheltered ravine, hidden by overhanging trees and carpeted by the dead leaves of a hundred summers. Duelling was frowned upon, so it was here, that the captain stood quiet and calm in the early morning sun, facing the still-angry lieutenant. The seconds took pistols and handed them to the duellists. His second, a doctor, whispered to the captain, "I tell you again, you have but one chance for your life. Fire quick. He's a dead shot, and if he misses you once, he won't the second time." "I shan't fire," came the reply, "He's a widow's son."

The signal given, the lieutenant fired and missed, the bullet just grazing the captain's collar, as he raised his weapon and fired into the air. "Load again, I say. Load again," shouted the angry lieutenant. Wishing to end the matter, the captain expressed himself satisfied, his honour vindicated. But they argued until he gave in, and the pistols were again loaded. Again his second whispered to the captain, "I tell you, unless you wing him first, you are a dead man."

"Ready, fire," came the command. The captain who had shot into the air now aimed to wing his adversary, but at that very moment the lieutenant jumped into the air discharging his gun wildly, and was shot dead through the heart. Horror descended upon the group as they stared silently at the body of the impetuous young soldier, until the doctor said hoarsely, "How terrible. Yet I acquit you, Captain. I do, from my soul. You fired that time to save your life. Now we must think of ourselves."

Furtively, they covered the corpse and crept away, hoping not to be seen. The doctor went immediately to Fort Townshend and reported an accident—a body lying in a little hollow just outside town. Soldiers investigated and returned, gently carrying the body of their comrade through the streets of St. John's. The fiction of an accident, of course, could not long stand. Even as the body passed bystanders watching the grim procession, the news spread that this man had been shot by a comrade, the man who had called out to his friend for some petty insult and then shot him through the heart.

This version of the event, like so many half-truths, incensed the crowd, and they yelled for revenge for what they called murder. Had the dead man been winged, or if the duel had been harmless, no one would have thought much about it, or would merely have considered the combatants romantic young fools. But this was different.

Soon could be heard the muffled drums and the sound of the dead march, as the funeral cortege wound down Garrison Hill to the old churchyard. The crowd that gathered were not friends—the dead man had few—but frightened citizens, sobered by sudden, uncompromising death. Then the other side of the story began to circulate, and the sympathy and pity of the crowd veered to the unfortunate captain.

The captain and the doctor were brought before court for the crime of wilful murder. The trial, said McCrea, was marred by the bias of the presiding judge, who in spite of the mitigating circumstances, summed up the case in virulent terms. "'Tis said," McCrea relates, "that having bidden the jury to retire to consider their verdict, the judge conspicuously turned the pages of the great law book, ready to pronounce the death sentence. The crowded courthouse waited in unbearable silence. This was something beyond the ordinary course of law in Newfoundland. This was something which bore on every man assembled. At last the jury returned."

"How say you?" asked the clerk. "Are the prisoners at the bar guilty or not?"

"Guilty, but without malice."

Down came the judge's hand, the desk shivering under the blow, even his wig trembling in anger. "What verdict is that? Who asked you to give anything but guilty or not guilty? Did you listen when I laid down what shooting a man in cold blood was?" Then he thundered, "Go back to your room and find a verdict in accordance with the law, or I'll keep you there until you do."

The prisoners' counsel, a distinguished and clever man, then rose and said quietly, "I must ask, my Lord, that you record the verdict just given by the jury."

"Certainly not. It is no verdict at all. I have refused it."

"I beg your Lordship's pardon, but it is a verdict. Guilty without malice is a verdict of not guilty of murder, which requires malice or aforethought. It is not possible now for the jury to bring in a verdict of guilty." Which is as obvious to you and me as it was to the jurymen, and the second verdict brought after a few minutes deliberation was "Not Guilty."

Never was there a more popular verdict. The crowd poured into the courtroom, clear up to the dock, and lifting the doctor and the captain on willing shoulders, they brought them triumphantly outside, up Garrison Hill, and back to Fort Townshend through a cheering mob. That night, it is said, the town celebrated in full libations of rum punch and whisky toddy.[50]

McCrea goes on to describe in detail his time in St. John's—little discipline, no tangible enemy to fight, very little social life and a vast deal of boredom.[51] The war with the United States over the *Trent* never did materialize, and at last came the order "to move on." McCrea's account ends as one morning in June, he stood on the steamer deck, "gazing up to the noble cliffs as she passed through the Narrows out to sea...and the purple cliffs of Fish-and-Fog-Land passed forever out of sight."

---

[50] In another duel in St. John's some fifty years later, Don Dooley and Augustus Healey fought over the hand of a Miss White. According to one version, the duel fizzled out, and the two ended up in a fist fight until arrested by the police. Another version relates that when the two duellists fired their pistols, Dooley fell to the ground. In shock, Healey cried out, "My God, what have I done?" However, since the seconds had loaded the pistols with blanks, Dooley had merely fainted and was quickly revived. To celebrate, they all went out for drinks!

[51] *Lost Amid the Fogs: Sketches of Life in Newfoundland, England's Ancient Colony.* London: Samson Low, Son, and Marston, 1869.

OUT FROM GREENSPOND
WITH JULIAN MORETON

Over the years, Newfoundland and Labrador benefitted from the efforts of dedicated men and women sent here to promote one Christian denomination or another. One who fascinated Ella was Julian Moreton, who pitched up on the shores of north-eastern Newfoundland as a Church of England missionary. His 1863 memoir, Life and Work in Newfoundland: Reminiscences of Thirteen Years Spent There, *describes life among the scattered population of Bonavista Bay.*

THE ISLAND of Greenspond had for some 150 years been a thriving community by the time the young Reverend Julian Moreton arrived in 1849. In fact my own ancestor, John Manuel, lived there on a piece of land granted by the Crown in 1732. All along Bonavista Bay and the Strait Shore, there were settlers, mainly of West Country origin, and there was much to-ing and fro-ing back and forth to England. Moreton found in Greenspond a neat village, a good church, a resident Justice of the Peace, and a Customs officer. For the previous twenty years, the village had had a school and a permanent teacher, as opposed to other settlements served by itinerants who spent a few months here and there. Moreton's mission, the largest in Newfoundland at the time, stretched along some seventy miles of coast from Bloody Bay[52] to Deadman's Bay, names enough to give any newcomer a chilly feeling. It included twenty-three settlements with 3700 people of whom eighty-six percent were of "my own flock."

Greenspond seemed quite a law-abiding, respectable place, though later it apparently fell on hard times. According to one historian, "Moral conditions left much to be desired. Drinking, swearing and adultery were rife." Indeed, as late as 1866, a Wesleyan parson described Greenspond as "Sodom and Gomorrah of the North." But though, during Moreton's time, it was a prosperous community, the outlying districts mirrored the times more accurately. If their stories had been written then, they'd have sounded pretty much the same. Their water generally came from the bogs or from rocky hollows after rains, and people considered themselves fortunate if in summer an iceberg grounded nearby, for melted ice water was much valued. "A bucketful of this Arctic water was often sent to the clergyman by some poor neighbour, and was counted no mean gift."

Moreton was always taken aback when, "Men would enter your house unasked, to light their pipes at your kitchen fire, and perhaps sit down to smoke and spit. Once Mrs. Moreton was surprised by a man thus entering her parlour, where she was sitting alone. He said nothing but coolly lit his pipe at the fire, then walked out again smoking it, without so much as a word."

Moreton wrote extensively about the bitter cold of winter and how it affected—and sometimes killed—settlers. Listen to him telling about trying to sleep in the bitter cold. "A remedy which I sometimes used and always found effectual, was to rise from bed and run twice or thrice with bare feet on the still colder floor. This excites circulation and soon a glow of warmth is felt which enables you to sleep. I believe now what I have often heard, that old people whose circulation is bad often suffer frost bite in bed." When writing, the ink would freeze in his pen so quickly that every few lines, Moreton had to stop and hold his pen in front of the fire to thaw it out.

[52] Now Glovertown.

As to their food supplies, I suppose it didn't matter very much if salt cod froze, and a carcass of meat kept much better frozen. Vegetables such as they had went in earth cellars with four-foot thick walls, but iced up the moment they were taken out. Milk froze so commonly that they used to put it on the table in a solid chunk to be sliced and slid into one's cup. And if you had the misfortune to spill your tea, it would freeze in the saucer and you'd lift cup and saucer together.

And bread? Well, you couldn't put this in the earth cellar because it would soon go mouldy. One stormy day when Moreton was visiting one of his "stations" he was invited to take some tea before setting out on his journey. While his hostess was cutting the bread and butter, she complained how difficult it was to keep the bread from freezing. "So I always put the loaf into the bed, and wrap it close up the minute the boys turn out." Rather horrified at the thought, he later discovered that in Greenspond his own maid always wrapped the bread up, and put it at the foot of her bed for the night.

Schools were few and far between, so how could people learn to read and write? Of the 334 people married in Moreton's parish between 1849 and 1856, only forty-nine could sign their names. Moreton asked one man if he could read and write, and he said, "No, I'm thankful to say, else I would be as big a rogue as them that can." Another man witness to a marriage, whom Moreton asked to sign the register, replied, "No, yer Worship, I can't write. I got to trust others, like most poor fellers. But I s'pose der will always be some smart enough to live 'longside their neighbours, and do nuttin' for their bread."

But they didn't all think that way. At Swain's Island, about four miles off the mainland where in Moreton's day the sealing vessels moored up the channel, there came to settle, years earlier, two families from the West Country. They worked hard from dawn to dark, with little comfort and less financial success. Finally, after several years the fishing improved, and one man began to prosper. By this time, there was a small host of children, none of them big enough to help with the fishing, but most of them big enough to be going to school if there was one. Well, the day came when the prosperous man called aside one of the hired fishermen and in his old-country accent said, "John, thee knows I cans't neither read nor write. Thee can read. Now it seems to me a sad, unchristian way for my boys to grow up without learning. Do thee stop ashore and teach our children, and I will pay thy wages as if thee went on the boat." And so he did, until a better teacher could be found, and John could go back to his fishing.

When Rev. Moreton arrived in Cat Harbour there was no school. They'd better get busy about it, said he, not understanding quite how much was involved in building a school there. So sixteen men, one from each house, decided they would get the timbers needed just as soon as they'd got their gear to rights after the fishing was over. They took two of the largest boats in the harbour and voyaged over sixty miles to get lumber to build their school. But bad weather came on. Strong headwinds blew continuously, and stirred up a heavy sea around Cape Freels, so the heavily laden boats struggled to make it. Three times they tried to sneak around the Cape, and three times they were driven back, but finally after an absence of twenty-two days they reached home, without enough timber. What a bitter disappointment, for now they had to wait another year before they would have time to repeat the arduous journey. Sure enough, the same time next fall, the same men set out again, and this time got enough to finish their school—this was in 1856.

I hope they behaved better in school than they did in church. The first minister in Greenspond complained that the rum bottle would pass around the upper gallery during the service, and once Moreton's own sermon was interrupted by a local lady crying out, "Gracious girls. I forgot the loaf. Julia, go next door and hang on the bakepot."

Moreton travelled back and forth across his mission, and, when at home in Greenspond, came to dread the appearance of visitors from the outliers of his district, for they would always "entreat me to go forthwith or name a time for going on a voyage to their distant places, while my duties elsewhere were claiming my presence." Much of his travelling was done during winter, when the backwoods were dotted with tilts—rude shelters—where families holed up while father cut wood. They would choose a site for their home and cut all the timbers, save for two opposite trees spaced far enough apart to make room for one dwelling. A thin pole called a lunger, stretched from one tree to the other, made the roof ridge. The four walls were made of tree trunks set close together, the floor of lungers and the hearth a flat stone. A chimney space was an uncovered spot at one end of the roof, and also served as a window. One end of this dwelling would be partitioned off with a punt sail, and that was home.

Along would come the minister, dressed in coarse cloth trousers, a reefer jacket, and a fur cap with earflaps—elsinores they were called—with a pair of blanket mitts and moccasins on his feet for easier travel on snowshoes. Thus was the Reverend dressed when he headed home one night from Deadman's Bay. He got as far as Seal Cove when he and his two companions broke through the "deceitful" ice. They pulled themselves out, but their outer clothes froze into a hard sheath. They were miserably cold and as they went on, the ice became thinner. They couldn't go back for it was too far, but ahead the ice bent under their weight as with weakened knees they got down and crawled. To their horror they soon came to open water between them and the shore. Not a thing moved on land, not even a dog to bark a warning of their approach, and shout as loud as they could, nobody appeared.

Finally, one of them spotted a few floating pans, and jumping from one to another managed to reach shore and find two boards. One he laid on the ice and crept across it, dragging the other board in his hand. And so the three of them managed to reach shore. When they reached the village, there wasn't a single change of clothing to be had. Nobody, but nobody had an extra garment. All they had to feed the minister and his companions was bread without butter, tea without sugar and a little molasses. Moreton said they sat up before the fire all night in order to keep themselves warm, though they were sick with fatigue. Later, when he visited this house again, Moreton was given good bread, butter and tea with sugar. He couldn't understand the improved circumstances, until he learned that the woman of the house, knowing he was expected, set out to walk the four miles to the nearest neighbour to borrow food fit to set before the minister.

So if Moreton had troubles, they were small compared to those faced by his parishioners. As the introduction to his book states, his aim was to give his readers "a plain, unvarnished account of facts, a humble and truthful picture of the difficulties and the encouragements of a devoted missionary." And this it does in spades.

JAMES LUMSDEN:
PARSON BUT NO SKIPPER

A quarter of a century after Moreton left Newfoundland, along came a Wesleyan missionary whose several parishes overlapped those of Julian Moreton. Here Ella tells of his nine years in eastern and northern Newfoundland.

ONE OF the more memorable of the nineteenth-century visitors was Scottish-born James Lumsden, who sailed into St. John's in September 1881 to be a missionary for the Wesleyan (Methodist) Church. After eleven years of work around Trinity, northern Bonavista and Notre Dame Bays, he retired to Nova Scotia, where in 1905 he wrote *The Skipper Parson on the Bays and Barrens of Newfoundland*. A parson he certainly was, but a ship's captain never: he had to rely on others to ferry him from one settlement to the next. Despite the constant sermonizing, his tales say much about the life and social customs   of his several parishes.

For example, I recall that in Lewisporte, where I grew up, we always flew the Union Jack when something pleasant occurred in the family—a success, a visitor or a birthday. I thought it a family custom until Lumsden set me right. "A pretty custom pertained generally throughout the island. Nearly every family had a flagstaff on its grounds, and flags were hoisted on national, local or family celebrations. Flags were called into requisition to announce to the world such important events as a marriage, a birth, the arrival of a friend, and the like. Neighbours rejoiced with rejoicing friends. And when a death and funeral occurred, many flags at half-mast were the silent but eloquent witnesses of a sympathy sincere and general. Churches without a bell substituted a flag, and here is how it works. The flagstaff, which is a high one, stands in a conspicuous place near the church, and the flag can be seen by all. An hour before the service, the flag is hoisted to full mast. A quarter of an hour before services, it is put half-mast, and as the minister enters the church it is taken down altogether."

Lumsden noted that Brother Blundell of St. Jones Without, in Trinity Bay, had neither bell nor flagstaff, so he would carry a horn which he blew with such vigour that its reverberations echoed and re-echoed among the hills. The first strong blast signalled an hour in advance, and the next told the village that Brother Blundell was about to leave his house for church, and they'd better follow immediately.

As Parson Lumsden himself said, his "knowledge of things in Newfoundland was often dearly bought." On his way by ship to his first mission to Northern Bight, on the shores of Southwest Arm of Random Sound, he encountered an "ominous circumstance. I saw an old man—a passenger—drinking spirits." Despite this alert to danger ahead, shortly afterwards his ship was wrecked on Shag Rock. He and his fellow shipmates barely escaped with their lives, finally reaching shore in a cranky punt. Lumsden lost all his clothes, books, and papers. When he arrived in Northern Bight, he was taken in by an old lady, who asked him if he'd saved anything. "Nothing beside what is in my head," he replied. To which she with kindly humour commented, "I hope you've got something in your heart, too."

Before long he was clothed with the best from local men's wardrobes, and later began to receive books from parsons all over Canada. I wonder how they heard about him from the place where he said "the isolation is terrible." As an example, Lumsden recorded that one day, a strange man, a railway surveyor, walked through Random, and a little girl spied him through the window. "Oh mother," she exclaimed, "who is that? He doesn't belong to this world."

But gradually the world did reveal itself, and James Lumsden played a part in opening it to the many hundreds of people along the coast. He was here, there and everywhere, by punt a-rowing, under sail, and in winter by snowshoes, made for him by local Mi'kmaq.

"Wearing long leather boots, I took my first lesson walking with the light and graceful snowshoes. The snow caked up on the heel of my boot, my feet slipped and down I sank in the snow. Up I got again and plunged headlong. Finally, disgusted, I took them off and beat my way through the snow to Lee Bight."[53] Once Lumsden tried them with a pair of moccasins, he was sold on snowshoes, especially with a pocket full of Hamburg bread to satisfy his hunger. This was hard bread, which when "boiled and served with pork fat and salt fish was a meal to nourish a strong and hardy race."

The strong and hardy race had their housing problems. The dwellings in which many coastal people lived were pictured thus: "Entering a low door, you are likely as not to stumble over a pig in the porch, to find frightened hens making desperate efforts to escape over your head, and when you enter the living room your eyes smart from the smoke of green sticks smouldering on the open fireplace."

Yes, they lived in tilts and ate Hamburg bread, but as Lumsden wrote, "a remarkable hardiness, robust vigour of manhood and womanhood is common. Longevity is often the reward of the simple outdoor life." Once, near St. John's, he found an old man of nearly 100 years lifting a huge sack of potatoes. "That's a heavy load for you," the Parson exclaimed. The old man doffed his hat, scratched his head and said, "I've just been wondering how it comes about that I can't lift it as easy as I used to." Forthwith he raised the load and staggered off, leaving Lumsden open-mouthed.

In Lumsden's time, the question of Confederation with Canada was a burning issue. One old boy told Lumsden that if the Canadians

[53] Now called Adeytown.

came down around Northern Bight, he'd go for them with his swilin' gun. When asked why, he said in deep anger, "Because they'll tax every pane of glass and make us all go as soldiers." And when one Canadian did come around, a bookseller who carried a good and wholesome cookbook, one woman in sorrow proffered, "You poor man. Did you come all this way from Halifax thinking we don't know how to cook?"

Parson Lumsden generally admired the people in his various parishes, especially if they were Methodists. He wrote that "Newfoundlanders are often characterized by emotionalism in religion, but they are usually intelligent; and when a warm heart is wedded to a clear head, something very near perfection is found. This is the character of Newfoundland Methodism in the main." Of the adherents of other religions he had little to say.

Of course, Lumsden has a chapter on sealing, for everyone who wrote in those days was an authority on the hunting of seals, and the hardships sealers faced. He described the arrival of one sealing steamer: "A great strapping fellow jumped out from deck to the wharf and immediately on speaking with his friends burst into tears, sobbing like a child. On learning the cause of his grief, I was not at all surprised at its intensity. He had come home empty handed to a wife and twelve children, and his old blind mother."

Lumsden wrote about men shipwrecked and saved, only to live out their lives as invalids. One such was Joseph Kean of Norton's Cove, near Wesleyville, bedridden for fifteen years, the result of exposure on the ice-fields. From his bed near a window overlooking the sea, he would while away the time with a looking glass, which he could manipulate to give a view of the entire harbour. One winter's day when the bay was frozen over, he spied a dark shape just poking through the ice. He knew what it was, and shouting to his family, who like everyone else was at dinner, he begged them to hurry, hurry—not a moment to lose. For their beloved pastor was walking across to Norton's Cove when the ice gave way. He clung to the edge, but being a very heavy man, he couldn't crawl out. He was about at the end of his tether when the villagers arrived with ropes and poles, and with much difficulty extricated him. Joseph Kean could never get over the wonder of his looking out at precisely the right moment.

Later, Lumsden went to Notre Dame Bay to more sophisticated and populous places, including Little Bay, with more than two thousand residents, some of whom lived in pretty little houses in a place called "The Park." Here they had created an orchestra of twelve instruments, and entertained the public with monthly musical and literary meetings. The rest of the people worked in the copper mine where, as Lumsden described, "The men formed a dismal procession coming out of the pit, their clothes wet with mire, a candle sticking in their caps. Working in the pit or half-stripped before a roaring furnace ladling the molten ore, shovelling all day amid sulphurous smoke, they were all sons of toil."

Farther along the shore, he came to Halls Bay: "Its lonely solitude unbroken by any sound except the shrill call of a bird or the low murmur of the water. Here the rocky battlements were high above the water and are broken into deep fissures, a miniature harbour, a dark cavern. Away on the other side the land slopes gently to the water, as if in friendly communion, and in a long stretch of unbroken coastline is one little bit of a clearing, with its tilled fields and curling smoke." Lumsden found here a tiny settlement, a dozen houses, a school chapel, and a little sawmill by the brook. The reason I am telling you about it is to set the scene that has haunted me from the moment I first read it.

In one of the tiny houses, a lone woman greeted him in the familiar accent of his native Scotland. His outspoken astonishment opened her heart, and she told him her story. In Glasgow, she said, she'd been content until poor health led her doctor to suggest a sea voyage. A friend got her a passage on a ship to America, which put in at St. John's. Someone there offered her a fine job as housekeeper, and she stayed. Not for long, she hastened to add, because she intended to return home as soon as she felt better. But the years slipped by, and before long she got married. Then, for a reason she did not tell, she and her husband came to this isolated settlement in Halls Bay. He was away all day, she was alone and her heart was "sore heavy, for she was city bred and used to much to do." And Lumsden says, "Her face, though marked with sadness and heart-hunger, showed unmistakable traces of refinement, and the story she told with inimitable pathos and sweetness, especially as I glanced around the bare and cheerless room, void of even the music of a child's voice, made a strong appeal to my sympathies. 'It cam up roond my heart.'" As it does to mine, and I keep wondering who she was, and what became of her? What mark did she leave on her village?

Lumsden closes *The Skipper Parson* with the hope that reading it will "stimulate an interest in home missions." Well, I don't know about that, but I'm grateful for his delightful word pictures of the old ways and old days of our people in Newfoundland.[54]

---

[54] And to honour him, a few years after his death in 1915, the village of Cat Harbour was renamed Lumsden.

DR "FITZ" OF THE *ALBATROSS*

About the same time as Lumsden arrived in Newfoundland, newly qualified doctor Conrad FitzGerald landed in Harbour Breton to attend to the health of people working for a company of fish and wine merchants along the southeast coast. As Ella relates, there were few medical men as tough and indestructible, and as self-effacing.

BORN IN England, the youngest of four sons of a doctor, Conrad FitzGerald decided early to follow in his father's footsteps. He apprenticed himself to a local physician, and within two years he was off on calls alone. In 1873, after several stints as ship's doctor on a full-rigger on the London to Melbourne run, he arrived in Harbour Breton. Here he was hired for three years by Newman, Hunt and Company, the prosperous West Country merchants who sent wines to mature in Newfoundland and brought back to England salt fish.

His practice covered so large a coastline, with settlements so widely scattered that he was continually on the move. His constant companion was the *Albatross*, a thirty-foot sailboat with two masts and a jib arranged so that one man aft of the mainmast could control the tiller, the mainsheet, the foremast and the jib. The *Albatross* became as familiar to Fortune Bay as the doctor himself. Whenever she hove in sight, men would swarm off in dories to help him anchor, and on shore men and women and children would greet him with all manner of ailments. For forty years he sailed her alone, or so it seems. But I know a woman who swears she more than once saw the *Albatross* bowling along while Conrad swam alongside, calling out at intervals to his dog on board, "Throw the tiller away from you. Now haul it back." And the dog would port and starboard the helm with precision and alacrity.

Conrad was a tough man who went swimming in November, sailed vessels in mighty storms and walked alone a hundred miles in midwinter. When he was an old, old man he would drag his bag behind him on a sled made of barrel staves, walking uphill and down on snowshoes. Once sailing on a sick call, alone as usual, the Doctor ran into a storm. The ship yawed, and when the boom swung it landed a vicious blow on the back of his head. When he regained consciousness, he staggered round to fasten the boom and get the boat into harbour. Here he managed to tie her to a tree stump, but in twisting around he heard a crack and realized he'd broken a rib. Slowly and cautiously he crawled back to the dory, rowed back to his boat where he strapped himself in plaster and bandages as best as he could. Then he sailed home another forty miles.

Another time, after three days watching over a sick man, Conrad walked twenty-two miles through slush and snow, cut the *Albatross* out of the ice and stood watch for the nine hours it took him to sail home. With barely enough time to swallow a cup of tea, he rushed to check on a woman ill with pneumonia. That required a four-mile row, walking across a neck of land, climbing into another punt, rowing another three miles before he could reach his patient.

At Fox Cove, Dr. Fitz had to remove a large tumour from the back of an old fisherman, without anaesthetics. The old man made no sound as the doctor made long incisions, until after the operation was over. Then he looked out the window and his only comment was, "I rather think we're going to have the wind out of the nor'east." Dr. Fitz was likewise a man of few words. On the night of his wedding to Katherine Partridge, from Nova Scotia, his diary entry read simply, "Wind from the north-east. Married,"

After attending a patient in Wreck Cove, Fitz was invited by a young woman who had just been married to attend a celebratory time that night. "In the house where the wedding party was being held a number of buxom maidens and tall, awkward youths danced to the strains of a 'Long Tom's' fiddle. The dance consisted of much swinging at a tremendous pace, preceded by stamping and various movements of the body. The bridegroom contented himself with drinking glass after glass of rum until he was completely intoxicated." As the guests sat down to a meal of fish and potatoes, the "bride disappeared to her chamber, the loft of the house, and shortly afterwards her more-or-less musical voice surprised the doctor by announcing 'I'm all in arder, Skipper Jarge!'" But by this time Skipper Jarge, the bridegroom, drunk as a lord, was sleeping it off.

Tough FitzGerald certainly was, but he could be gentle and understanding when required. He distributed medicines free, and made some money trapping foxes and selling their pelts. Once he quarantined a whole community for three months when smallpox broke out there, and he nursed his own family through diphtheria when there was such panic that you could hardly get anyone to bury the dead. And when the epidemic was nearly under control, he had to sail off for Jacques Fontaine where a man had blown his hand off with a gun.

According to his grandson, Dr. Fitz "attended patients at the risk of his life, beating up and down the treacherous, cruel, rocky coast alone in his *Albatross*, or battling his way on snowshoes across a desolate land in blizzards, to reach some isolated spot where were people in pain. His practice was so large, and the settlements which constituted the practice so scattered, that in order to visit all his people he was almost continually going from place to place. He was indeed glad to spend his time among men and women who underneath their crude, primitive outer surface possessed qualities which have been essential to the maintenance of empires, and through no fault of their own had been forced to obtain a livelihood in settlements where medical aid was unknown."[55]

---

[55] C.T. Fitz-Gerald, *The 'Albatross', being the Biography of Conrad Fitz-Gerald, 1847-1933*. Bristol: J.W.Arrowsmith, 1935.

When he was seventy-seven and the Newfoundland Medical Association called him a hero, Dr. Fitz said he felt an utter fraud, for he'd done only what any man would do who liked boat work. A fine man who came for three years and stayed a long lifetime in Newfoundland.

MACDERMOTT OF FORTUNE BAY

Another missionary of sorts, this one with a medical wife, was the Rev. Hugh MacDermott. He arrived, in 1904, not far from where Dr. Fitz was working, though the one seems to have written little about the other. Ella's story of the man once described as "to Newfoundland what Grenfell has been to Labrador" is based on his 1938 memoir.[56]

HUGH MACDERMOTT came to Newfoundland not because he was drawn to it but because he was sent by the Congregational Church in England. He arrived with his head stuffed with stories of fogs, bogs and dogs, and was agreeably surprised at the balmy summer weather that greeted him. This gave way to some alarm as he discovered the fiords and cliffs of his Fortune Bay parish-practice, and the rocky coast without harbour for fifty miles. Had he returned home when his time was up he might have been forgiven, but he stayed for more than thirty years.

A woman who in her youth worked under him as a teacher-missionary told me, "He was a big man and bluff, with a red face and a quick temper. He'd say to you, 'Good Morning. How is your soul?' wanting an answer. He was hard to get to know. He didn't talk much,

---

[56] *MacDermott of Fortune Bay told by Himself.* London: Hodder and Stroughton 1938.

but my dear, he was a saint. Nobody knows the good that man did."

If he couldn't do what he wanted, MacDermott would do the next best thing in a place where nothing had been done to help people for a good many years. He brought out from England a supply of footballs, cricket bats and tennis racquets, but when he found that there wasn't a big enough level space for a playing field, not in miles around, he packed the sports equipment away, his heart aching for the children who had no childhood, who went to work before sun-up and did a day's work before other children were going to school. One of his favourite memories was distributing a huge crate of dolls from abroad to children who never before had a toy.

He learned to adapt himself quickly. On one of his first voyages when they ran short of food he was given the only egg, poached. He took one look at the revolting bright red yoke and pitched it overboard, only to learn that hens fed on lobster laid red eggs! He learned not to be disturbed when in the middle of his evening sermon the sexton would stand on a chair, take the chimney off the lamp, balance himself on one foot and strike a match along his raised trouser leg. The matches, very sulphurous, locally called "stinkers," would slowly burn while the sexton gazed round the congregation, and when it flared he'd light the lamp. So the moment he could, MacDermott he got a lighting plant for the church. In fact he built the church with the help of fishermen, good carpenters all, and the things they couldn't make, like windows, cement and nails he begged from rich friends.

Soon MacDermott had a house built for himself, shot his first moose and sent for his fiancée, an English nurse. As soon as they reached the new house from the wedding, she was called to a maternity case. It was early winter, a calm night and the men couldn't row the boat fast enough to prevent her from being frozen in halfway across the bay, where Mrs. MacDermott spent the night sitting in an open boat. At the same time her new husband was on call in a small vessel becalmed on a pitch-black night. She began to drift with the tide, nobody knew where, until cliffs blacker than the night loomed on her bow. They escaped only to be caught in a high wind and had to make six attempts to get into port in driving snow. Another time

MacDermott crossing the bay on thin ice fell in and with the tide running and a thick overcoat he was unable to get out. Luckily two men happened by and managed to rescue him, only when he'd lost his mitts and his hands were frozen to the ice. And there was the time his hair froze to the side of a tent, and he had to be thawed out before he could rise to breakfast. These were things that often happened to Newfoundlanders—a part of their lives they couldn't avoid. But that an Englishman should choose to run such risks trying to help them, they thought a great sacrifice.

MacDermott built schools and churches. He attended the sick for miles around and he fought against disease, dirt and malnutrition, always with new ideas about what to eat. Then came typhoid, and although the people were mortally afraid of it they nursed Mrs. Mac through an almost fatal attack, because they simply couldn't do without her help.

It was about this time that the MacDermotts realized that making do and patching up wasn't enough: they had to break the circle of poverty somehow. It wasn't much use preaching to people with cold feet and empty stomachs. They knew that men who could build their own boats, rig and sail them the world over could do anything with their hands, and that women who could shear a few puny sheep, card and spin the wool and supply their families with clothing could make anything, given the wherewithal. So when one day the governor's wife sailed in on the *Nonia* along with samples of work done by her countrymen in the Scottish Highlands, MacDermott called his people together, got some wool, and before he knew it was sent off to St. John's with a suitcase full of sweaters. The knitters had no idea what they'd be paid, neither did he. But he related, "When I gave the payment to the first knitter, her eyes filled with tears. Later I asked her if she was satisfied with the ten dollars and she said, 'I don't know how I got home, on my head or on my feet. My Bill hasn't made a cent this year, and we hadn't a thing in the house. Now I could buy flour and the other things we needed.'"

Somehow word got around what the MacDermotts were doing, and they were sent for the summer from Canada a weaver with a loom. A loom was set up in the church and one minute, you'd see a woman at the hay, the next she'd catch sight of the teacher going to the church and she'd stick her pitchfork in the ground and run to be in time for the weaving class. Women came from other villages by dory, and if the weather was too bad, they'd send the men back with the finished garments and stay for the next lesson.

They couldn't afford to buy looms so they drew a picture of the one they had before it was returned to Canada and copied it. They ended up making and selling looms to Canada. They wove, knit, hooked rugs, and the men made looms and chairs. I might say that the fabrics from these looms were wonderful: I've a suit made of Fortune Bay weave that I've been wearing for sixteen years and it still looks new!

Soon people who came to help in the summer went back with reports on malnutrition, the lack of dental care, and the shortage of nurses. Because the MacDermotts had helped their people to realize some of their potential, assistance came in. They lived to see a floating medical clinic, visits from American specialists, occasional dentists and as many nurses as needed.

But the Macs were fighting pretty tremendous forces. They tried to improve the breed of animals, to introduce goats, to get people to grow vegetables, but then the War came. Fishing was neglected by the far more lucrative rum-running from St. Pierre and Lunenburg. The money came easier, and people became "embittered, their lives coarsened and they were hard and cynical." This did not please MacDermott, so it is no wonder that some do not wish to be reminded of him, even years later, for they must have felt the rough edge of his tongue on occasion. Yet he cared for them. Wherever he was he was wanted somewhere else, to bury the dead, to marry, to hold a church service, or to give medical aid to someone desperately ill. And so he lived for more than thirty years, another of the small company of men who changed the lives of people in outport Newfoundland.

OF SAILORS
AND THE SEA

THE *NEWFOUNDLAND* AND *LABRADOR* PILOT

Ella takes a bemused browse through a copy of an old guide to sailors in Newfoundland waters.

NOW THIS isn't a person: it's a book. It is a compilation of directions, noted by mariners from Captain Cook to masters of all kinds of vessels at the end of the nineteenth century, directions that you could still follow today and safely come to harbour. My copy, given me by my father, who first went to sea in the late nineteenth century, is battered and sea-stained. It was published by the British Admiralty in 1897, the third edition, compiled by J.R.H. MacFarlane, who set out to assemble a simple, direct, and as near as humanly possible, infallible guide to our coast. This was accomplished with astonishing clarity, poetic rhythm, and what I can't help thinking of as "elegant economy of speech."

I give you first my favourite entry. "St. Shotts is an open, exposed cove where a few families reside on its eastern side, and are always ready to assist the shipwrecked and distressed mariner. A melancholy interest is attached to St. Shotts on account of the many shipwrecks which have taken place in its vicinity. It is seldom that a year passes without a wreck taking place in the neighbourhood, and in most cases, these wrecks have occurred during foggy weather with a neglect of the use of the lead, and a want of attention to the ordinary set of the currents."

And another, which concerns Fleur de Lys: "There is never any sea at this anchorage, but after a strong breeze from the north round by east, the sea breaks with fury on the outer coast, while the foam stretches across the entrance, looking like breakers. This phenomenon has been observed to follow a northerly gale at an interval of one day, after the wind has completely fallen, when the sea rose in one hour."

In many places, the naval gentlemen who compiled the *Pilot* apparently believed that houses, churches and trees stood eternal. "Now, entering Fortune Harbour, care should be taken when turning around Sweeney Island to shut in the house with the diamond on the door at Davis Point with the east end of Sutton Island."

Another direction: "The Episcopal church with a square tower and a Roman Catholic church with a spire on the dividing point of the bends of the harbour, and westward a barn on the north shore opens east of a shoal around which a safe passage may be made by keeping the north shore aboard."

Ships passing Fox Island are informed that "on the western slope is a large pine tree that towers considerably above the rest of the woods and shows conspicuously from the eastward." And on Goat Island "there is a remarkable tree, one hundred and eight feet above high water and no passage for a stranger."

"No passage for a stranger." I cannot tell you how many times that ominous but evocative phrase occurs. How much of the history of our province is buried in these words!

In Famish Gut "beware of a rock called Winging, near Shag Roost, not far from Sly Boots." And "Come by Chance harbour gives anchorage for lesser vessels, but it must be borne in mind that the water shoals rapidly off Molasses Point."

Famish Gut, Molasses Point, Bareneed, Sweet Bay and Bloody Bay and Damnable Bay, Angel Harbour and Civil Cove and Isis Cove are all part of the litany of names along our Newfoundland coast. Mon Jambe becomes Mose Ambrose, and Bande de l'Arier becomes Belleoram. And everyone knows of the wanderings of Bay d'Espoir—from hope to despair and now back to hope again!

Belleoram, incidentally, has "an iron head rising perpendicular from the sea and to the east a semicircular beach forms a snug harbour for large vessels." Could anything be more succinct?

Another entry: "Small vessels should be careful not to leave Little River when the wind is against the tide, as a confused sea soon gets up." I do not know whether I am more enamoured of the confused sea or the bone-clean prose which tells me perfectly what I, a sailor, should know.

"Naked Man dries at three feet at low water! Old Man is a peaked hill where for about two hours near noon the sun is shining, a shadow on the cliff forms a curious resemblance to the figure of a man."

"Heart's Ease is a long narrow inlet. A hundred feet up the hill over it is a church in the form of a large, ordinary house, isolated and conspicuous." Never before did I understand the vast difference in meaning between the word "remarkable" and the word "conspicuous."

"Off Cape Anguille, the coast curves back. The tops of the cliffs are densely wooded, as are also the slopes of the mountains behind, and during spring months, waterfalls mark the mouths of several gullies. At the entrance to some of the gullies, there are small clusters of rude huts which are used by fishermen, temporarily living there during the summer months. A narrow bush trail originally for the benefit of persons shipwrecked on this inhospitable coast, runs parallel with the cliffs and connects Ship Cove."

My particular piece of coast is described thus: "Northwest winds, blowing with strength, throw a heavy sea on this shore and during these periods, landing with safety is almost impossible, except in a few places where there is a little indifferent shelter. The large quantity of driftwood along the whole coast is suggestive evidence of the violence with which this sea rails on the shore."

Such were the directions to mariners, and so they were used until 1952, when a new edition of the *Pilot* was issued. Mariners also had charts marking shoals, lighthouses and aids to sailors. However, they were warned "that instead of considering a coast to be clear unless it be shown to be foul, the contrary should be assumed," and "that the ten-fathom line is often on rocky shores"—another warning, especially for ships of heavy draught. Furthermore, "it is manifestly impossible that any reliance can be placed on buoys always maintaining their exact position. Nor can the lights shown by gas buoys be implicitly relied on as, if occulting, the apparatus may get out of order."

This *Pilot* has what Joseph Conrad called "the clearness, precision and beauty of perfected speech... created by simple men with keen eyes for the real aspect of the things they see in their trade." To me, it is poetry, full of lovely images, haunting and beautiful. Someone should put it to music! [57]

---

[57] Years after Ella wrote this piece, the 1897 *Pilot* was reprinted by the British Library. For some time it was listed under their catalogue heading "Fiction and Prose Literature"—a most appropriate recognition of the elegance of its language.

SHIPWRECKED OFF
GREEN GARDENS

Among the nineteenth-century seamen who recorded what they saw and heard during their voyages to Newfoundland and Labrador was Lieutenant Edward Chappell. His 1818 book describes the cruise five years earlier of the H.M.S. Rosamond to Newfoundland and Labrador "of which countries no account has been published by any British traveller since the reign of Queen Elizabeth." While visiting southern Labrador, he wrote, "We were much surprised, on visiting our good friend Mr. Pinson, to find a handsome female seated at the head of his table. The sight of a white woman was now a real gratification to us all; and our officers were anxiously desirous to discover by what means she had been thrown upon the savage territory of Labrador." Chappell recorded the strange tale told by "Mrs. E." as he called her. Here, in the voice of the young woman herself, Ella retells the story with some artistic license.

I HAVE always loved the sea and ships. My earliest memory is of my father, a Quebec merchant, taking me down to the river and aboard the foreign vessels that crowded our dockside. My strongest recollection is of my father and my mother standing on the dock to wave farewell when I sailed down the river with my husband. It was his first long voyage since our marriage, and despite warnings from my family that the journey would be long and hazardous, I was determined to accompany my husband in the little brig of which he was captain.

It was on December 2nd, 1812, that we set sail, bound for Labrador to load a cargo of dried cod, and thence for Liverpool. The weather was calm and for the first three days, we had a comfortable passage. But when we reached the St. Lawrence Gulf, we ran into a tremendous storm which lasted for a day and a night with thick snow adding to the darkness. When we were driven far off course, my husband showed some concern to which the mate, who knew this passage well, added by declaring, "If this wind does not abate, we shall drive straight unto the Newfoundland coast." My husband thought we might find anchorage in a cove and there wait out the storm, but the mate warned him: "There is neither harbour, nor creek nor habitation for a hundred miles on that Godforsaken coast. I know—I have seen that cruel land!" How cruel it was, we soon discovered.

With sails in shreds, poles bare, we were hove to when the wind shifted and in wind and darkness, we were driven ashore. I can still hear the crash—still see the lantern's feeble gleam as we forced our way over smashed timbers awash on the deck. I can still remember how the darkness was torn briefly by the moon's light. Only by that single, brief flash were we able to find the shore and to row our little dory to it.

I remember a feeling of great thankfulness that we were still alive, every one of the crew, and that we had the upturned boat and a shred of canvas to shelter us against the freezing wind. The long night wore on in silence, nor again did we see the moon. And when the day dawned, not with sun but with a cold grey light which reflected from a steely sea, we drank a mouthful of brandy and looked about us.

There, by Heaven's mercy, was our ship, high on a jagged rock, stranded by the receding tide. Behind us and reaching almost to the water's edge, smooth-faced mountains hemmed us in. Snow covered all, and the silence was as deep as the snow. Before us, the sea heaved in great, unbroken waves with only a thin line of foam to mark the shoal which had caught us.

We launched our tiny dory and hastened to remove whatever we could before the tide rose. When it did, and sucked our little vessel under, we turned from the horrid sight, sick at heart, our last link with humanity so rudely broken. But we were grateful for what we had saved. We should not starve, not for some weeks. We had nails, canvas and planks with which to build shelter against the intolerable cold. My husband climbed through the deep snow to the mountain tops, seeking where we might build a hut further inland. He returned to say that as far as one could see were plateaus and peaks, and in valleys were frozen lakes and streams and dense woods.

It was clear that we should have to remain for some time on the thirty or forty feet of shore between mountains and sea. So there we built two huts, one for my husband and me and the mate, which would also contain the stores and our tiny supply of gunpowder; the other, a little way off, for the crew. Against the further end of our hut, I hung a piece of canvas to afford some privacy, and at night we slept on the bare floor in the clothing we wore all day long.

We built a fireplace under a hole in the hut's roof, but the burning of the sodden, green boughs that we had gathered with difficulty from under the snow banks, made so acrid a smoke that we found the cold more bearable. However, we were able to build a sort of fireplace on the beach for the cooking of our food.

Then, when everything possible was done for our comfort, we took stock of our situation. The mate who, as I have said, had sailed along this route many times believed that we were on the barren coast north of Bay of Islands and south of the bay which the French call "La Belle Baie," where for many miles mountains rose sharply from the sea and fell away inland into woods and ravines, inhabited only by wild animals. A few people lived by the shore during summer, but when autumn storms came, they moved inland, how far and in what direction, we did not know. We knew that it would be folly to attempt moving over that desolate land through snow that piled sometimes to a depth of ten feet, perhaps to find nothing in the end.

We were imprisoned between mountains and sea, but we hoped there was a chance that the sea would bring us rescue. Although the mate said that small vessels would not come within two miles of the shore, so confused was the sea and so full of reefs, yet we hoped that some vessel bound south from Labrador would pass by and sight us.

The days crawled on. Dirt and dampness affected us disagreeably. Our faces were caked with ash, our eyes red and inflamed from the constant smoke. My hair, of which I had been so proud with its golden sheen and soft curls, was now matted with icicles that did not melt, even in the warmth of sleep. That was to me a source of torment. One day when my husband went to search for firewood, I cut my hair close to the scalp. So small an act it was, but how forlorn I felt; no longer was I a bride to be cherished, but an unkempt derelict. My husband wept that night when he saw what I had done.

It was about this time that we gave up hope of rescue, for no ship would sight us now in the dead of winter. The ice grew thicker and stretched as far as one could see. At night it groaned and creaked like some giant tree in the frozen woods. I was often utterly spent and often longed only for the oblivion of sleep. But I would not, for pity's sake, let my dear husband see how badly it went with me. While I could, I accompanied him on expeditions for firewood and to set snares for animals that never came.

One day, when nauseated and weak, I lay wrapped in a cloak before the smoky fire, and felt obliged, for his peace of mind, to tell my husband that I was with child. How happy I am to recall that moment. I had withheld the news from him, believing that it would only add to his burdens, but I was wrong, for now we were spurred to hold to life and to greet each day with hope. And I will confess to you that when the sun shone on that white world, the austere beauty of the mountains, carved with black shadows, lifted our hearts. Life was precious. It was lovely when such moments of pure delight blotted out pain and hunger.

Still, such moments were few, and hope we needed now. Our crew became more and more sullen and troublesome. They hounded us for more food, more brandy, and we could not make them understand that we shared alike in food and drink, and in risk of using all our stores before help came. I could not be left alone with these men so that when I was forced to remain in the hut, my husband or the mate kept me company, and none of us had a moment's peace.

I do not think that these men were evil, not all of them, but I do believe that one among them urged the others to rebellion. One night of wind and terrible cold, we were waked by the sound of footsteps outside our hut. As we listened in the silence, we were aware of a penetrating odour of smoke coming from the corner of our hut where our stores were piled. We barely had time to remove the gun powder before the flames reached it. We put out the fire, and next day we learned that it had been started by a drunken sailor tossing a brand into the hut. After that we set a watch nightly, and daily went in fear of our lives.

Thus, the weeks passed in hunger and cold and pain, but sometimes with sights of such unearthly beauty that we were stirred to wonder and awe. My husband and I looked forward to our child and we were happy just to be alive, though often we were anxious about our dwindling stock of food.

Then came a day when the wind shifted and the ice moved from shore. The snow melted and poured in torrents down the mountain sides. Spring was upon us. The mate formed a party to explore the coast and search for fish and game, and my husband and I were alone with the day stretching ahead full of the promise of pleasure in our being together. As we sat in the weak sunshine, enjoying its feeble warmth, we saw a black spot on the water about half a mile from shore. My husband seized his spyglass, and his hands shook with excitement as he whispered, "I think it is a cask from our wreck: it may be food."

Without another word he pushed off the little boat and rowed away. I picked up the glass and marked his progress. He leaned over the barrel, turned and waved to me with a reassuring smile. Then I saw the boat rock, and overturn. My husband disappeared beneath the water. I remember no more of that day. When the men returned, hours later, I was sitting on the beach with the glass in my hand. I was alone. The boat was gone. No words were needed to tell them what had happened, and of words to describe the horror, I had none.

Many days must have passed, but I do not remember them, before the mate came to me and for the first time talked to me of our situation. He spoke of my husband, of the child I was bearing, of home and of my parents. He said, "We must go now; we must travel inland. We must find food, shelter and help."

His words gave me strength, hope and courage. We set out, feet almost bare, clothes in tatters, and we climbed the mountains and turned our backs to the sea. All day we walked through a wild landscape. Brown, scarred, barren hills were to the right of us, like pictures I had seen in the Bible of the Holy Lands. To our left, as if the hills had been cut cleanly with a knife, the verdant green of spring grass sloped up to softer hills. We must have walked through that wide valley for ten miles or more. We slept beside a stream that night, eating the soft, frostbitten red berries we found in profusion.

Late the next morning we saw smoke rising in the distance, and we came finally upon a cluster of houses along the shores of a wide bay. Outside one house a man stood. He looked at us briefly, then intently. He turned his head and shouted, "Virtue, come quickly. We have some shipwrecked people, a woman, too." Oh, the wonderful sight of that lady with her starched white apron, her neat hair, her clean smooth face. And how she cared for me! She brought me water in which to bathe, milk to drink, and then she wrapped me in her best linen sheets. That was my undoing. For the first time since my husband left me, I wept. And then I slept for a day and a night, and another day.

While I slept, the kindly folk of Jersey Rooms—for that was the name of their village—had cared for the crew and had arranged for them to go north in some fishing boats to Labrador, where they would find ships to take them to their homes. Virtue would not let me accompany them, for she said I must rest and regain my strength, so I lodged several weeks with her before a passage was found for me to Forteau in Labrador where, they said, I would quickly find a packet bound for Quebec.

Virtue's husband charged the skipper of the little vessel I sailed in to lodge me with a friend of his, a man with whom I should be comfortable. But when we came to Forteau, the friend had gone and I was put to lodge with a Guernsey fisherman. He was an evil man and I was in peril, alone and without a friend.

Help came, as it always seemed to do, through the kindly, nay almost saintly, people it was my good fortune to meet. Mr. Pinson, the planter in the village, offered me hospitality. He was a widower, but his house was large and filled with servants, and I was an honoured guest. I recall the night when Mr. Pinson asked me if I would dine with him and his friends, English naval officers from the cruiser *Rosamond*.

"They would be delighted with a lady's company," he told me. I was vain enough to dress as well as I could and to arrange my hair which had grown quite long and curly again, and I thought myself quite presentable. So did young Lieutenant Chappell, I am sure, for he plied me that night with many questions about my adventure, and said he would write it down in his journal for all to read.

That was my last night in Forteau. The next day I sailed for Quebec and arrived well in time for the birth of my son. My parents, who had mourned me dead, poured on me the love and care that had been pent up in them these long months. They said to me that I should tell my own story, lest the young lieutenant make me out more of a heroine than I am, my adventures more tragic than they were. For am I not alive? Do I not have my son, so like his father? Someday I shall go back to Newfoundland to visit my dear Virtue and to thank Mr. Pinson for his kindness and to see the land which, despite its cruelty, still haunts me with its beauty.

So ends the tale of the lady known only as Mrs. E. She never returned to Newfoundland. Her friend, Virtue, lies in the old cemetery by the seashore in the village of Jersey Rooms that we now call Woody Point, in the bay the French called "La Belle" but which is to us "Bonne."[58]

---

[58] From Chappell's record, it seems likely that the wreck occurred off Green Gardens, between Bonne Bay and Trout River. Having survived the winter on the narrow coastal terrace there, the survivors eventually walked out through the Trout River Gulch, and down the hills to Winter House Brook and Woody Point. Who Mrs. E. was and what became of her are unknown. Ella imagined the reception in Woody Point and the person named Virtue.

MURDER AT SEA: OR WAS IT?

Around 1900, John Pittman of Rocky Harbour disappeared under mysterious circumstances. Here Ella recounts what might have happened to him.

I WILL never hear a tale that has haunted me more than the one Stephen told me that evening, as we fished the placid water and watched the sun set over the bay.

"Now mind you don't go round telling this for a good long spell," Stephen warned. "Some of the people I'm telling you about are still alive, and they mightn't like it if you went airing this around to everybody, like you do with your yarns."

Well, it is a good long spell since that day, so now I can tell it.

"It's about a murder," Stephen began, "about my uncle who disappeared. He just vanished right off the face of the world, and we never found the rights of it, though it happened almost fifty years ago."

As Stephen told it, the story began with an American banker loading salt herring in the Bay of Islands, late in the fall. She delayed leaving just a day too long and was caught in the ice, just outside the bay. Being unfamiliar with the coast and quite without experience of early winter ice, the crew feared what they didn't know. They attempted to free themselves, but with windless days and nights and falling temperatures, the ship was only trapped tighter. Driven with the ice steadily north along the forbidding, harbourless coast, they finally came in sight of Trout River, hardly a dent in the coastline, but showing a few houses. The men turned their backs on the ship, walked ashore over the ice, and went home—out of this story.

"Now," said Stephen, "here was a sound vessel, loaded with good salt herring, standing out there alone and drifting north. And here were the b'ys on shore with nothing to do but watch her. Fishing was done for the season, and 'twas too early for logging. Nobody in Trout River paid much heed, 'tis true, but when the ship drifted up across Bonne Bay, and they could see her from Woody Point, somebody said, "Come on, let's go out aboard of her.""

"Were they just going for the hell of it?" I asked.

"Not exactly. I think they must have been thinking of salvage. They figured, if they stopped to figure at all, that they could get their boats within a half mile of the ship and then walk across the ice to her. They would stay on board 'til she was free, and then bring her back. Anyhow about a half dozen men started out. They put in for a few hours at Rocky Harbour, where they met up with me uncle, a big red-headed feller he was, and always ready for a bit of fun, despite his awful temper. They persuaded him to go along, to sort of liven up the party. Anyhow, off they went.

"For about a week, we could still see the ship way out, still stuck in the ice. Then the wind hauled round and drifted her out of sight. More than a month went by and we didn't hear a thing about her. I can mind me father talking about it—I was five or six then. He said there was no use worrying, because we couldn't get out to her, not rightly knowing where she was.

"Finally, she drifted toward shore, up there by Cow Head, where the land leans to the westward. Pretty soon she was off the Arches, just past Parson's Pond. Then some fellers came down to Bonne Bay by dog team, and told us they had seen the vessel. So we decided to go and get my uncle to bring him home. They took me with them, so now I'm telling you what I saw and done.

"We harnessed the dogs and drove up over the coastal track 'til we came to Parson's Pond. We got the loan of a dory, but we had a bit of trouble getting right up to the ship, because of the drift ice and slob and patches of open water. When we got to the vessel, she looked empty. I minds I had a cold, knotty feeling in the middle of my stomach, and I can see my father's face now, all screwed up and anxious. Anyhow, soon as we got to the boat, we saw a man coming up out of the forecastle. His head was bandaged up so's we could hardly see his face. He was a Bonne Bay man—never mind his name—said he was acting cook, and he looked over the side, down on us, with a gray, sick-looking face and shifty eyes. We asked him, hearty like, 'Well, b'y, how're you getting on? And where's our man?'"

The cook stared. Then he said, "Ain't you seen him yet? He left here last Friday to walk ashore. Said he was anxious to get home and see how you were all getting along."

"When they had digested that information, they wondered where on earth me uncle'd got to. Was he lost? Had he started to walk along the bleak coast alone and been caught in a blizzard? Perhaps he had broken his leg and was at this moment cold, hungry and suffering, off in the bush by himself.

"So we went right back to Parson's Pond," Stephen continued, "and the people there told us he couldn't have walked ashore on Friday because there was open water between the vessel and the shore. And he couldn't have come ashore in a boat, else someone would have seen him, which nobody did. So all we knew was that he wasn't lost in the woods.

"Then my father said, 'I wonder what happened to the cook's head.' Nobody said anything to that, but we were all thinking of me uncle's terrible temper. Anyhow, my father got three men from the village—he left me ashore this time—and rowed out to the ship again. When they got there they could see all the crew on the move, opening hatches, clearing the decks and tidying up the gear. They were getting ready to bring the vessel back to port, now that the ice was breaking up. They were a quiet lot, Father said, never saying a word when they went on board."

The crew offered no resistance, and no hospitality, which was strange for people usually friendly. The visitors asked the normal questions. What kind of a time did they have? Was it cold on the vessel? Had they plenty of food? And talking thus they worked their way slowly from deck to forecastle, eyes everywhere. They were looking for something, but they did not know what, just that they would recognize a sign when they saw one.

The forecastle was empty when Stephen's father, ahead of the others, climbed down the ladder into the crew's quarters. He returned, in his hand a torn bit of sail in the middle of which was a deep stain of blood, stiff and dry now, but unmistakably blood.

"I found it under a bunk," he whispered to his friend, "stuffed in tight against a plank. It looked strange, so I pulled it out. Look!" He showed the deep stain.

"I'll hold them here," the friend whispered back, "while you go and have another look." And he kept the crew on deck telling them a long, drawn-out story of what occurred at a dance in Woody Point when the magistrate got roaring drunk. This served to keep the crew together for ten minutes, giving Stephen's father time to investigate and to discover carefully stowed under a bunk a belaying pin which was also blood-stained.

A Parson's Pond man who had been poking around on his own muttered, "Queer t'ing. They got ne'er kedge anchor nor jib sail." An explanation was then demanded. The crew, to a man, related that the cook and the redhead had been at daggers drawn from the beginning of the voyage. One night they got into a proper row, and the cook called Red a nasty name and got a wallop on the head with the belaying pin for his pains. Oh, it was a bad knock enough to make him bleed like a stuck pig! In fact, he had a huge gash in his head that moment under the bandage. The blood on the piece of sail was due to the cook's dripping all over it as he waited to be bandaged. Cook looked such a ghastly sight that Red took fright and made off in the dory for shore. And of course as it was night, the Parson's Pond people couldn't see him row ashore.

But where was the little anchor? They had lost it one night in a gale. How did it happen that the rope attaching it was cut? That was just the way it looked—it broke off clean. So what happened to the jib? They didn't know. Maybe the Americans had lost it. Anyhow it wasn't there when they came aboard.

Stephen's father and his friends left the vessel and went ashore. They organized search parties that scoured every foot of the shore and inland between Parson's Pond and Rocky Harbour. Never did they see sign of Red or anyone else. They waited. He did not turn up. Every living soul along that coast kept a sharp lookout for months. The devil-may-care red-headed fisherman, who took life so easy and laughed so much, despite his villainous temper, was never again seen.

Stephen's father bided his time. The ship was brought back to Woody Point. The Americans came back to claim her and paid good salvage money. Then Stephen's father struck. Gathering a few friends for moral support, he went to the magistrate and demanded the crew's arrest for murder. The magistrate is reported to have said, "You haven't got a body, so how do you know it's murder?"

And that was the end of it, until several years later. Then a rumour spread after one of the ship's crew fell ill. Before he died, he is said to have confessed to helping kill the redhead after a tremendous row. They didn't mean to kill him, only to give him a good fright, but when they found he was dead they panicked. So they sewed him in the sail, weighed him with the kedge anchor and threw him overboard.

"Mind you," said Stephen, "'Twas only a rumour, but even to this day one old man will whisper, "Murder," and another will shrug his shoulder and, "Poor feller must'a lost his way."

While Steve was yarning, the sun had set and a little breeze blew up to ruffle the glassy surface of the bay. The moon stood on top of Gros Morne then leaped off into the sky. The little gasoline engines that generated electricity for the big houses began to chug, and lights came on as tiny pin-points along the shore. We piled our catch in a heap, shipped our oars and rowed home for a glass of beer before the cafe shut.

"What do you think, Steve?" I asked.

"Oh, I think they done away with him. But 'tis a long time ago, and there's no good holding it against them people. We got to live with them, so we might as well forget about the past. Still, I'd like to know for sure."

And so would I.

AROUND THE ISLAND
FOR 75 CENTS

This is the story of how a man from Labrador became an unintended prisoner on a coastal steamer in the 1950s.

UNCLE ALBERT had come into the wharf from his morning's fishing, and in the windy sunlight, he was standing between his beached dory and a cleaning table, his knife flashing as he split the cod and tossed them into a barrel.

"Nearly done," he called as I came down the path. "Wait a spell, and we'll have a yarn."

I found shelter from the wind by the door of his shed and made myself comfortable on a warm, flat rock. I could have waited happily all day, so pleasant was it in the sun with all the beauty around me. Presently, Uncle Albert joined me, filling his stubby pipe.

"Shift over a bit," he ordered, "and I'll sit on the rock besides you. I never told you about the time I went right round Newfoundland island for seventy-five cents, did I? Well, wait now, 'til I gets to rights. If I'm not comfortable, it puts me out of mind of what I'm going to say." He settled himself with his back against the door of the shed and puffed until his pipe glowed merrily.

"Well, 'twas when I was a young feller, and we lived in West St. Modeste, down on the Labrador. It was the first year I went teaching. Them times you didn't have to have as much learnin' to be a teacher as you do now. Anyhow, I was teaching in Henley Harbour, about fifty miles north 'long shore from Modeste. It came Christmas holidays, and the coastal steamer was due by then, so I was going home on her. I had me suitcase all packed and waiting when she blew, fit to split the rocks, and I ran down to the wharf and got aboard. I wasn't much surprised when I was the only one got on the boat, but I thought about it a bit when I saw I was the only passenger on her. Then I thought—Oh well, nobody goes to Modeste this time of year. They all go the other way, so I went and got me ticket.

"Seventy-five cents, the purser charged me. Mind that, now, seventy-five cents."

I said I'd mind, but that surely seventy-five cents was quite a lot of money in these days.

Uncle Albert retorted, "Not so much when you consider what I got for it. Anyhow, when the purser give me my ticket, he said there was ice outside and it might take us a good spell to get down to Modeste. But I wasn't fretted, because I had five days to Christmas and a week or more afterwards. So I settled down. I fair loves to watch the land slide by and me, comfortable like, not having to make any effort to get along."

He sat on the deck in the lee of the smoke stack, on the little steamer that carries freight up and down the coast of Newfoundland and Labrador, a cosy, warm and clean little ship on which New-foundlanders loved to travel because it had the air of wealth and good living compared with their usual situation. He watched and soon he saw the ice. Miles of it, thick and rolling. The steamer hit with a crash, went astern and hit again. She shivered from stem to stern with every crash, and Albert was relieved when she backed away and turned in a wide circle, back the way they had come. Then he heard footsteps on the bridge ladder and turned to see the mate com-
i   n   g
off watch. The mate stared at Albert.

"Didn't know we had a passenger," he said. "Where you going?"

"Modeste," said Albert.

"My son, we won't get to Modeste, not this year. See that ice? You better get off this craft soon's we tie up, and walk home."

"Yes sir, that's what he told me," Uncle Albert said, "but now you knows I wasn't going to walk home like a common workman with me pack on me back. Damn it, I was a teacher! So I told the mate we'd get to Modeste all right. I told him I never heard tell of ice making this early, and I been on the coast all me life.

"Then the mate said—oh, he was a terrible big man, did I tell you? Must've been seven feet high and as big as a puncheon. Anyhow, he said as how he'd been on the coast a good long spell too, and he knew there was a first time for everything, and 'twas my bad luck I picked on it."

When the steamer tied up back at the wharf in Henley that night, after bucking through the film of ice on the harbour, Albert chose a warm cabin with an outside porthole, with clean sheets and plenty of blankets and he slept like a log. Around daylight, he heard footsteps overhead and presently the mate's voice, "Let go the ropes."

Naturally, Albert thought they were on their way to Modeste, but to his astonishment, when they steamed through the headlands they steered north. The wireless operator told him they had received a message from a schooner in distress and they were going to the rescue. Edging her way between the ice and the shore, the steamer made her way to the next harbour in which lay the schooner, caught fast.

Finally, after much bucking and churning, a channel was cleared and the schooner followed them out into the Gulf and away south. The steamer set her bow south once more.

All day long they fought the ice, advancing yard by yard. As darkness fell, the burly mate swung down the ladder and made his way to the mess room. Albert followed. The mate turned and eyed him speculatively.

"Come in, me son, and let's you and me have a mug-up," he invited, "Take off yer coat, 'cause I wants a long talk with you."

On the mess-room table there was hot coffee and buns. Albert sat on the bench as the mate tossed his beret on a hook and unwound his muffler. Then he settled his huge bulk in a chair and said, "Now, we made less than three miles in the last three hours. You made one big mistake not getting off in Henley when you could. We're going over to Port Saunders now, if we can get out of this mess we're in. There's schooners froze in, all down the coast, just like the one we got out this morning, and the ice is making fast. If we can only get out without smashing our propeller or twisting our tail-shaft, we'll be in Saunders by tomorrow noon. That's pretty far from Modeste, now isn't it? And what are you going to do?"

Albert was distinctly unhappy. He wished he hadn't been so cocky, but he didn't intend to give up. In answer to the mate's question, he said, "The thing is, I paid my passage to Modeste and it's up to you to get me there."

The mate's big mouth fell open. "Well, blast it. If that's the way you feel, the best thing you can do is settle down for a nice long cruise. We might get back north again the winter; we might not. And how you're going to get from Port Saunders to Modeste without sproutin' wings is more than I can tell."

By noon on the following day, Albert was two hundred miles from home and feeling very lost. True, he slept warmly and ate well, but he was consumed with anxiety. Each time the steamer left the wharf and poked her bow far enough into the Gulf to see what the ice looked like, his heart leaped, only to fall lower and lower each time they returned. Christmas day came and went, but apart from a large figgy-duff and a rabbit stew—the rabbits snared by the cook on the hills behind Port Saunders—Albert did not celebrate.

Ice was now forming along the shoreline, blocking the coves and harbours in its grip; clearly, it would not unblock them before spring. It was a matter of hours until the steamer, if they wished to escape, would have to hurry south. Watching Albert closely, it was plain that the mate was taking a morbid interest in him. Sometimes he'd grin, sometimes shake his head, as if he couldn't quite believe Albert was real.

After they been four days in Port Saunders, the mate sought Albert out and said to him, "Now, you'll see the sights, me lad! We're going to Humbermouth, We're getting short of coal and grub, and anyhow, we got to do something—can't stay here all winter. I hope you got some money, because when you get to Humbermouth and see all the shops and taverns, my son...," his voice trailed off.

"Had you ever been to Humbermouth?" I interrupted Uncle Albert.

"No, my maid, that's what I hadn't! I thought 'twould be some fun, if I had a bit of money. But all I had was five dollars, and I told the mate that."

"I'll never forget him then," Albert laughed at the memory. "He sat there with his great elbows on the table. Then he put his ugly chin between his hands and looked at me and grinned, a dirty grin 'twas, only I didn't think about that until afterwards. Anyhow, he said to me, slow like, "I s'pose you're a good Government man?"

I said certainly I was, and how did he s'pose I got my teaching job if I wasn't?

Then he leaned over to me and he said, "I'll tell you what to do. You send a telegram to your Member and ask him to lend you fifty dollars—that'll do you. Tell him to wire it to Humbermouth."

Uncle Albert said he was sure the mate was fooling him and didn't really mean it, but it was an idea. So the next time the steamer tied up in Port Saunders, Albert streaked up the hill to the telegraph office and sent his message. He said that it came to him much later that it was a pretty daring thing to do, considering he'd been eating off the government for seven days now and sleeping in the government's warm bed, all for seventy-five cents. Asking for a loan on top of all that was going a bit far; but it was done, and no use worrying.

When they arrived at Humbermouth, Albert had just time to collect his money at the telegraph office and to buy a bottle of Christmas cheer before the steamer's whistle brought him back on the run. The mate was waiting.

"Hoping I'd miss the boat, I daresay," said Uncle Albert, "and when he seen me with the bottle sticking out of me pocket, he fair stamped his feet, he was that mad. He began to curse and swear something awful. And you know why? This is the best part of it altogether—the government man what sent me the money, guess who he was? The mate's father. Wasn't that a good one?"

"So here was I with the old man's money in me pocket and he without even a penny, not enough for a glass of beer. 'Twas his own fault, anyhow. He shouldn't have put me up to it, only he didn't think I'd do it."

"Anyhow, when he got his breath, the mate says to me, 'Now you're in for it, me boy. Now you're going to be some sick and tired of us before you're done, because we're going all down the west coast, around Cape Ray, along the south coast, past Cape Race and clear round the ruddy island.' He said I'd be lucky if I got home for Easter, so I offered him a drink."

The steamer bucked and rolled, pitched and tossed along the south coast for thirteen days, rounding Cape Race, passing St. John's, and Cape Freels. Albert was mortally seasick, and the sicker he got, the more jubilant was the mate. Finally, they arrived at St. Anthony, not many miles as the crow flies from Modeste, but as far as transportation went, it might have been on the moon, at least until spring.

"We tied up," Uncle Albert said, "and the mate come alongside me. He said, 'Now, me son, off you git. Unless you want to spend the winter freightin' in the Gulf.' I couldn't give up tormenting him just a little bit more so I said to him, 'What'll I do now?'"

"He looked like he'd like to choke me, but all he done was say, 'Oh, for Lord's sake, go up to the Grenfell mission. They're used to looking after lost souls up there!'"

"So that's what I done." Then Uncle Albert commenced to laugh. Tears poured down his whiskery cheeks and he gasped for breath. I waited patiently for the denouement. When it came, it was more than I expected.

"I went up to the mission," he said, when he finally caught his breath, "and I told the doctor there about the trouble I was in. And he said, 'My son, you're some lucky. We just got an airplane come in from St. John's, and 'tis going up to Modeste to fetch old man Barnes—he's pretty sick. That is, if they can land on the ice. So you can go up along with it.'

"Honest, I was afraid to go back to the steamer and tell the mate. I thought he'd burst, or something. So off I went, and I was some proud to come home in an airplane. 'Twas worth missing Christmas and all."

"Did you ever see the mate again?" I asked.

"Hold on, now, I'm comin' to that. I forgot all about him for a long spell, and then after I was down here, I heard he'd given up the sea and was living down shore in Cow Head. Then, it come to me mind about the fifty dollars. So, know what I done? I paid it back to him, two dollars a month I paid him. And I'm sure that every time I went, the old feller got one step nearer a stroke.

"I never let him forget how mad he was the time I went round the Island for seventy-five cents."

THE SKIPPER ON
THE BAIE VERTE RUN

In the early 1960s, Ella journeyed around the Northern Peninsula by coastal steamer, then the only public means of moving people and goods from one isolated outport to another. Her account of one trip around western Notre Dame Bay and the Baie Verte Peninsula tells of her conversations with the ship's captain.

IT WAS late summer, when I boarded the coastal steamer on a calm, moonlit sea. When we were away from land there came such a creaking and rolling that I couldn't sleep, so I watched the dawn break from my window on the boat deck. We were heading for the Baie Verte Peninsula. I was eager to see something of the outports in and around the serpentine western coast of Notre Dame Bay, full of inlets and islands linked to each other and the world only by boat. Growing up in Lewisporte, I had heard of many of these from my father who had travelled this way on his mercantile rounds.

Although his black hair was turning grey, the skipper's face was as round and unlined as a child's, except for the squinting lines around his deep-set grey eyes. His only concession to weather was a pair of sheepskin-lined boots, than which nothing could have been more incongruous.

"Starboard a quarter, me dear!" he was saying to the helmsman as I reached the top of the ladder, and I heard a curious little sigh which was his punctuation to every order.

"May I stay up here to watch you dock?" I asked, for we were approaching Little Bay Islands.

"Sure, but stay over in the corner of the bridge because we've got some job getting her in, and I moves about a lot."

The passage into the harbour was hardly wider than the ship. As we slipped through, we could almost touch land on either side. I said to myself, "All very well, getting in, but what about getting out again?"

In that harbour and later in many others, I watched the enthralling game between ship and crew against wind and tide—a game played with different rules for each port. Sometimes we would steam in with the wharf-face open to our bow, heave a line and finish with engines. In other ports we would literally slide in, bow on, and warp her round. Then going out, we would inch ahead, swing the bow round, go astern a few yards, and do it all over again until we were heading for open water. If the tide was running out, we would use the anchor to hold the bow off the rocks until the precise moment when the bow swung. And sometimes we could not enter a harbour, but would anchor outside and send the loaded mail boat ashore.

When we had tied up, the skipper said, "We've got an hour or more here. We have to unload lumber and take on fish. Why don't you go for a walk and I'll blow the whistle in plenty time for you to get back."

I went into the village where the sun poured down on houses strung along the beach and higgledy-piggledy up the cliffs. I do not know how many backyards I trespassed on before I found the road over the rocky, turfy land. A few trees grew: in one garden were aspens, juniper, damson and two dogberry trees loaded with scarlet berries. Forget-me-nots grew in a ditch along the hillside, on the top of which I had a breathtaking moment. I saw a fish shed across a narrow gut, perched on the water's edge and backed by rocky cliffs. The shed's six windows caught the sunlight, reflected into the wind-disturbed water and caught the reflection back again in a moving curtain of ebony and silver.

The whistle recalled me. I joined the skipper on the bridge. The mate came up to report that the radar had gone "on the blink," to which the skipper replied, "Ah, t'row the damn t'ing overboard. I can smell land quicker'n that t'ing can see it." He hated modern aids to navigation and mistrusted them almost as much as he did landsmen, a little more than he did his fellow seamen.

"Once," he told me, "we were coming across the Gulf from Sydney with a load of coal, me and another boat. I had radar and the other feller didn't, so when I seen this big liner bearing down on the two of us, I called to him to come up 'longside of me so we'd both be in the clear. So he hauls in close aboard, and didn't that great leviathan steam down between us and sweep the coal clear off our decks with her wash!"

He blew his nose, gave a direction to the helmsman, sighed and continued: "Out there in the Strait of Belle Isle, I can tell you I wouldn't poke me nose out for anything, if there was one of them big cargo ships in sight. They wouldn't change course for little chips of t'ings like us, not if we had all the right-of-way in the world." I said it must be hard on his nerves, and he swore a most satisfying oath that you couldn't be skipper these days and have nerves too.

All day long the sun shone and everything was blue—from deepest indigo to the blue-grey of islands smudged on the horizon. A rainbow clung to our bow, a miracle no matter how often one sees it. We steamed for Snook's Arm to pick up a hundred barrels of salt fish, but when we arrived there were only twenty-three, and the skipper swore because someone lied to get him off his course to an unscheduled port of call.

We put into little coves, anchored off islands, and wherever we went people in their best clothes came to see us, for we were strangers and might have exciting news from outside. Sometimes they joined us for a little cruise, but one man was obviously leaving it all for good. He had five tin trunks and a wooden tool chest arranged on the wharf under a tarpaulin anchored with beach rocks. When the trunks were put into a canvas sling and hoisted into our hold, he solemnly shook hands with a knot of tobacco-chewing men and climbed our gangway. No women in his life? Well, perhaps he was going outside to find one: he hadn't much choice in this tiny settlement.

The skipper called, "Come here and see this." A small tanker on the horizon, wallowing in the swell, was washed over with fire from the setting sun and as she rolled, something on her deck gathered the sun's rays and sent them flashing to us like a gigantic red star. Then the fire died as the sun sank, muted red and gold, into the sea, and for hours after the northern sky was softly bright.

I asked the skipper, "Is it true that waves come in cycles—a few small ones, then one big one?"

I was confounded when he quoted, "Send me a ninth great peaceful wave to drown and roll me under / to the cold tunny-fishes' home where the drowned galleons are."[59] He loaned me his copy of John Masefield so I could read the rest of the poem.

"But you don't want to drown?"

"Drown!" he said, "No I don't s'pose I do, but I daresay I will, just the same. I hope it won't be soon—there's so many ports of call to make." Then, quick as a flash his head I swivelled round, and he shouted, "Look out, Jim. Watch what you're doing with that chain!"

To me he remarked, "Them young sailors. Got to watch them every damn minute." And he did. He watched them as I would a three year old crossing a busy street. In his tight little world, circumferenced by wind and centred by the watch bell, he actually brooded over his thirty men.

We hauled round Cape St. John and headed for La Scie. Here, three calves and a cow went over the side in a crate. As soon as they were released they careened up a grassy bank in ecstasy, with the village children in full cry behind. It was night now, and the fish plant loomed butter-yellow in the moonlight. On the wharf had gathered a crowd of people from which four little men disengaged themselves

[59] From "D'Avalos' Prayer" by John Masefield. *Salt-Water Poems and Ballads.* New York: Macmillan, 1916.

and, one after the other, walked up the gangplank, across the deck and up the bridge ladder. I heard a murmur of voices—quiet, portentous—and I saw in the light of the chartroom a paper change hands. The four little men climbed down and disappeared. The skipper, behind me, said, "What man proposes—you know the rest! Just got a message to take a feller to hospital. Got his face smashed with a mallet." The man, swathed in blankets and followed by his wife, was brought on board and put in the best cabin. We cast off and steamed through the moonlit night to the nearest hospital, and back again around Cape St. John to Springdale we headed. Back to the soft moonlight on the wooded arms of Green Bay.

Sometime during that passage, I remembered that my father and grandfather and great-grandfather—yes, and further back than that—had sailed these very waters in their homemade schooners. The ghost of my great-uncle Jonathan Manuel came to keep me company; he who had seen this same moon, felt the heave of these waters, watched these stars swinging round a mast, and his voice echoed to me, "My maid, you're just like us. Can't stay away from the water," and I replied to him, "I'm glad of it."

The skipper was on the bridge by the time I had finished breakfast. "Did you have a good night?" I enquired.

"Finest kind. We got good mates on this boat. Some though, I wouldn't trust. I'll never forget one night when I had a new third mate on. 'Twas clear and fine and we were hauling through the bight, so I thought I'd have a nap. I told him to keep a straight course and to call me if anything happened. Well, I hardly got me boots off when in he rushes. 'Skipper, get up, get up,' he yelled in me ear, 'We're in somebody's backyard.' And, so help me, when we got on deck, there on our port bow was a house, curtains all up and everything. I nearly choked, 'til I seen it was somebody launching a house, floating on empty oil drums, and being towed from one side of the bight to the other. Being a fine night, the fellers towing her went ashore for a mug-up and, not expecting us, left her right in the run. And all the time the mate was blabbing, 'I couldn't figger how we was going to get out of that garden?'"

We steamed past Calvary Hill and Cape Brulé, at the entrance to Pacquet harbour, and came to Coachman's Cove, called by the French *Havre du Pot d'Étain*—a lovely little cove formed by a narrow peninsula on which stood a tiny white lighthouse. The air was crystal. Smoke rose straight from little houses, newly washed-looking, scattered along the beach in front of hills rising soft and smooth. There were nets on the fences, fish drying on the flakes and whiskered old men in homespun jerseys sculling black punts.

The skipper said, "Wonder those people don't move to bigger places. All this money wasted sending a steamer for a few families."

"With all the money we're wasting on destruction," I shot back, "surely we can afford to link with this little pocket of serenity."

"Serenity!" he snorted. But the way it looked that morning, I could have spent the rest of my life in Coachman's Cove, with the island called *Gentille* to protect me from the sea.

The skipper leaned over the bridge and shouted to a sailor on deck, "Mind you don't part that cable," just as the wire broke with a vicious snaking in the air an inch from the skipper's head. He looked startled for a moment, then let out a great gusty bellow of laughter that reverberated the length of the ship.

"You nearly had it that time," I said, my knees trembling.

"Guess my time isn't come," he shrugged. "Fate? A miracle? Some think one way, some another."

Then he told me: "Once we got into a terrible storm when we had a deck-load of full oil barrels and the hold full of machinery. And there was I with a hundred people and probably a million dollars' worth of cargo. I thought about it, and then hove over some of the oil barrels that were rolling around. Then I thought about it some more, and I figured I'd done what I could. So I prayed."

"Don't you pray when you're not in trouble?"

"I don't even think about it when I'm not it trouble. But it's awful lonely being skipper sometimes, 'cause you got too much responsibility for one man to carry. It's black outside. You know there are rocks about, and shoals, but you can't see them. You get scared—no, not scared, exactly, just awful anxious. Then you pray. And I don't believe God minds helping a seaman any time. Anyhow, what else can you do? No power on earth can help you." He looked away to the horizon for a moment then added, "Anyhow, I prays, and just as sure as you're there, He helps me."

"In the old days, they called up the Devil."

"Yes," the Skipper said, "and I've heard them dare God instead of praying to Him. I seen my old father, when I was fishing the Labrador with him, stand by the wheel in a gale of wind and tell God to come down and take the wheel, if He thought He could do any better. My father gloried in a storm. 'Twas his vessel, his cargo, and most of the crew was his family. Now 'tis different, different altogether. 'Twouldn't be much sense me paying the Devil to call up wind; with steamers we don't want that, and that's all the Devil is good for—a wind. Anyhow, where did you hear about that?"

"I had a friend who used to live on the south coast," I replied. "She told me she was coming around a headland one day in a small skiff. It was dead calm and the two-man crew was pretty tired of rowing. So one fellow took a twenty-cent piece out of his pocket and threw it into the water saying, 'Now then, Old Boy, send us some wind to sail home.'"

"Did the Devil send it?"

"Not that day, they rowed home safely, but the next day the same two men were drowned on their way back from the fishing ground—drowned in a sudden squall off the headland, while the dories ahead and astern didn't even see a cat's paw on the water. They found the two bodies exactly where they sank."

"I daresay. Yes, I daresay," mused the skipper. "Queerer things have happened. But mind you, whether God or the Devil, you got to know how to help yourself before you start asking for it from either one of them."

He told me, then, how he was once involved in a quite unjustifiable stranding, surrounded by shoals and hidden dangers: "I didn't pray then, I worked." He eased the steamer's bow off the rocks only to nuzzle her stern against mud. He threw out anchors and warped her round. He ran engines dead slow, but still churned rocks and mud with his propeller clear up to the bridge. And so he worked all through the night. Daylight brought the lighthouse keeper in his dory to the beleaguered steamer. Skipper and lighthouse man held a conference, and the lighthouse keeper boarded his dory and with a twelve-fathom line, sounded a passage and got the ship to open water.

"I'll never be the same again, though," said the skipper, "because I can still taste the danger in my mouth. I'd have been disgraced for life if I'd lost my ship in there—and that would be worse than drowning."

I told him, "You know what Richard Gordon said about you seamen? He said, 'Their sense of values in human and elemental behaviour is unblunted, and they look upon their existence as a long, uproarious joke relieved by not unentertaining interludes of necessary tragedy!'"[60]

"Yes, I know Gordon. Now, take me brother. He'll never be skipper now, 'cause his eyes have gone on him. Yet, he despises sailing under men not so old nor as experienced as he is. So I told him to go ashore."

"What did he say to that?"

"He said, 'Eight hours a day in one job? Eight hours in a bed. The same rocks and trees every damn day. I'd rather die.' And I don't blame him, poor feller."

And so, talking thus, we came to the port where I was to leave the steamer. Walking uphill from the wharf, I turned to watch her sail away, tossing her saucy little black stern in the swell. And I thought, to warp a little iron steamer into a lonely wharf in starlight, to feel the hull respond to the twist of the wheel, to beat to windward in a gale and to sit in a tight company of seamen in a mess at midnight— without that, a seaman might as well be dead.

[60] From Richard Gordon's *Doctor at Sea*. London: Michael Joseph, 1953.

SIX MONTHS
ADRIFT ON THE ICE

During the long history of Arctic exploration, of expeditions that disappeared and of the many attempts to find them, one in particular stands out for its connection with Captain Isaac Bartlett of Brigus. Here is Ella's retelling of the rescue of shipwreck survivors from a southward-drifting Greenland ice floe.

RECENTLY I was reminded of a yarn—one of those I was brought up on—about how skipper Isaac Bartlett rescued some of the survivors of the ill-fated *Polaris* expedition. As my father said, "It wasn't so strange, his rescuing them. What was so strange was his being where he was at the time that they were: almost an accident, you might say."

Now, Isaac was from the wealthy town of Brigus, where seafaring captains lived in high style. They were among the toughest old salts that ever our island bred, and to them Labrador and Greenland waters were as familiar as the coves where their ships lay at anchor. They'd push their prows wherever seals or whales could be found, and if any adventurous gentleman without the necessary knowledge wished to penetrate the unknown, a Bartlett could always be signed on as skipper. The best known is Captain Bob Bartlett, who accompanied Peary on his North Pole explorations.

It was in the spring of 1873 that Isaac took his vessel, the *Tigress,* on the annual seal hunt. He brought home a bumper crop without much effort, and when he had unloaded and the season was still in full swing, he cruised north along the Labrador coast to look for another seal herd. All was well as they picked up seals here and there, until a day came when all thought of seals was driven far, far from their minds.

April 30 was a day like any other, foggy and not very windy, when suddenly the lookout shouted. The crew tumbled to the rails, Captain Bartlett picked up his glass. There was something moving out on the ice. The dark specks came into focus, moving, but not like seals, or anything else they had ever seen on an ice floe. Isaac stared and stared. Then he put down his glass and gave the helmsman an order. The *Tigress* moved ponderously through the ice floes and as she closed in, what they saw left the crew speechless.

Now, I must go back and sketch in light strokes the background to this story. In 1860, American newspaperman Charles Francis Hall, long driven by an obsession about the lost Franklin expedition, set sail for Greenland to find it. Over the next decade he attempted twice to find traces of Franklin, but to no avail. With these Arctic experiences and valuable contacts with the Inuit, Hall persuaded the US Government to back yet another expedition, this time to reach the North Pole. He managed to acquire an old ship, which he renamed *Polaris*, and in June 1871 headed north again with a full crew. They reached northern Greenland, but only after much argument and dissension among the crew and officers. Following an exploratory sledging journey, Hall returned to the ship and shortly fell ill. Before he died, he accused members of his crew of poisoning him. Though the general interpretation at the time was that he had had a stroke, nearly a century later his body was exhumed to discover that, indeed, he had ingested a large quantity of arsenic in the last two weeks of his life.

During the winter, as the ship lay frozen in the Greenland waters, they took on two Inuit men, their wives and little children. The next summer, with Hall now dead, the decision was made to return home. However, as Bob Bartlett, a generation later, wrote out of bitter knowledge, "You can make all the plans you want in the far North and write them out in hundreds and hundreds of pages, using all the words in the dictionary. But the finer the plan you have, the worse it will go to smash when wind and ice and drifting snow take charge." And that's what happened to the *Polaris* and the plan for her.

Shortly after she started to head south, the *Polaris* was caught, moving helplessly among the grinding, crushing ice. For two months, all aboard lived in terror, shuddering at every loud noise, wondering from moment to moment when their ship would be crushed. Just when they thought they had survived the worst, a fierce storm blew the *Polaris* against the ice and a huge piece penetrated her hull. In the twilight, the howling wind and vicious snow squalls, they began to heave what they could onto the ice. With despair to lend them strength, they threw boxes, barrels, cans, beds, coal and clothing overboard. And as the ice climbed up and over the ship, they moved the women and children to the safety of the floes. Suddenly the ice began to crack. Those on the pans, clawed and thrust at their gear and crawled to the comparative safety of a large ice floe. Then, more and more open leads appeared and the ice divided. The ship lurched, a mighty gust of wind took her, as lightning swift the ice pressure shifted and she broke free. Through the darkness of the Northern twilight, those still on board watched the floe with its human cargo break into smaller pieces. They saw one of the Inuit rush to pick up his baby, and saw men leave the floe in a desperate attempt to return to the ship. They tried to launch their boats to pick them up, but in vain.

That was October 15, 1872. Official records give us the story of what happened from then on. The *Polaris* found anchorage, and her men lived comfortably, with help from friendly Inuit, until the spring when they were picked by a whaler, and returned home via Scotland.

Meanwhile, on the ice floe were George Tyson, the assistant navigator, who quickly took command, the ship's steward, seven sailors and the two Inuit families, without whom they would likely not have survived the ordeal I am about to relate. They found the ice floe was about five miles around, with plenty of room to build snow houses, which they did. There was very little food on the ice: fourteen cans of pemmican, eleven bags of bread, a can of dried apples and fourteen hams, all to feed nineteen people, including the three-month-old baby of Hans Hendriks, the Greenland Inuk. There were two whaleboats, two kayaks, a small canvas tent, a compass and a chronometer. Hans and the other Inuk, John, who came from the Canadian side of the Nares Strait, built three snow houses, and went hunting in their kayaks as the group drifted helplessly in darkness, wind and snow. To begin with they had little luck hunting, and Tyson said that the first seal they caught they ate uncooked, skin, hair and all. The next seal they managed to cook, making a small fire with the bones and blubber of the first one. Once, Tyson wrote, "I have dined today on two feet of frozen entrails and a little blubber. I only wish we had plenty of that."

The ice they were on was part of a pack drifting south with the Labrador Current, and as they well knew, it was a race between the gradually lengthening days, the increase in temperature, and the chance of sighting a boat. After eighty-three days, surviving on seals, birds, and even one bear the Inuit shot, they were threatened with a break-up of the ice, so the people remained awake and dressed, keeping all their necessities ready in case of sudden disaster. Fortunately, the ice houses proved to be on the thickest and most solid part of the floe, and they had two comforts: "good health and a speed of 23 miles a day, bringing them closer to the haunts of men."

The ice pan got smaller and smaller, and then separated entirely from the pack and drifted toward the open ocean. On April 1, said Tyson, "It was necessary to abandon the floe, which was now wasted to such an extent that it was no longer safe." So they took to the one boat they had left. Built to hold six to eight men, it now carried twelve men, two women and five children. They kept only their tent and a little meat, bread and pemmican, and went floe to floe, moving by boat when one after another pan became uninhabitable.

Having now drifted 2900 km in six months, on April 28 they saw their first ship, but she did not see them. Next day another, but as they watched, she disappeared beyond the horizon. On the 30th a fog blotted out their surroundings. Suddenly it cleared, and there in front of their eyes was a ship. Isaac Bartlett in his *Tigress* had spotted them. He hauled them on board, all nineteen of them, and not an hour too soon, for Isaac's log revealed that for the next two days a storm of extreme severity raged incessantly. Their last floe could not have survived this gale.

Of course everyone on the *Tigress* wanted to know their story. One incredulous sealer asked, "And was you on the ice day and night?" Eventually the story was told, and the *Tigress* sailed homeward, stopping only to collect more seals. Every man jack of them survived, to be wined and dined in the fabulous Brigus homes before they were speeded on their way, to families who had long since given them up for dead.

As we say at home, "Trust those old swilers. They'll fish anything out of the sea."[61]

---

[61] For details see *Arctic Experiences. Containing Capt. George E. Tyson's Wonderful Drift on the Ice-Floe, a History of the Polaris Expedition, the Cruise of the Tigress and Rescue of the Polaris Survivors*. E. Vale Blake (Ed). New York: Harper and Brothers, 1874. Shortly after the party rescued by Isaac Bartlett had returned home, the US Navy purchased the *Tigress* and sent it north to search for the *Polaris* crew left behind in Greenland. Eventually it was discovered that they had been picked up earlier and taken to Scotland, and the *Tigress* was re-sold—at a handsome profit—to its owners, Harvey and Co.

WHEN SHIPS WERE SHIPS
AND NOT TIN POTS

Ella delighted in discovering the tales told by old salts like Bill Barnes, the wilder the better.

HERE IS a story about a Newfoundland sailor long since dead, but whom I have loved for his strength and humour and his deep love and knowledge of the sea. Though I never knew him in life, I have grown to know him in the tales he told in his memoirs, when he was eighty years old. His name was Barnes, William Morris, after his father's cousin, the great English painter of the same name. He was born in 1850 and brought up in St. John's. He sailed every kind of craft afloat in the days when Newfoundland 'fish boxes' were the hardest-driven ships afloat, when Oporto and Alicante were home to our sailors, and when Rio knew them well.

Barnes introduces himself. "My head is sculpted, every inch all over, behind and in front, on top and all. I've been struck by a hammer that knocked in my skull, and shot in the back of the head. There's a hole gone through from the right side of my cheek and out through the left side, and a tooth gone with it on both sides. It was caused either by a bullet or a piece of shrapnel, I don't know which, because I hadn't time to run after it. You'll find a mark on the back of my left hand where a fellow nailed me down with a sheaving knife to the cover of a sailor's chest. I had a great mind to stick it back in his belly:

if I done right I should have, but I changed me mind. I have only a few little tattoos on me, and half an anchor on my left arm, which would have been finished only I got a heavy kick on the backside from my father and the anchor never got finished—one of the flukes broke off in a squall. I've been in every bloody rig that's afloat, fore and afters, full-rigged ships, brigantines, barkentines, tops'l schooners, jackass brigs, steamers large and small, a decoy duck during the War, and once I made a short journey in a horse and carriage in a gale of wind."

In December 1875, the ship *Silver Sea*, Captain James Day and Mate Will Barnes, put out from Alicante with a load of salt bound for St. John's. New Year's Day found them off the southern end of the Grand Banks. The wind blew, then calmed, then blew again, a strong head breeze. They beat back and forth from Cape Race to St. Pierre, and as they were getting more and more fed up with it, there came a howling gale. "Well," says Barnes, "we'll have to take off the topsail and reef the mainsail if it comes any worse. We won't round the Cape this way."

It did come worse. The heavy laden *Silver Sea* was rail under, making three miles an hour and well off course. The glass plummeted, and it began to freeze, ropes and rigging stiff as boards on her myriad of sails. "We needn't get frightened 'til daylight, the rate we're travelling," Barnes told the crew. And hardly had he said it when began a hurricane of wind. Canvas reefed hastily, shouts and orders in the midnight darkness, and a growling, smashing sea knocked in the galley, broke the skylights and almost carried the helmsman overboard. Then, they hove to.

Of course it got worse; else this wouldn't be a story. It got worse all through the long wet day. At dark, the crew took off the jib and upper topsail and clewed up the foresail. "Keep a sharp lookout," the captain warned Barnes, and all the black night he stood watch, peering ahead and around. Suddenly to the helmsman, he sang out, "Look, do you see anything there? By heavens, breakers, I see them plain."

It was the dreaded Shingle Head, just southwest of Cape Race. Barnes roused the captain. All hands were called out of their sodden sleep. They stumbled around half conscious, tore at the frozen ropes, loosened topsail, and sheeted it home. Now the thing was, said Barnes, "Will we have room to come round and get stern in before she strikes?" Fateful minutes, then a shout. "She's clear." A near escape. They sigh relief. The skipper says, "We'll fetch up around Cape Pine" on the west side of Trepassey Bay. "We'll never sight Cape Pine with this wind," Barnes told the skipper, "We'll hit Powles Head."

Half an hour later came the helmsman's shout. "Look there under our lee bow, breakers again, breaking mad!" Urgent terror in his voice, the captain said, "It must be Powles. Barnes, keep cool, we're in Mutton Bay, and we can't get out." Well, that was a situation. Mutton Bay, at the top of Trepassey Bay, wasn't wide enough to manoeuvre the ship, so full of rocks and reefs as to attempt an anchorage almost suicidal. Keep cool, indeed.

The *Silver Sea* did her master's bidding. She came round, head pointed straight for a jagged reef, seas boiling mad, then she cleared, stern into the wash. She tore up Mutton Bay, as if she meant to run clear up on the rocks waiting to rip her to kindling. The anchors went out precisely the right second, exactly the right length of chain following, and she brought up clean, with no engines, only miles of wet, stiff, billowing canvas. Twenty-foot seas rolled down over them, rocks astern foamed madly, her bow plunging under, then rising as the chains went taut. They prayed the chains would take the strain that the windlass would hold.

Now it was dark again. Fires from those watching on land gave them courage, though they knew if the ship went, the sea and rocks would claim them too. The night wore on. Barnes went below and took from a tin his mate's certificate and put it in his pocket, for being parchment it would resist the water and tell a rescuer that this mangled body was once Will Barnes of the *Silver Sea*. Then, as if by the hand of God lightly laid, the wind slackened, only for a moment, but long enough for these master seamen to beat it out the bay to safety.

Now in St. John's, people were just going to church when the news flew around them. "A big gale yesterday. A barkentine looking like the *Silver Sea* anchored on the back of Trepassey. If the chain parts, none will be saved." A message then came from the Trepassey people. "We stayed on shore all night, waiting. But when daylight came, the ship was gone. They must have broken their hawser, the chains must have sawed the wood down to the water and the ship must have sunk with all hands."

It was night, three days later, when the *Silver Sea* put into St. John's. Says Barnes, "I got home late. There was my wife sitting there mourning for me. She thought I was a ghost, but I gave her a smug and one thing and another, and that was the end of that."

Once though he really frightened her, when he came in with the brig *Plymouth*, of which he was skipper. A day or two earlier, the wind had freshened and he went forward to take in the sails. The mainsail swung around, hit him on the jaw and split him from lip to chin. He swore, and held his jaw together with his hand until he found the mate and cook and demanded that they sew him up. But, quaking at the sight, they refused. So he got a needle and thread and a piece of leather and, with neat overhand stitches, sewed himself together. He finished the job with sticking plaster and Friar's balsam. Then he wound bandages around his head, and that is how he appeared before his wife. The doctor said he'd done as good a job as a surgeon.

Of the more disreputable incidents in Barnes's life, let us not talk. After all, what sailor worth his salt hasn't painted some seaport red, or gone slightly berserk with the heady freedom of dry land and a release from danger? But once he almost caught it. His skipper was a drunken sot, arrogant too, and one night in a foreign port as Barnes and the cook were in the galley, they heard him fumbling his way on board. Barnes said in disgust, "Aw, grease the ladder and let the old bugger go overboard and drown." Next day, the skipper, having heard this remark, hailed Barnes before the English consul, demanding he be punished. Barnes turned to the skipper and bellowed, "Where were you, when we were in the breakers off the coast, and I had to put sail on the ship to drive her off the rocks? In your bunk, drunk! And I stood on the bridge for thirty hours without food or sleep. Take away my certificate? Not you!" And the skipper beat a hasty retreat.

Another time, heading for St. John's from Bermuda with a ballast of stone, they ran into a storm. The very same skipper refused to shorten sail, the ballast shifted, and the ship began to list sharply to one side. "We've got to do something quick before another sea catches her," warned Will Barnes, "else she'll go bottom up. We've got to cut her masts and cut them quick." So he crawled along the deck, unable to stand upright with that list, then he balanced on the bulwarks outside to reach the mast. One eye on the seas, one on the job at hand, Barnes began to chop, crouch down, grab the shrouds and wait for the sea to go over him, then chop again. When the mast went down, they had to crawl into the hold and right the ballast. All night it took them, Barnes leading the effort. Then, he discovered that the skipper was "full to the chin" as he elegantly put it. That did it, Barnes took over.

They rigged a sea anchor and the ship swung to it fine. Then, the crew hove ballast again until they could barely move. The vessel was by now a wreck, so when a steamer hove into sight, the crew signalled, and full sea running, clambered into the lifeboat. Still on board, Barnes turned and with a sick heart set fire to his ship, then he too went overside.

Well, everything went wrong with the steamer that rescued them. It took eight days to reach Hull in England, by which time the steamer itself was almost in two pieces. Barnes went passenger on a ship going to St. John's, and it took seventy-five days to make the voyage. The water gave out after sixty days and they drank the cargo of Irish porter, until they decided it was more pleasant to die of thirst. And so they got home, and Barnes walked into his house with his belongings tied in a bandanna. All that agony and nothing left. But his wife said, "Ah, what odds, as long as you didn't lose yourself."

When he was well over sixty, the First World War began. Being in England at the time, he wore down the entire Admiralty until they accepted him into the Navy. He was shipwrecked three times, and just as the War was ending the little fishing boat dressed up as a decoy got a direct torpedo and disintegrated under his feet.

At sea, Barnes was a great man, but on land he made a mess of things. He couldn't live the cramped, confined life of a landsman, and after his wife died he came less and less ashore. Then, waiting in Cardiff for a ship, he fell in love. The crusty, hard-living sailor met a woman who tangled herself so inextricably into his life that he never forgot her. She was a lady, he said, fine and lovely, educated and witty. She fell in love with him too. She knew the strength and poetry of him under the salt-caked skin. That they never married must have been a grief to Barnes, for twenty years later as he writes his memoirs he is talking of her as if he had loved her only yesterday. Whatever fate waited for her, Barnes never knew, for she simply disappeared: the rumour was that she was shot as a German spy.

Somehow that is all of a piece with the rest of Will Barnes's story.[62] He knew the best of life, from the old Newfoundland boxes, through the graceful clipper ships, down to the navy ships he so aptly called "tin pots," in which he spent the last years of a wonderful career. He had the sailor's religion—"a clear conscience, and a knife ready to cut the lines at a moment's notice."

---

[62] *When Ships Were Ships and not Tin Pots: The Seafaring Adventures of Captain William Morris Barnes.* New York: Albert and Charles Boni, 1930.

FINIS

Here is Ella signing off at the end of a series of stories told on the CBC.

"AND THIS dear listeners, is the last of my tales. I am sorry, for I have so enjoyed telling them. I do thank you all for your kind letters to me telling me how much you enjoyed them. There is no greater joy to a teller of tales than to know her favourite stories reach the hearts of listeners. I hope that they have brought you the pleasure that I have had in the telling. And so may they linger long in your memories.

"This is Ella Manuel, teller of tales of yesterday, speaking to you from CBY in Corner Brook."

Ella and
Louise Manuel
(1914)

The R.W. Manuel hotel and general store, Lewisporte, in the 1930s

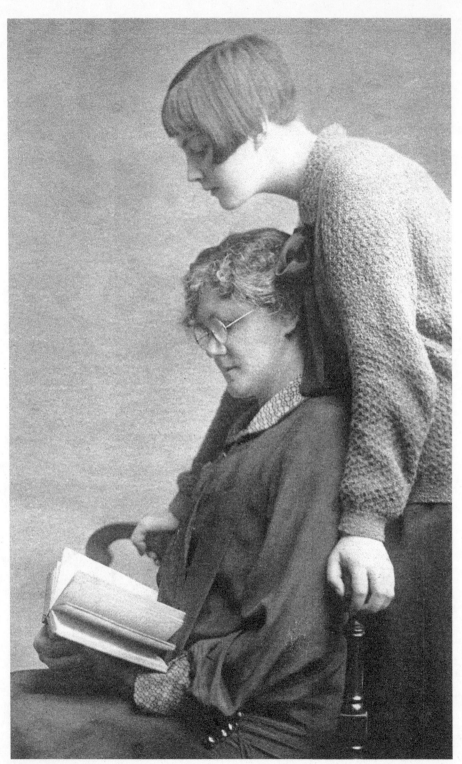

Ella and her mother

Ella in Boston

Joe, Ella, Antony, and Jonathan
in Madison, Connecticut (1941)

On holiday in France with Joe, Lee, and Peter (1936)

Ella and Lee Wulff, Western Brook Pond (1946)

Ella as "Gram" with "Kate" from *All Aboard* (1978)

Receiving the Persons Award from Governor General Schreyer (1980)

Ella's "girl-guide," Em Tapper, on the Lomond River

Ella on the beach near Sally's Cove

Killdevil Lodge in 1946

The view from Glenburnie on June 13, 1886. The house is almost certainly that of Hugh McKenzie. Modified from a watercolour by French Lt Koenig. Original in Library and Archives of Canada.

Ella's little house overlooking Bonne Bay

In the Antarctic during Scott's Last Expedition. (TOP) The Northern Party at Cape Adare. Victor Campbell front center. (BOTTOM) Three of them after nine months in the ice cave.

Missionaries and medics (clockwise from upper left): three Wesleyan missionaries fitted for winter travel, Dr. "Fitz" of the *Albatross*, James Lumsden, and Hugh MacDermott of Fortune Bay.

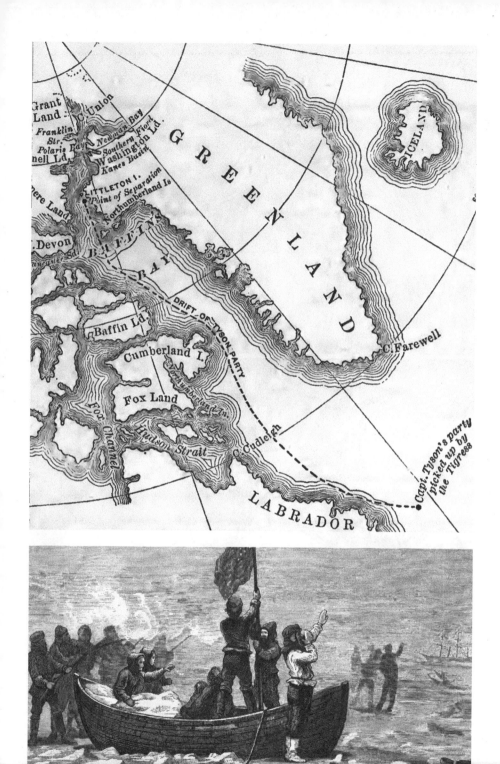

Six months adrift. (TOP) The path of the drifting ice floe. (BOTTOM) The rescue.

Will Barnes
remembering
his many
vessels

ACKNOWLEDGEMENTS

My greatest debt is, as always, to Carol Harris, who encouraged me to plough through and organize Ella's jumble of scripts and scraps, and to bring out her feminism. Her keen and critical eye was essential to shaping Ella's own story. I thank my brother Jon, Lee Somerville, Judith Love, Jeanie McFarlane, and Gisela Westphalen for their comments on early drafts. Tim Babcock and Christina Roy helped me to puzzle out Ella's pre-war days. Notwithstanding my scientific and other academic publications, my reticence in taking on this very different writing project was eased by encouragement from Annie Proulx and from Elizabeth Hay, who both read through a late draft of Part 1. I thank James Langer at Breakwater for his sound editorial advice. I am also grateful to listeners to the Voice of Bonne Bay community radio who repeatedly asked for more of Ella's stories, which I read out from the Woody Point house of Mike Madigan and Kathy Lepold.

CBC radio was always important to Ella, not only for bringing her own work to the public, but also for the way it engaged rural listeners, in those days when local radio was still viable. It seems fitting therefore to acknowledge here the encouragement she received from many at the CBC who more than sixty years ago helped to open a space for her in national broadcasting. These included Elizabeth Long, Marjorie McEnaney, Dick Halhed, R.S. Lambert, Fred Scott, Helen Carscallen, Helen James, Bob Weaver, Harold Hatheway, Catherine MacIver, and Jimmy James.

You can listen to Antony Berger reading most of these stories on a podcast series *Down to Sally's Cove*, now available on Buzzsprout, Spotify, Apple Tunes, etc. Included is one story recorded by Ella Manuel, the only radio broadcast in her voice still in existence.

ANTONY BERGER is a geology graduate of Dalhousie, the University of Melbourne, and Liverpool University and has lectured on every continent except Antarctica. The author and editor of numerous scientific books and articles and more recently *The Good and Beautiful Bay* (Flanker 2014), a history of Bonne Bay, Newfoundland, he divides his time between Woody Point, NL, and Wolfville, NS, where he is a keen choral singer.